Arctic Gardens: Voices from an Abundant Land

ENDORSEMENTS:

John Bodley, Human Ecologist, Applied Anthropologist, author, Washington State University, Pullman, Oregon.

"The best way to grasp the realities of a complex and unfamiliar region, like Arctic North America, is to find long time local residents with long term interest in the region, and get them to tell you about the realities of their lives, their concerns about the present, and how they feel about the future. Arctic Gardens is a compelling collection of just such personal realities. It is a rich cross-section of personal experience and outlooks told in the words of men and women, young and old, Native peoples with families rooted in the remote past, and relative newcomers from the South, teachers, ministers, bush pilots, guides, and researchers, all tied to this remarkable land and waters.

Here are vivid life stories told by the Athabaskan speaking Gwich'in, whose lives revolve around the caribou, and the Inuvialuit and Inupiat Eskimo whose livelihood depends on whales as well as caribou. The unifying theme of all these personal stories is the mixed benefits and immediate threats posed by the on-going development of fossil fuels in the Alaskan and Canadian Arctic.

This development drives the greatest threat of all - global warming which is already causing massive disruptive changes in these fragile Arctic regions. Chapter Five makes it clear that the ongoing melting of sea ice and permafrost accelerates global warming. Every political decision-maker in Ottawa and Washington, D.C., should grasp the Arctic realities contained in these personal stories, because everyone's future is linked to what happens in the Arctic."

Mark MacDonald, National Indigenous Anglican Bishop of Canada, Toronto, Ontario

"Modern mass society, even with its glorious technology and science, appears to have lost the capacity to understand the critical intimacy God gave to the relationship of humanity to the earth. Without an awareness of this relationship, most people seem unable to comprehend even the elementary dynamics of the balance of life in the North. Such ignorance is deadly beyond words to describe, but here is a resource that may provide an alternative - some life-giving light.

The Indigenous sage, Vine Deloria Jr,. was extremely critical of the frequently damaging relationship of anthropologists (the church, too!) with Indigenous Peoples. A longtime friend of his said that this was because he felt these disciplines had wasted their potential to offer constructive help to the people of the land. Arctic Gardens- Voices from an Abundant Land begins, I think, to display what that help might look like."

Al Corum, Irish/Chippewa, Boone, North Carolina

"It has been said that those who control the language, the evidence, and the ritual also control the power. For many years, Dr. Harvard Ayers, a forensic and cultural anthropologist, has helped Native peoples gain a grip on the levers of power over their own lives.

Now the battle has shifted to the land of the Gwich'in, the Inupiat and the Inuvialuit, who have lived in the Arctic North of Alaska and Canada and been sustained by the caribou and the whale for 20,000 years. In the profound text and photographs of Arctic Gardens, the authors have brought to life their desperate fight against the "carbon barons."

Harvard Ayers, Landon Pennington, and Dave Harman have stood with the Native peoples in Congressional hearings, courtroom testimony, and strategy meetings. If the power brokers turn a deaf ear, the dreadful prediction of Dennis Allen, a Native person from Inuvik, Northwest Territories, could come true: 'When two worlds collide, there is nowhere else to go.'"

Arctic Gardens:
Voices from an Abundant Land

A story of the Gwitch'in, Inupiat and Inuvialuit peoples
of the Alaska and Canada Arctic

by

Harvard Ayers, PhD
Dave Harman
Landon Pennington

Tom — Enjoy reading as
we do researching. Thanks Ayers

Arctic Voices
2010

Published by:
Arctic Voices
346 Fieldstream Drive
Boone, NC 28607

www.arcticvoices.org

This book is produced on paper with 30% PCR content
using soy-based inks in the USA by
BookMasters, Inc.

Authors: Harvard Ayers, Landon Pennington, Dave Harman
Editorial assistance by: Laura Anne Middlesteadt
Cover design: Landon Pennington
Book design and layout: Judy Geary
Map: Chris Badurek

ISBNs:
Paperback - 978-0-9843947-1-5
E-book- 978-0-9843947-2-2

Library of Congress Control Number
2010908390

First Edition published November 15, 2010 by Arctic Voices
Printed in the United State of America

Arctic Gardens:
Voices from an Abundant Land
is dedicated to two people who have
greatly inspired our effort:
Jonathan Solomon & Studs Terkel.

Jonathan Solomon, a Gwich'in Indian from Fort Yukon, Alaska, was a long-time protector of the calving grounds of the Porcupine Caribou Herd in the Arctic Refuge coastal plain. In 1988, he was appointed for life to the Gwich'in Steering Committee, which is charged with obtaining federally protective Wilderness status for those calving grounds which would prohibit petroleum exploitation. Until his death in 2007, he fought tirelessly for that charge. This dedication is made for his indomitable spirit and inspiration for all who have aspired to help achieve that goal.

Chicagoan Studs Terkel spent his illustrious literary career championing the life of the common man and woman. As an oral historian, he had no equal when it came to getting  to the heart of the lives of his subjects, no easy feat. He proved through the popularity of his books, especially that of *Working*, that we all have lives that are informative and, indeed, fascinating. We authors of this book have striven mightily to approximate his expertise and insight into the lives of the people who acceded to telling us their life stories. We never had the pleasure of meeting Studs, but we hope that from his vantage point above, he will smile when he sees our work.

Table of Contents

The Brooks Range in the fall-- no trees, lots of lichen

Thomas R. Berger

Foreword

This book is about a region of the Arctic that many of us have read about, but few of us have seen. It extends from Point Hope on the Chukchi Sea eastward to the Mackenzie Delta, where Canada's greatest river reaches the Arctic. It concerns both Canada and the United States, and its future depends on the United States and Canada.

Harvard Ayers, Landon Pennington and Dave Harman have chosen the title *Arctic Gardens* for the book. It is a title well chosen. The land and the waters, the lakes and the rivers, the mountains and the valleys of the region are the dwelling place of the original peoples of the Arctic, and provide critical habitat for the Arctic species on which they have for centuries depended.

In this book we hear from the people who were born there, who will spend their lives there, and will die there. They are the indigenous peoples of the region: the Inupiat, the Inuvialuit and the Gwich'in.

My experience in the region goes back to the mid-1970's, when I conducted the Mackenzie Valley Pipeline Inquiry. The proposed pipeline was to bring natural gas from Prudhoe Bay along the Arctic coastal plain of Alaska and across the Arctic coast of the Yukon to the Mackenzie Delta, where it would pick up Canadian gas and then transport the gas from both frontiers along the Mackenzie Valley to Alberta and then to metropolitan centers in the United States and Canada.

The Gwich'in and the Inuvialuit argued that a pipeline along the Arctic coast from Prudhoe Bay would drive the Porcupine Caribou Herd from their calving grounds along the coastal plain. The wintering grounds of the herd are mainly in Canada while the calving grounds are mainly in Alaska along the coastal plain, though they extend well into Canada. But Gwich'in villages on both sides of the boundary depend on the herd. The case they made was altogether convincing. In 1977, after two and a half years of hearings throughout Canada's Western Arctic, I recommended that no pipeline be built until land claims of the Dene and the Inuvialuit had been settled and measures taken to protect critical habitat. I urged especially that critical habitat along the Arctic coast of the Yukon extending south to Old Crow be set aside as wilderness to protect the calving grounds of the Porcupine Herd and the staging area for 500,000 snow geese, as well as other species.

And that is how it turned out; Canada decided that no pipeline was to cross the calving grounds, and that no pipeline was to be built along the Mackenzie Valley until land claims were settled.

When the Inuvialuit and the Gwich'in settled their land claims, they provided in their land claims agreements for the establishment of two wilderness parks: Ivvavik, to protect the Yukon coastal plain, and Vuntut, to protect the lands extending south towards the Porcupine River, for the protection of the caribou herd and the snow geese. Together with the Old Crow Special Management area, five million acres were brought under federal protection.

I also urged the United States to protect the contiguous area of Alaska, where the calving grounds of the Porcupine Herd are more extensive than in Canada. I went to Washington, D.C., in 1978 to testify before Senate and House committees to argue for international cooperation in protecting the herd. Those were the days of the Carter administration, and I received a sympathetic hearing.

The United States established the Arctic National Wildlife Refuge in 1980. In 1984, Canada signed a treaty with the United States to protect the caribou calving grounds on both sides of the international boundary. But critical habitat along the coastal plain of Alaska, encompassing much of the calving grounds, was still subject to the possibility of oil and gas exploration. This question is not yet resolved. It is one which has engaged the Gwich'in on both sides of the international boundary.

In Canada my work led to the settlement of land claims. In Alaska of course they had been resolved in 1971 by the Alaska Native Claims Settlement Act. In 1983 I was asked by the Inuit Circumpolar Conference to go to Alaska to conduct the Alaska Native Review Commission, which was to examine the 1971 settlement. Having held hearings in the late 1970's in all the Arctic Gardens villages on the Canadian side of the border, I then held hearings in the 1980's in all the Arctic Gardens villages on the Alaska side of the border. What Alaska Natives had to say closely resembled what I had heard from the Inuvialuit and the Gwich'in in Canada's Western Arctic a decade earlier. They affirmed the importance to them of a way of life based on the land, a culture centuries-old.

Since then the settlement of land claims has made the Dene and the Inuvialuit the owners of hundreds of thousands of hectares of land, including surface and subsurface resources, and has provided guarantees of their right to hunt, fish and trap. The land claims settlements have also provided for setting aside protected areas for caribou, migratory birds, and other species. Moreover, the Dene and the Inuvialuit are important players in working out the choices that face the region. They will have an influential – if not decisive – voice in determining whether a Mackenzie Valley gas pipeline is to be built today. They are no longer spectators in their own drama.

In 1985, after I had completed my report on the Alaska Native Claims Settlement Act, I was testifying in support of my recommendations for changes to the Act before the Interior Committee of the United States House of Representatives. When I talked about the importance of hunting and fishing to Alaska Natives, about what Alaska Natives call the subsistence economy or subsistence, Congressman John Sieberling said to me, "That's all very well, but how are we to bring Native people into the modern world?"

I tried to explain – how successful I was, I do not know – that in the Arctic and sub-Arctic regions of North America, subsistence hunting and fishing is actually a part of the modern world. Here the traditional economy of the Native people has not been extinguished. They still occupy the land and use it as before. In many places in North America the subsistence economy is still important to Native people, but this is especially so for the Native people of the Arctic and sub-Arctic in Canada and the United States.

As for "bring[ing] Native people into the modern world," the Gwich'in are in the thick of it. For two decades the Gwich'in from villages on both sides of the border have travelled to Washington, D.C., in their campaign to achieve Wilderness status for the Arctic Refuge coastal plain in Alaska. Getting up petitions, buttonholing members of the House and Senate, never giving up. All of this is part of the modern world: using the newspapers, television, and the internet, and the Gwich'in have mastered it. And so far they have been able to prevent drilling in the calving grounds.

As Ayers, Pennington and Harman have told us, *Arctic Gardens* "puts a human face on energy's front line."

It is not only the Gwich'in who regard subsistence as their birthright. This is true too of the Inupiat and the Inuvialuit.

Wherever I went in the Mackenzie Valley in the 1970's and wherever I went in Alaska in the 1980's, I saw the equipment used for subsistence – snowmobiles, skiffs, nets, sleds, snowshoes, oil drums – and the products of subsistence – racks of drying fish, skins being scraped, smokehouses full of meat. Everywhere the cry was for the defense of subsistence.

The scope and intensity of subsistence hunting and fishing activity in the Arctic and sub-Arctic always comes as a surprise. In both Canada and Alaska its prevalence has been demonstrated time and again. It is their sole occupation for some. But for virtually all it is important to their well being and their way of life. Yet there remains a seed of skepticism which sprouts again and again each time we learn of another survey, anywhere from Alaska to Nunavut, which reveals that harvests have not diminished but have even in some instances actually increased. We are surprised once more – yet why should we be? Only because there is no place in our idea of progress for the concept of a viable hunting and fishing economy.

In 1975, Gabe Bluecoat of Arctic Red River (now Tsiigehtchic), speaking to the Mackenzie Valley Pipeline Inquiry, said:

The land, who made it? I really want to find out who made it. Me? You? The Government? Who made it? I know [of] only one man who made it – God. But on this who besides Him made the land? What is given is not sold to anyone. We're that kind of people. What is given to use, we are not going to give away.

Richard Nerysoo of Fort McPherson, a young man in his early 20's, speaking in 1975:

It is very clear to me that it is an important and special thing to be an Indian. Being an Indian means being able to understand and live with this world in a very special way. It means living with the land, with the animals, with the birds and fish, as though they were your sisters and brothers. It means saying the land is an old friend your father knew, your grandfather knew, indeed your people have always known....we see our land as much, much more than the white man sees it. To the Indian people our land really is our life. Without our land we cannot – we could no longer exist as people. If our land is destroyed, we too are destroyed. If your people ever take our land, you will be taking our life.

In the *Alaska Native Claims Settlement Act* of 1971, Congress abolished the aboriginal rights of Alaska Natives, including their aboriginal rights of hunting, fishing and trapping. Congress had spoken. Yet when I held hearings in Alaska in 1984, Alaska Natives defended these same rights. Their defense was best made by a 14-year-old, Teddy Coopchiak, Jr., at Togiak:

How should Natives give up their hunting rights? It is well hidden in our mind, and nobody could take it away, like a bird who flies, and nobody could take it or boss it around.

Congress should let Natives boss themselves, because they have survived during the past. Had to make their own laws then, make their own decisions. That is why they are known to be smart people. That's why they survived in the Arctic for so long.

Zacharias Hugo of Anaktuvuk Pass: "We need that land to subsist, we need that land to find our food, we need that land for our children someday, so that they may use it."

Lori Kingik, a young woman, at Point Hope:

We, the Inupiat people, have always shared and divided our food, and that is our way of life. I do not want to lose our cultural lifestyle, because it is so precious. Our Inupiat lifestyle from time immemorial has been utilized and it is still prevalent today. We have practiced our whaling traditions and we are still using them today...The whaling tradition is the most precious in my life.

The ancient art of whaling exists alongside many examples of government-supplied amenities – the school, the welfare office, the water truck. The people here use snowmobiles. They play basketball. They watch television. Like all cultures today, theirs is changing, but their ancient beliefs and values persist. The Inupiat in the whaling villages asked, "Why are we here, if not to take whales?"

Basketball in Point Hope, Alaska

These were people who spoke when I traveled in the Arctic more than 20 and 30 years ago. Yet these same voices may be heard today in Arctic Gardens. A generation has passed away, but these same ideas endure.

Harvard Ayers, Landon Pennington, and Dave Harman have included in *Arctic Gardens* contemporary voices raised in defense of subsistence, offering a defense of a way of life. In the midst of the tumultuous changes in the Arctic over a generation and more, these voices speak to these same values.

But, of course, there has been movement all along to drill in the calving grounds in Alaska. The idea of drilling for oil and gas in the calving grounds represents a kind of technological manifest destiny.

The struggle to protect these lands has been a joint struggle, led by the Gwich'in on both sides of the international boundary, and by their allies in the United States and Canada, some of them, people from the Lower 48, who have made Alaska their home, and who speak for themselves in this book.

In summer, 2005, traveling with David Suzuki and *The Nature of Things*, we camped in the Arctic National Wildlife Refuge, south of the calving grounds, as the Porcupine Herd was leaving the calving grounds on the coast and beginning its migration back into the mountains. We could see them in their thousands on the slopes, and sometimes, with their calves; they came very near to the creek where we had pitched our tents. It was solemn, stunning, and stirring. To the Gwich'in this has always been a sacred place. And so it should be to all of us.

In North America a particular idea of progress has become fixed in our consciousness, but Canadians and Americans nevertheless have a strong identification with the values of the wilderness and of the land itself, a deeply felt concern for the environment. Americans invented the idea of national parks. In the United States this goes back to the establishment of Yellowstone in 1872. Just more than a decade later, in 1885, Canada established the Rocky Mountain (now Banff) National Park, Canada's first national park. In recent years we have seen the growth of ecological awareness, a growing concern for wilderness and wildlife and environmental legislation that parallels – although it does not match – the increasing spread of our technology and the consumption of natural resources.

All of this is occurring in a suddenly altered Arctic landscape. The Arctic is the epicenter of global warming. The shrinking of the Arctic ice represents a threat to polar bears, seals, caribou, the whole range of Arctic marine mammals and wildlife – a threat to the traditional way of life dependent upon these resources. The evidence of climate change in the Arctic is accumulating day by day. The permafrost is melting. The ice in the rivers goes out earlier; greater snowfall is impeding the migratory routes of the caribou. If present warming trends continue, the Arctic landscape could be greatly altered within our lifetime. It makes it all the more necessary that we hear the voices raised in this book, voices of both Native people and respected scientists.

Harvard Ayers, Landon Pennington, and Dave Harman offer us all an opportunity to listen to these voices and their stories, stories that are engaging at all levels and that enable us to get to know these people and the gardens of the Arctic.

Thomas R. Berger, QC
Vancouver, B.C.
September, 2009

Acknowledgements

Many people have contributed to the creation of *Arctic Gardens*, but two stand out: Charles Little and Leigh Ann Henion. Charles is a well-established author of books on environmental topics. He was my partner in the conception of the book and in the writing of its initial prospectus. His intellect and ability as a writer were indispensable ingredients in the first six months in the life of the book. A long weekend at his and his wife Ila's beautiful home in Placitas, New Mexico, followed a months-long gestation and resulted in the book's basic concept.

Leigh Ann is an Appalachian State University English professor who planned and discussed the book concept with me for several months, and I greatly appreciate her enthusiasm and insistence on high literary standards.

Landon Pennington is one of us, the authors, as is Dave Harman. Both have brought tremendous energy and ability to our final product and of course, there is no adequate way for me to thank them for their indispensable role in bringing my dream to fruition. The final product is without doubt a collaborative ef-

Landon learns dry-fish making

fort; without Landon or Dave, it could not have become reality. Judy Geary, publisher, author and Appalachian State University professor, and Gabe Ayers, web-master and my second cousin, have also played indispensable roles in helping the three authors to bring the paper book and e-book to fruition, respectively.

While funding for the book was perhaps predictably difficult, we have had the generous funding support of several individuals. Dave Harman, Hanes Boren, Leigh and Pam Dunston, John Cooper, my daughter and her husband, Pam and Mike Reed, and I have all made significant contributions to the book's cost. The cost of travel to the far-flung villages, none of which we reached by ground travel, was the greatest expense, followed by honoraria paid to the large majority of people who opened their hearts and their lives to us in their interviews. Of course donor Dave Harman has taken on the role of co-author as well, and Leigh Dunston has graciously acted as advisor and logistical supporter over the book's three-year creation.

I want to thank the advisory committee for the book: Thomas Berger, Lenny Kohm, John Bodley, Darius Elias, Luci Beach and Erica Heuer have all freely given the considerable benefit of their thoughts in all phases of the book's production. Of these, Thomas, Lenny, John, and Darius have played additional important roles.

Thomas Berger's involvement from when I first met him on a visit to Vancouver in 2007 to his creation of an outstanding, contextualizing Foreword for the book has given the authors the critically needed encouragement at the most important time. To have the moral and creative support of the most accomplished figure in modern time in bringing justice to the Native people of the Arctic of North America has been inestimable.

Likewise, to have my respected anthropological colleague John Bodley of Washington State University on our team has been a great plus. His advice on how to structure interviews in the Native communities, and ultimately his creation of a very strong written endorsement for the book, have been greatly appreciated. His expertise in applied, or what some call action anthropology is legend and gave us considerable confidence as we proceeded into the field.

Also of considerable help in the fieldwork phase of interviewing was my Appalachian State University anthropological colleague, Susan Keefe. She graciously allowed me to take her graduate course in ethnographic interviewing the spring of 2007 just before we began the interviews, which provided indispensable knowledge of how the process works. My background as an archeological anthropologist had given me scant preparation for the detailed ethnographic work that followed. Due to Sue's excellent instruction, I now have cultural anthropologists coming to me for advice on interview techniques!

Many people in Alaska and Canada have been of help along the way with introduction to people we interviewed and logistical advice and support. David Case is an Anchorage-based attorney who has written the authoritative book, *Alaska Natives and American Law,* and has provided invaluable insights on working with a client community of his, Anaktuvuk Pass, Alaska. Also from Anchorage, Dalee Dorough is a Yupik Eskimo attorney who worked closely with Thomas Berger in his studies of Native views of the Alaska Native Claims Settlement Act, and she has provided useful perspectives on Alaska Native politics. David Smith, tribal administrator in Nuiqsut, Alaska, provided lodging and office space and much more. Lily Tuzroyluke was our enthusiastic supporter in Point Hope, Alaska. Sarah James was our supportive host in Arctic Village, Alaska, as well as our interviewee. Larry Burris, likewise, was interviewee and host in Anaktuvuk Pass, Alaska.

In Canada, Mary Jane Moses and Joe Tetlichi of Old Crow, Yukon, gave us helpful assistance in finding contacts in Inuvik, Fort McPherson and Tsiigehtchic, Northwest Territories. Paulo Flieg of the Aurora Institute of Inuvik was very helpful in obtaining the licenses to conduct our work in these communities. Alestine Andre provided lodging and much logistical support in Tsiigehtchic, while Dennis Allen provided introductions to potential interviews in Inuvik.

Two indispensable supporters in the book's creation were my wife Mackie and Landon's wife Cassie. Both joined us on part of our journeys to the Native communities, and in so many ways supported us in following our dream of creating the book. Cassie became part of the team on our return from the Arctic as she did the majority of the drudge work of transcribing the interviews. Other valued transcribers included Savannah Haas and Nathan Barnes.

Laura Anne Middlesteadt has done yeoman service in copy editing. It is so hard to see your own work when you write it, rewrite it, and proof it. She added a pair of fresh eyes and a superior sense of grammar, spelling, and punctuation. In terms of hours spent on the project, she was right up there with the transcribers. Only the authors devoted more sweat and blood.

No doubt saving the best for last, I must thank the people who played the most important role in making this book possible, the people who gave of their time to tell us about how it is in the Arctic. Indeed these people are the very reason for the book's existence. Arranged by date of interview from first to last, they include Shirl and Bill Thomas, Dirk Nickish, Jules Lampe, Dave Harman, Lenny Kohm, Robert Bruce, Roger Kyikavichik, Glenna and Joe Tetlichi, Stanley Njootlee, Edith Josie, Darius Elias, William Josie, Alice Vittrekwa, Steven Tetlichi, Abraham Peterson, Herbert Firth, Neil Colin, Sue Oliver, Rebecca Blake, Elizabeth Colin, Gladys Alexie, Daniel Andre, Itai Kah, Frederick Sonny Blake, Doug Kendo, Noel Andre, John Norbert, Dennis Allen, Freddie Rogers, David van den Berg, David Bobo, George Paneak, Rachael Riley, Paul Hugo, Raymond Paneak, Andrew Hopson, Rhoda Ahgook, Johnny Rulland, Laura Beebe, James Nageak, Vernon Weber, Maggie Robert, Ellen Henry, Louise Frank, Abraham Henry, Jonah Nukapigak, V. Matthew Gilbert, Geoff Carroll, Robert Nukapigak, Trimble Gilbert, Margaret Simple, Donald Firth, Fannie Gimmill, Lydia K. Sovalik, Thomas Napageak, Faith Gimmill, Rosemary Ahtuanganeak, James Taalak, Ruth Nakapegak, Martha Lampe, Robert Lampe, John Walsh, Clarence Alexander, John Thomas, Ed Alexander, Caroline Cannon, George Kugik, Issac Killigvuk, Alfred Steve Oomituk, Luke Kosrvook, Jack Schaffer, Kristi Frankson, Donald Frost, Eyvi Smith, George Moses, Jeffrey Peter, Alestine Andre, Agnes Mitchell, Charlie Swanea, Li C. Tritt, Lorraine Peter, Jerry Garmott, Sarah James, Larry Burris, Rev. Scott Tisher, Peter Solomon, Baker Perry, Mike Mayfield, and George Woodwell.

Harvard Ayers, PhD
Boone, North Carolina
October, 2009

A startled fox in the fall in the Arctic Refuge

Preface

Many of you reading this book have no doubt been to Alaska or Canada as visitors. Some may have even toured the Arctic of one of the northwestern Canadian villages of the Yukon Territory or Northwest Territories, such as Old Crow, Yukon Territory, or Inuvik, Northwest Territories. I'd be willing to wager that few of you have visited in far north Arctic Alaska, for instance Barrow or Anaktuvuk Pass. They and other Native communities are indeed the focus of Arctic Gardens. If you are unsure where these places are, check out our regional map at the beginning of Chapter One.

In reality, only a few visitors traveling to Canada and Alaska ever see any Arctic destinations. In fact, few who reside in Canada and Alaska ever see them.

But they are there, way up there. And they are different from anything in the South--way different! They are in essence, another world altogether.

It is widely understood that much of the United States' domestic oil comes from northern Alaska. Similarly, Canada has long hoped to exploit the natural gas and oil of the Mackenzie Delta. But there is no pipeline to the south from the Canadian Arctic.

For both countries, environmental damage in the fragile Arctic is a great concern. In fact, the United States Congress has struggled mightily to decide whether to allow drilling in the coastal plain of the Arctic National Wildlife Refuge in northeast Alaska, as oil supplies and corporate profits have been pitted against caribou and other wildlife of this de-facto wilderness.

However, the area cannot be understood simply as a disembodied collection of environmental and economic issues. This region is also home to an abundance of cultures and distinctive voices including those of the Gwich'in Indians, the Inuvialuit and the Inupiat Eskimo, recreationalists, and others who make their home in, or visit, this oft-politicized place.

For the Inuvialuit, Inupiat, and Gwich'in people who live a subsistence lifestyle, the land and the sea are their gardens that provide nourishment, thus the title of this book. But these same gardens also hold energy and other resources that are in demand worldwide. This project's underlying assumption is that when citizens of non-Arctic regions of the United States and Canada hear the individual voices of the Arctic, the speakers will be transformed from abstract others in a distant, almost incomprehensible land, into what the Inuvialuit call themselves, "the real human beings." The voices included in Arctic Gardens

Gwich'in girls and Myra Keeter in Old Crow, Yukon

are those of the people who live, work and play in the Arctic, those who truly have the most to gain and lose from what nations choose to harvest from their homeland. Arctic Gardens puts a human face on energy's front line, and gives special attention to the human rights aspect of the ongoing debate concerning Arctic energy extraction.

Given the rapidly changing state of all printed matter in 2009, you are reading this book in a format of your choice, either as an e-book or a paper copy, or perhaps both. The e-book obviously presents the opportunity to provide a broad range of experiences for the reader. At the click of a mouse, you can see some pictures not in the book or see those that are black and white, in color. With another click, you can go to one of the web sites we have listed that give you further information. You can see maps of countries/states/provinces, and zoom-in on photos of the community of the person interviewed.

But what if you prefer to do it the old-fashioned way, the paper copy book? Both have all the words of all the six chapters listed below. It's your choice. If you don't have both e- and paper book, you may want to consider it.

Chapter One: "Beyond the Northern Divide." This chapter is the only one researched and written exclusively by the authors, in this case Harvard Ayers. It is meant to familiarize the reader with a little-known landscape and its human component. Most people are familiar with the Rockies and Appalachians and their outliers, but few know about the other divide that defines the hemisphere. In this perspective-building chapter, the authors will describe the geology, the ecology, the human cultures and the recent history of this land of north-running rivers, from the Kukpuk at Point Hope in western Alaska, clear to the Mackenzie in Canada, a distance of almost 1,000 miles.

Chapter Two: "Caribou Nation." The Gwich'in people, some 8,000 of them, who spread out over thousands of square miles on either side of the U.S. and Canadian border, are literally the "People of the Caribou." Their 15 villages are strategically placed along the migratory routes of the 120,000-strong Porcupine Caribou Herd. The bulk of this chapter will be the story of the Caribou Nation as told by the Gwich'in themselves. We have visited villages as far west as Arctic Village, Alaska, and the eastern-most Gwich'in town of Inuvik, Northwest Territories. The chapter consists of the voices of the Gwich'in people from these two communities, and also from Tsiigehtchic (previously called Arctic Red River) and Fort McPherson in the Northwest Territories, Old Crow in the Yukon Territory (www.oldcrow.org), and Fort Yukon and Venetie in Alaska.

Mt Chamberlin, Brooks Range, 9,020' elevation, Alaska

Chapter Three: "The Gardens of the Inupiat and Inuvialuit." While most of the Inupiats and the Inuvialuit (the Alaskan Eskimos and Canadian Inuit) also count on caribou for subsistence, theirs is a vastly different relationship with the natural environment. They are a people of the sea as well as of the land, traditionally taking a living from the bowhead and beluga whale, seal, walrus, and fish, as well as caribou, moose, Dall sheep, and other land-based wild-

Kaktovik Whale Hunt–Isaac Akootchook and James Lampe offering a prayer, Kaktovik, Alaska
Photograph Subhankar Banerjee, 2001

life. The Inupiat settlements stretch all across the length of Alaska's northern coastal plain from Point Hope on the Chukchi Sea to Kaktovik on the Beaufort Sea. The Inuvialuit are centered on the Mackenzie Delta of the Northwest Territories. One exception to this sea-oriented subsistence practice is the Inupiat village of Anaktuvuk Pass, Alaska, located in

Permafrost–in this case, white ice layer–melts and the
Coleville River bank cave in near Nuiqsut, Alaska

the largest pass through the Brooks Range. These people are 200 miles from the ocean and hunt primarily the caribou that migrate through the pass. For most of these Native people, then, their gardens are in the sea and on the land. Our interviews emphasize their whaling, fishing and hunting pursuits.

Chapter Four: "Those Who Come for Business and Pleasure." Each year, droves of people come to the Arctic to hunt, fish, raft, and backpack. We have interviewed these visitors, and those who guide and fly them, to get varied perspectives on the tourism industry in the Arctic. Since these people return in most cases to the Lower 48 and southern Canada, the opinions they take home with them are particularly influential in the political decisions made about this vast land.

Chapter Five: "The Warming of Arctic North America." Climate change is the joker in the deck in any contemporary analysis of an Arctic or Antarctic region. For the region covered in Arctic Gardens, the issue is significant enough in social, economic, and ecological terms to demand a chapter of its own. According to a recently completed international scientific panel, global warming in the Arctic is occurring at several times the rate of the temperate zones of the planet. Native residents speak of sinkholes in the tundra and river bank erosion caused by melting permafrost. They have also reported the early breakup and late refreezing of lakes and rivers, which cause all manner of modifications of human and animal movement. Thus, our selected voices will include the equally valid perspectives of both the scientific community and the Arctic's Native residents. This chapter is written and organized by Dave Harman.

Chapter Six: "This I Believe." This concluding chapter reprises the issues of the previous five chapters. What are the common threads, both for voices in the same chapter, and between voices crossing chapter lines? What are the fault lines of differences between them? Clearly, this area of the Arctic is a complex place, and our ability to understand it depends on our careful listening to its many voices.

Because the Native people are the main source of information about the Arctic Gardens, the authors will contribute about 10% of the proceeds of the book to two Native non-profits. Ten percent will be donated to REDOIL (Resisting Environmental Destruction on Indigenous Lands), a non-profit organization dedicated to protecting Alaskan indigenous ecosystems, and 10% to the Gwich'in Steering Committee of the U. S. and Canada, dedicated to protecting the ecosystems of the coastal plain of the Arctic National Wildlife Refuge by establishing it as a Wilderness Area.

For single copies, discounted class sets, and access to the related e-book, visit our website:

www.arcticgardens.org

Arctic Gardens is distributed to the trade through Atlas Books

About the Authors

Harvard Ayers is a retired Professor of Anthropology and Sustainable Development at Appalachian State University in Boone, North Carolina, who retains the position of Professor Emeritus. He teaches several courses including Arctic Anthropology, which is composed of a two to three-week field trip to the Arctic area covered by the book. Arctic Gardens is Ayers' second project of this type. He was senior editor of *An Appalachian Tragedy* (Sierra Club Books, 1998), with text by Charles E. Little, and photography by Jenny Hager. He made two trips to the Arctic in 2007 and one in 2008 to conduct interviews for the book.

Landon Pennington (right) is a Professor of Spanish at Caldwell Community College in Boone, North Carolina, holding an MA in that field. He participated in the Appalachian State University Arctic Anthropology field trips of 2004 and 2008, and continues to maintain his knowledge of the many issues involving the Arctic of Alaska and the Canadian Arctic in the Yukon and the Northwest Territories. He made four trips to the Arctic over 2007 and 2008 to conduct interviews for the book.

Dave Harman is a retired businessman and a visitor to the Arctic of Canada and Alaska who is keenly interested in Global Climate Change, especially as it applies to this region. He is the lead author/editor of Chapter Five, "The Warming of Arctic North America." He is a lifelong resident of Blowing Rock, North Carolina. He participated in the 2004 Appalachian State University Arctic field trip.

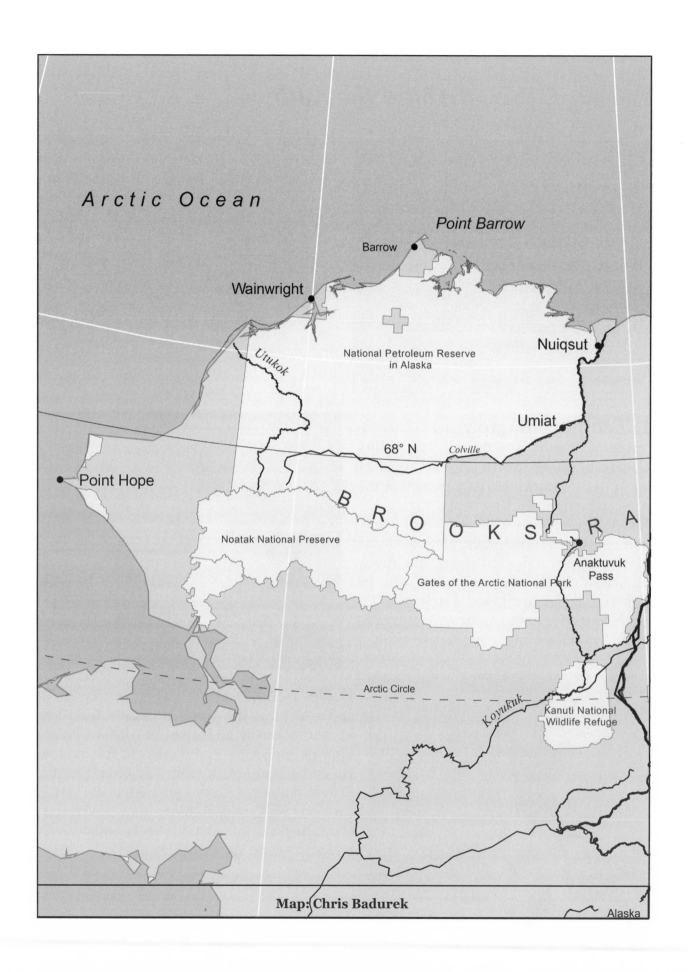

Arctic Ocean

Point Barrow

Barrow

Wainwright

National Petroleum Reserve
in Alaska

Nuiqsut

Utukok

Umiat

68° N   *Colville*

Point Hope

B R O O K S   R A

Noatak National Preserve

Gates of the Arctic National Park

Anaktuvuk
Pass

Arctic Circle

Koyukuk

Kanuti National
Wildlife Refuge

Map: Chris Badurek

Alaska

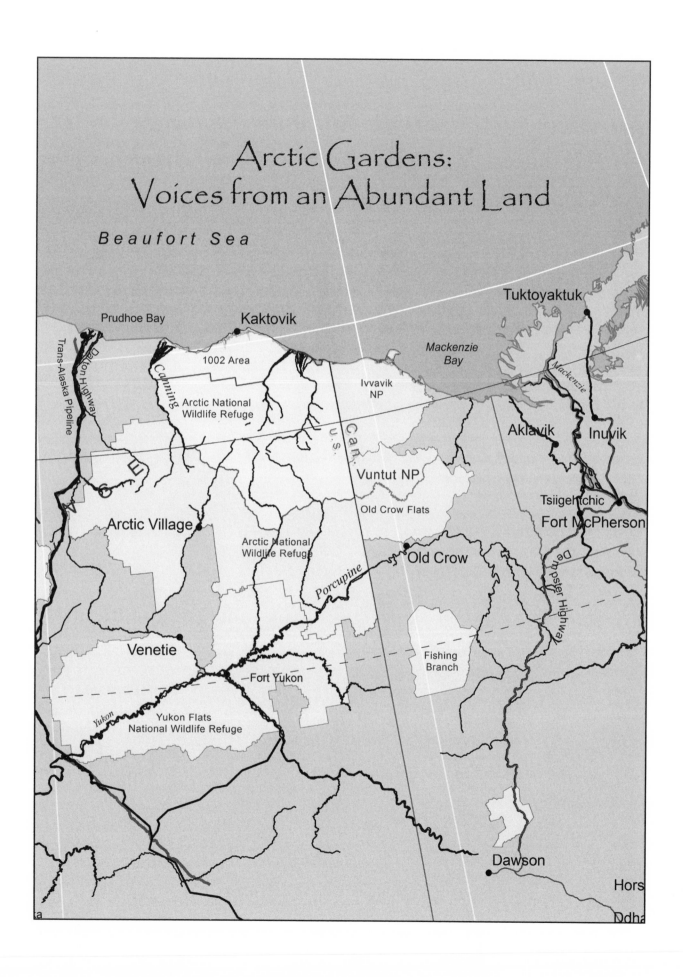

Arctic Gardens:
Voices from an Abundant Land

Beaufort Sea

Tuktoyaktuk

Prudhoe Bay   Kaktovik

Mackenzie Bay

1002 Area

Arctic National
Wildlife Refuge

Ivvavik
NP

Aklavik   Inuvik

Vuntut NP

Old Crow Flats

Tsiigehtchic

Fort McPherson

Arctic Village

Arctic National
Wildlife Refuge

Old Crow

Porcupine

Venetie

Fishing
Branch

Fort Yukon

Yukon   Yukon Flats
National Wildlife Refuge

Dawson

Hors

Ddha

Chapter One
Beyond the Northern Divide

In North America there are three Continental Divides. We are familiar with two of them: the chain of mountains, the Rockies and their outliers, that separate the waters flowing eastward toward the Atlantic Ocean or westward to the Pacific; and the Appalachian chain which divides the Atlantic-flowing rivers from the ones flowing into the Gulf of Mexico. Few know about the other divide that sends its waters northward into the Arctic Ocean, which also defines our hemisphere. This chapter will describe the geology, the ecology, the human cultures, and the recent history of this land of northern-flowing rivers, as well as the South Slope of the mighty Brooks Range, an important part of the land area above the Arctic Circle of our region, which stretches from the Kukpuk River at Point Hope in the west to the Mackenzie River on the east.

The Brooks Range was created by tectonic movements and other geologic forces that are not as well understood as are the forces that created mountains more accessible to academic geologists. The geologic forces not only created peaks and crests and rocky slopes, but also flat areas of importance to the caribou and millions of migratory waterfowl. Meanwhile, offshore a bit, other forces created what is called the "Barrow Arch," a rich, oil-bearing formation as well as an environmental attraction to whales that come close to the shore during their annual migration. In between the shoreline and the mountains is the vast tundra, daunting to humans, but ecologically rich.

Arctic Refuge coastal plain with Beaufort Sea 20 miles distant, principal calving grounds of the Porcupine Caribou Herd

Does anyone live up there today? Many of us might know that Eskimo or Inuit people do. Some of us might know that Indian people do as well. What we might not know is that the ancestors of these Native Americans or First Nations people were the first residents of all of the Americas, North and South.

Archeologists have found that the ancestors of the modern Indians such as the Gwich'in tribe may have been in the Arctic country as early as about 15,000 years ago, migrants across the Bering Strait from Russia. This migration is generally agreed upon by the scientific community, although disputed by traditional Gwich'ins, who assert that they have lived in this place forever.

In either case, these people were in every sense of the word pioneers, following as closely as humanly feasible the retreating glaciers of the last ice age or else following the strip of un-glaciated land along the Pacific Ocean. Some of the earliest evidence comes from near the Porcupine River community of Old Crow, Yukon. These people in all likelihood came up the mighty Yukon River from the Pacific several hundred miles and thence up the Porcupine another 300 miles to the well-known archeological site of Bluefish Caves.

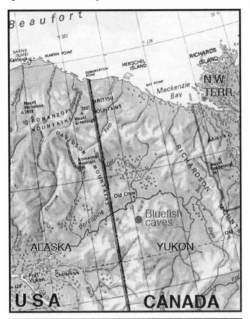

Bluefish Caves- courtesy of www.andaman.org

From this time on, people lived sporadically in ice-limited parts of Alaska and adjacent Canada. They left behind only a few clues of their lives. But we know from geologic studies that the door from Russia to Alaska slammed shut by 12,000 years ago. The climate was warming, glaciers were melting, and oceans were rising. The Bering Strait land bridge was flooded, and what scientists call *Beringia* ceased to exist.

Thus, whoever was in the Arctic of Alaska and Canada and indeed in all the Americas at that time were the only ancestors of all later Indians and Eskimo people. Nobody else could have gotten here until much later (the last one or two thousand years) when the technology of boat travel began. Both before and for the next 7,000 years (12,000 to 5,000 years ago), the people of the Alaskan and the adjacent Canadian Arctic had no access to the frozen coastal environments and were limited to the inland areas.

In any case, people's adaptation to coastal environments resembling the modern-day Eskimo of our region was not seen until about 5,000 years ago. It is likely that coastal areas in the Arctic were not glacier-free until then. Thus the hunting of sea mammals such as the seal, the walrus and even the whale probably began about that time or somewhat later.

To me as an anthropologist, the Eskimo Inuit and Indian people of the North American Arctic are some of the most amazing and interesting in the Americas. Their story is indeed one of high risk and high reward. The risks are obvious. Mainly, they face some of the most extreme climates anywhere in the world. Indeed, humans did not develop the technology to live in these climes until perhaps 25,000 years ago.

Periodic glacial advances and retreats had resisted human adaptations for more than a million years after our ancient ancestors first walked the earth. Our existence as humans began four to five million years ago in the permissive climes of the tropics as the

Breaks in the ice called "leads," and a bowhead whale
-courtesy of the International Whaling Commission

Eskimos, The First Whalers

It is quite possible that the ancestors to the modern Inuit of the North American Arctic were the first whalers in the world. Artifacts found in the coastal areas of northern Alaska indicate that whaling was present as early as 2500 years ago in the Alaskan/Canadian Arctic. It may have started as whaling from land (actually, ice) where the whales pass through an interconnected system of narrow cracks in the spring ice called leads. That was no doubt followed by whale hunting from sea-going canoes called umiaks, the less well-known cousin of the kayak.

With such a time depth of hunting such a charismatic animal, it is not surprising that the modern-day Inupiat and Inuvialuit peoples have at the center of their subsistence practice and indeed of their entire culture, the technology, art and even religion of whaling.

To understand the complex history of Eskimo whaling, we will flash back to 1848, when Yankee Captain Thomas Roys discovered the rich bowhead stocks in the Bering, Chukchi and Beaufort Seas of the Arctic Ocean. The population of this whale that spends its entire life in the icy waters of the far North was estimated at that time to be about 60,000 animals.

But over the next 60 years, that number dropped radically. Heavy whaling by commercial crews interested primarily in the bowhead's large yield of whale oil, caused the population to crash. By about 1910, bowhead numbers were estimated to be somewhere between a few hundred and 2,000 animals, which along with a declining world-wide market for whale products, was the most important factor in the complete shutdown of the commercial exploitation of whales around the world.

This crash was a great blow to the Inupiat, who had benefited from their involvement in commercial whaling. After the bowhead crash, they had in fact become partially dependent on imported goods they bought with the cash they earned from whaling. Thus, they chose to return to subsistence whaling, which put some food on the table, but not nearly as much as before due to the large reduction in the bowhead numbers.

Fast-forward to the late 1960's. Enter on the Arctic stage the oil industry, which provided cash wages never before known to the Inupiat. Many Inupiats invested thousands of petro-dollars in whaling boats and gear and gathered crews. But the flush of new Native whalers brought with it inexperience. The number of whales struck with harpoons but lost, soared. In the spring hunt of 1977, 111 strikes were made, but only 29 whales were killed and landed. This meant many whales were killed or gravely wounded, but not caught. This resulted in the International Whaling Commission halting even this subsistence hunting of the bowhead in 1978.

Today, the Inupiats are whaling again, having over the years successfully proven through their own scientific research that bowhead numbers were around 10,000. Their quota, all used for subsistence, is high enough that they can essentially take as many whales as they need. No more are large numbers of whales lost, as the quota is for whales struck. If you strike one and lose it, it still counts. Stay tuned as the evolution of Inupiat subsistence whaling continues.

For further information on Eskimo whaling, see the web sites of the International Whaling Commission and the Alaska Eskimo Whaling Commission: www.iwcoffice.org and www.uark.edu/misc/jcdixon/Historic_Whaling/AEWC.htm.

**The skin-covered umiak,
big brother of the kayak**

genus *Ardipithecus*. Perhaps a million years ago we spread to temperate areas with the appearance of *Homo erectus*, the first member of our own genus. But not until well after the appearance of own species, *Homo sapiens*, did we make the big move to the far north.

And the rewards? The cold waters of the Arctic are blessed, from the point of view of meat eaters like us humans, with teeming fish populations, and more importantly for the Eskimos, sea mammals. Can you imagine, for example, how long a 50-foot whale would last for a small group of perhaps 50 people? And unlike other climes, their land has a built-in freezer. Even though summer temperatures may reach the 70's F and even 80's F on occasion, your freezer is only three feet down in the ground in the appropriately named permafrost.

For the Indian people who concentrate in inland areas, there are very similar rewards. Besides fish, some of which come up the numerous rivers from the Pacific and Arctic Oceans, these people have an incredibly abundant resource in the caribou herds which pass by the thousands by their strategically-located villages twice a year on their annual migratory path back and forth to their birthing grounds in the coastal plain of northeast Alaska and across the North Slope. Like the Eskimos, they have the built-in freezers in the permafrost.

And how did humans solve the puzzle of Arctic living? First and foremost, you have to survive temperatures well below what your body itself can stand. This of course involves both housing and clothing. For the Eskimos, this means not only the famous igloo, frequently temporary in nature, but more importantly the sod houses; and it means the equally famous parka, perhaps of caribou; and it means staying dry in a coastal environment with the use of sealskin and other water-proof clothing and foot-wear. For the Indians, this means much the same: sod houses, and caribou and other animal clothing.

One major challenge down and at least one more to go. Especially for the Eskimos, almost all their sea mammal prey had thick skins. How do you get close enough to a whale to touch him, and once there, how do you get your weapon into the whale's vitals? First, you tether him with a barbed harpoon you have thrown by hand. But that probably doesn't

Yukon River at Fort Yukon, Alaska

kill him. Next, you tire him out by attaching a series of floats and drags, also allowing you to track him as he dives and resurfaces to get a breath of air, as you see the floats. After a few hours of this, assuming that he is more tired than you, you get close enough to apply killing jabs from a lance.

But he can swim in this bitter cold water and you can't. You employ a multi-man, sealskin and driftwood, canoe-like boat called an umiak. One man in the better-known kayak would be no match for the multi-ton beast. Each person

The Inuvialuit blanket toss in Inuvik, Northwest Territories.
When practiced on the beach, the man tossed up in the air gains enough height to see a distant whale at sea.

has his assigned task, the most important people being the boat owner and the harpooner.

Eskimo land travel was by the famous dog sleds, which could carry cargo and limited human bodies much more quickly than walking over vast distances. And if an unexpected winter storm caught you away from home, your dogs could keep you warm at night in your hastily-constructed igloo.

For the Indians, the task is perhaps a bit less daunting. Sometimes, the caribou were taken by driving a herd down vee-shaped fences and into a stockade of rocks and branches. Sometimes they were ambushed. Sometimes they were taken as they swam the rivers. Keep in mind here, that unlike for many, not all, of us in the South, hunting is not a sport here. It is exciting for sure, even more so when your food for the next six months or longer depends on it.

Herds don't always follow the same migratory paths every year, and they may not come close enough to your village next time. So you make it as easy and thus successful as possible. But when you get enough to last for the next period of time, you stop. Relax for a while. Or catch up on all the things you've neglected for weeks. Bows and arrows and spears, stone or bone-tipped, were the weapons of choice in prehistoric times. Winter travel, as with the Eskimos, was made much easier by dog sleds.

So, these were the breakthrough technologies thousands of years ago that allowed these human beings to live here. In some ways, their technologies had to be the most advanced on Earth. But once the inventions were made, these technologies made not only life in the cold climates possible, but certainly unintentionally opened up the potential over many generations to inhabit a new world-- in essence, the New World of all of North and South America.

Fifty year old Presbyterian church in Anaktuvuk Pass, Alaska, Winter and Summer

How about today? Bows and arrows and spears are replaced by high-powered rifles. Harpoons are similar to those in the past, but the killing lance is replaced by a big gun. Traditional land and water transportation systems are partly replaced by fossil-fuel-driven motor boats. Winter travel for both Indians and Eskimos has been revolutionized by snowmobiles. Sure you can't eat them if you break down or get trapped due to bad weather, but they travel at unimagined speeds for dog sled travel, extending your reach many times over. Four-wheelers have likewise revolutionized summer travel. Housing is now almost exclusively of modern, frame construction. Foundations in the permafrost present challenges, but provide a much more secure environment.

Turning now to modern Indian and Eskimo villages, we will look at the location of the communities where our interviews were done. These communities are the source of most of the voices of our book. They span an east-west distance of almost 800 miles, stretching from the Mackenzie River of Northwest Territories, Canada, to the Chukchi Sea of Alaska.

Going east to west, we begin in the Northwest Territories of Canada, where Inuvik, Fort McPherson and Tsiigechtchic (pronounced Tsi'-ge-chick) are located. All three are on or very near the mighty Mackenzie River, the largest northern-flowing river in North America. Fort McPherson and Tsiigechtchic are occupied by the Gwich'in Indians who, in the past, were heavily dependent on the Porcupine Caribou Herd. Inuvik has been built up in recent years as an oil and gas center, and serves many governmental functions as well. Both Gwich'in and the western Canadian Inuvialuit, live here in larger numbers than they did in the past. All three are connected to the south by the Dempster Highway, which was constructed in the 1960's and 70's.

Just over 100 miles to the west is the Gwich'in village of Old Crow. It is located along a Porcupine Caribou migration route, where that route crosses the Porcupine River, after which the herd was named. It is isolated in that no roads lead to it. One must either fly or take river travel -- boat or in winter snowmobile-- to reach it.

Having left the four Canadian communities and crossed the international boundary into Alaska, we traverse an imaginary but highly significant line. The line itself was drawn as an even more significant boundary in the past, as Russia claimed Alaska until its purchase by the United States. The Tsar of Russia instructed his minister to the United States

The Dalton Highway and the Trans-Alaska pipeline in Alaska

A Tale of Two Highways

Most of us are used to having roads to almost anywhere. But in the Arctic of North America before the 1970's, there were no roads, period. Zero! Air travel, mostly bush planes, boat travel in the rivers in the summer, and dog sleds in the winter were pretty much it. Not only were there few people up there, but building and maintaining paved roads on tundra with its permafrost make for an all but impossible technological challenge.

But then in the 1960's came the Alaska/Canada northern gold rush -- black gold that is. Oil. Natural gas. And billions of dollars for the taking, if you could get it back to "civilization." You see, it was almost all in the Arctic. You needed pipelines. And the construction and maintenance of pipelines requires a road.

In the summer of 1974, construction of the gravel "North Slope haul road" of Alaska was begun. It runs north for 414 miles from the end of the Elliott Highway north of Fairbanks to Deadhorse, near the oil port of Prudhoe Bay. Later it became known as the Dalton Highway, named after ace Arctic engineer James W. Dalton. This amazing feat of highway engineering, which includes a crossing of the Brooks Range and hundreds of streams, was done not in two, or even three years, but in four summer months.

The classic slogan for full-time, "twenty four and seven," was coined in English for this project, as the months between April and August see little if any dark. Rumor has it that there is such a phrase in Eskimo, given that they have lived in the "land of the midnight sun" for millennia and never stop until they succeed at certain forms of seal and other hunting, even in winters with their constant darkness. In any case, the Trans-Alaska pipeline was built along the haul road, and was completed from Prudhoe Bay to the Pacific port of Valdez in 1978.

The Dalton Highway has only two towns with services between the Yukon River crossing at the beginning and Deadhorse at the north end. Cold Foot and Wiseman are so close they may be considered sister cities. The highway averages about 200 commercial trucks per day over the year, and these trucks were the only traffic until 1995, when the public was first allowed to use the road. Needless to say, it's a rugged trip from Fairbanks to Deadhorse. Any prospective traveler would want to go to numerous web sites which describe the adventure. It seems as if there is one website for every person who has ever tried. http://en.wikipedia.org/wiki/Dalton_Highway; http://traveler.nationalgeographic.com/drives/dalton-highway/2.

The other North American Arctic road is the 736-kilometer (457 mile) Dempster highway of Yukon and Northwest Territories, Canada. This all-

The Dempster Highway snakes across the fall landscape of the Arctic of Canada

A Tale of Two Highways - cont.

gravel road even allows travel to the ocean in the winter on an ice road that begins in Inuvik and ends at the Inuvialuit coastal village of Tuktoyaktuk. It has a very different history from the haul road of Alaska, although both were built on the prospects of oil and gas exploitation along and near the Beaufort Sea of the Arctic Ocean

The Dempster was actually begun on the very front end of the oil rush in 1959, 15 years prior to the Alaskan haul road. Canada was already exploring for petroleum resources north of Inuvik, which town was under construction at that time. Construction of the Dempster began near Dawson City, Yukon, of Klondike gold-rush fame. As estimated costs for the highway escalated over the first two years, federal versus territo-rial squabbling led to slow if any progress, and the construction was abandoned in 1961. Only 115 kilometers had been completed. More oil discoveries occurred in 1968, and construction was resumed. The road all the way to Inuvik was not opened, however, until 1979, a year after the Dalton Highway was completed.

The Dempster has always been a public road. It passes through several First Nations Gwich'in communities including Fort McPherson and Tsiigehtchic. Ferries run across rivers including the mighty Mackenzie. You haven't lived until you have hurtled down this gravel road at 110 km/hour (69 mph), following a local Gwich'in driver. Fortunately it's pretty straight, so the author's white knuckles turned back to pink not too many hours after the 125-kilometer (75 mile) drive.

to enter negotiations with Secretary of State William Seward, which negotiations were said to have continued until the signing of the treaty at 4 a.m. on March 30, 1867.

As interesting as this bit of trivia may be to U.S. historians, the line itself has proven a significant annoyance to the Gwich'in, who have lived on both sides of the imaginary line for thousands of years. Different governments, different government programs, and different currencies are only a few of the problems imposed on the tribe.

In any case, three Gwich'in communities: Fort Yukon, Venetie and Arctic Village are grouped within an approximately 100-mile-diameter circle which has as its southern boundary the area of the Yukon River and as its northern boundary the southern slope of the mighty Brooks Mountain Range. As with Old Crow to the east, there are no roads leading into these communities, bearing testament to the difficulty of building modern roads on the mostly frozen tundra. Indeed, as previously described, the only two roads into the North American Arctic would never have happened but for the lure of natural resource riches.

The nearest road to these and other Alaskan Arctic communities

A cabin in Nuiqsut, Alaska, with caribou antlers and whale baleen.

is the Dalton Highway, constructed in 1974 as the so-called "North Slope haul road" from Fairbanks up to Prudhoe Bay, the farthest north center of the Alaskan oil and gas industry. It is paralleled by the Trans-Alaska pipeline.

Four Inuipiat (Alaskan Eskimo) villages round out the 11 Native communities visited by the book researchers. About 200 miles nearly due west of Arctic Village is the community of Anaktuvuk Pass, which is situated in the largest pass in the 700-mile long Brooks Range. Kaktovik is about 150 miles north of Arctic Village, and is situated on an island just a few hundred feet out in the Beaufort Sea of the Arctic Ocean. Two hundred miles west of Kaktovik is the relatively newly established community (early 1970's) of Nuiqsut, which is on the Coleville River only a few miles inland from the Beaufort Sea. Finally, and furthest west, Point Hope is located on the Chukchi Sea on the westernmost point in northwest Alaska.

While the focus of *Arctic Gardens* is on the voices of the region's Native people, others have played an important role in the region's history, and we present some of their voices as well. We have interviewed some of them in Alaskan communities such as Fairbanks as well as when they have visited the Lower 48. They include a bush pilot, a wilderness guide, an environmental activist working to protect the Arctic National Wildlife Refuge from oil drilling, a biologist and various others who have a close relationship with the region. In addition, to gain perspective on the issue of global climate change, which is affecting the region more than any other part of the world,

A grizzly contemplates another meal

**The Arctic in the fall —courtesy of the
Gwich'in Steering Committee**

we have interviewed Alaskan and other leading scientists on that subject. Their interviews, as explained in the Preface, appear in Chapter Five, which is only devoted to that subject.

The physical beauty and ecological worth of the Arctic Gardens region is incredible. From the Mackenzie River and its delta to the Chukchi Sea 800 miles to the west, this sprawling and rugged region contains high elevation mountains such as the Brooks Range, which rises from the sea level of the coastal plain to glaciated peaks like Mount Chamberlain that exceed 9,000 feet in elevation. From the Yukon River, North America's second longest, on the south to the coastal plain of the Beaufort Sea on the north, the land goes from a spruce forest near the river and on the South Slope of the Brooks Range to a treeless tundra on the North Slope.

Beginning in the early spring, a great river of a different sort begins to form, with small tributaries at first, which then combine into a broader current flowing toward the north. This is the migration of the Porcupine Herd of caribou, more than a hundred thousand of them, moving toward their calving grounds on the eastern Alaskan coastal plain and its foothills. This and other caribou herds, including the smaller Central Arctic and Lake Teshekpuk Herd, and the larger Western Arctic Herd, occupy the entire coastal plain of the region at various times of the year.

The Porcupine Herd spends its winters to the south and east of the Brooks Range in both eastern Alaska and western Canada, the location of the six Gwich'in villages we visited. All the caribou herds are hunted as well by the people of one or another of the Inupiat villages of Alaska and the Inuvialuit of Canada.

This coastal plain and the adjacent foothills and North Slope teem with many other wildlife species such as the grizzly bear, polar bear, wolf, marmot, Arctic fox, Dall sheep, bald and golden eagles and even the shaggy, buffalo-like musk ox. And in the late spring and early summer, the area is the temporary breeding and hatching grounds for many of the migratory waterfowl species that winter in the Lower 48. These include many species of ducks, geese and swans, who, like the caribou, come to the coastal plain to feed on the many high-protein grasses and other plants. Rivers and lakes have many fish species such as the Arctic grayling and the huge lake trout, and also spawning populations of perhaps the most delectable species in the region, the Arctic char.

Other biological wonders of the Arctic region include the large numbers and wide variety of sea mammals. These include the seal, the walrus, the sea lion and the most charismatic of all Arctic sea creatures, the whale. The larger of the Arctic whales is the bowhead, which can reach lengths of 60 feet. The smaller Arctic whale is the beluga, which reaches lengths of about 15 feet.

Much of the eastern half of this Alaskan Arctic region has been put in various categories of protected status as part of the Arctic National Wildlife Refuge, which covers 19.3 million

Oil well on east bank of Coleville River near Nuiqsut, Alaska

acres, an area the size of the state of South Carolina. The southern perimeter of the Arctic Refuge is bounded by the 9 million-acre Yukon Flats National Wildlife Refuge. Almost half (8 million-acres) of the Arctic Refuge is permanently protected from exploitation as Wilderness. Another half is in an intermediate status of protection, but 1.5 million acres, known as the coastal plain of the Arctic Refuge could, with Congressional approval, be opened to petroleum exploitation. There is no apparent exploitation pressure on the Yukon Flats Refuge.

Most of the area west of the Arctic Refuge on the North Slope is open to petroleum exploitation. A large area of state lands is just west of the boundary of the Arctic Refuge, and an even larger area west of that is designated as the National Petroleum Reserve - Alaska. The latter is 23 million acres. One particularly environmentally sensitive area within the Petroleum Reserve is protected, that around Teshukpuk Lake. The area south of the Brooks Range crest to the Arctic Circle is generally in protected status. East of this area is the 8.2 million-acre area of the Gates of the Arctic National Park. To its west is the 6.6 million-acre area of the Noatuk National Preserve.

On the Canadian side, one finds lower elevation mountain ranges such as the British and the Richardson Mountains. But this region is dominated by low elevation, lake-filled areas such as Old Crow Flats and by the huge delta of the Mackenzie River. This delta is a landscape created by the river's near-coastal braiding. The land here is warmed by the flowing river, which rises from the Great Slave Lake a thousand miles to the south, creating a region with a longer growing season than any other along the coastline of northern Alaska and Canada's western Arctic.

Not very far upriver are the beginnings of the tree covered taiga, much closer to the sea than in other places in the region, resulting in a transitional zone, an area containing 25,000 lakes that support a large variety of fish, waterfowl, and mammals not normally seen at these latitudes. Muskrats, beavers, black bear, and moose are particularly abundant, plus the snowshoe hare that the Gwich'in call "the little man who feeds everybody," since many predator populations are strongly dependent on hare population cycles.

Canada, in conjunction with the Inuvialuit and Vuntut Gwich'in, has established three protected areas along the U.S. border. The most northerly of these is Ivvavik National Park. The name of this park means "nursery" or "birthplace" in Eskimo. Immediately to the south is Vuntut National Park and the Old Crow Flats Special Management Area. Collectively, these three areas contain 22,830 square kilometers or about 5 million-acres of land. These three areas together protect much of the wintering grounds and migratory path of the Porcupine Caribou Herd in Canada.

From the point of view of Arctic Gardens, the common denominator that links the 11 Native communities is the exploitation of the oil, gas and perhaps in the near future, the coal of the region. The Mackenzie Delta is especially rich in natural gas, while the Alaskan villages are affected in one way or another by the region's oil and gas resources. Known coal reserves are located along the North Slope of the western portion of the Brooks Range, but have not yet been exploited. Offshore oil potential exists from Point Hope in the Chukchi Sea and along the northern perimeter of Alaska and northwest Canada in the Beaufort Sea and Arctic Ocean.

While Native people have their own rich history described briefly above, perhaps the best-known history of the entire region covered by the book is related to oil and gas exploitation. The current relationships of the people in the Arctic to each other and to the Alaskan and United States governments cannot be understood without briefly describing this

Anaktuvuk Pass, Alaska

The Caribou and You

Do you believe that your heart is half human and half caribou? The Gwich'in Indians do. We all know the importance of the heart. We have phrases in English like " the heart of the matter," and "in her heart of hearts." And our body is directed to turn all its attention to the heart if the body's existence is threatened. The body always tries to keep the "core" warm if we are threatened with freezing to death. That's why the extremities are most susceptible to frost bite. The heart, and to a lesser degree, other organs, are the last to go. Even the critically important breathing function goes first.

Bull caribou in the Arctic Refuge coastal plain, Alaska

Let's look at why the Gwich'in have chosen to elevate the status of the caribou to such a lofty place in their lives. A friend of mine from the Lower 48, Lenny Kohm, was out caribou hunting near Arctic Village, Alaska, with a Gwich'in friend, Louie John, some years back. Louie asked, "Lenny, do you care about money?" Lenny said "Sure, everybody cares about money, worries about it really. It's the way we put food on the table, buy our clothes, send our kids to college, it's how we live. Yep, money's pretty important all right." Louie said, "So, you worry about money. It's kind of like your bank, your trust fund." Lenny replied, "Yep, that's about it." Louie then said, "Lenny, you see, with us it's a little different. We worry every day about the caribou. We worry about the calving grounds up in the Refuge. It's like our bank, like our trust fund. We worry every day about it."

When I take my college students up to the Gwich'in villages, we see the importance of the caribou every day. These generous people have served us caribou many different ways. We've eaten caribou stew, caribou spaghetti, caribou jerky, caribou and eggs, and my favorite, caribou tenderloin grilled over an open fire. In fact, about six caribou are needed for every Gwich'in man, woman and child, each year.

The Gwich'in have for many thousands of years placed their base-camps along the favored migration routes of the Porcupine Caribou Herd, where the animals pass twice a year: in the spring on their way north to the calving grounds, and in the fall, on their way back to where they spend the winter.

One fall (August in the Arctic), my students and I happened to be in Old Crow, Yukon, when the caribou were about to arrive from the calving grounds. The excitement was unbelievable! The village had scouts out looking from mountain tops for the approaching herd. They could see many miles from certain vantage points and reported that some caribou were crossing the Porcupine River up above Driftwood River. So one of my friends, Peter Jossie, whose caribou camp was 60 miles up the Porcupine just above Driftwood, agreed to take me and one of my students hunting. We were told we could watch but couldn't shoot.

From his camp, a couple of small cabins along the Porcupine River, we saw a small group of about five to seven caribou swimming the river. We almost fell flat of our faces as we raced down to his boat at the river's edge. Unfortunately, we were a few seconds late, and just before we could get in range, they had exited the other side of the river and melted into the willows. Going back to Old Crow the next morning, my student and I heard from Peter endless stories about every mile of caribou hunts past, when luck was with him, or not.

Because the caribou have half a human heart, they allow the humans to take them. But the people have obligations as well. They must be careful the way they butcher the caribou and the way they prepare it for eating. It's a matter of thanks. It's a matter of respect.

Protecting the Porcupine Herd's calving grounds is another important thing the people do as their part of the bargain. The Gwich'in village leaders from Alaska and Canada go every year to Washington, D.C., and other places in the Lower 48 where they can petition US leaders to help them protect their heart. They find it incomprehensible that someone could care more about profits than a people's very lifeblood.

50-year history. Canada has its own history of dealing with the Yukon and Northwest Territories First Nations people and the petroleum resources in their homeland. Since fossil fuel resource exploitation is indeed at the heart of those dealings in both countries, the Canadian time period covers about the same 50-year span.

In 1953, a fateful event took place in Alaska, on the Kenai Peninsula more than 800 miles to the south of the Arctic region. A group of California investors filed a large number of oil leases at the instigation of President Eisenhower's Secretary of Interior Douglas (Giveaway) McKay, who decided the leases should go for 25 cents an acre.

Eventually, some oil was found on the peninsula, but the larger importance of this event was to set in motion an oil-leasing frenzy that reached, finally, the North Slope of Alaska. This resulted, 15 years later, in the Atlantic Richfield and Humble Oil fields (1968) of Prudhoe Bay and later the Trans-Alaska pipeline.

As a further result of the oil frenzy, two major acts of Congress were passed which are directly relevant to this book. The Alaska Native Claims Settlement Act, Public Law 92-203, was passed in 1971 to finally quiet claims made by one Alaska Native group or another to all 366 million acres of Alaska. While these Alaska Natives got about 44 million acres ceded to them, the remaining roughly 90% of Alaska was then firmly in private, state, and federal hands. Also, the act allowed Alaska Natives to form corporations which would deal with other corporations to exploit the natural resources of the region (www.alaskool.org/projects/ancsa/ancsaact.htm).

The second act was the Alaska National Interest Lands Conservation Act passed in 1980 at the end of the Carter Administration (Public Law 96-487, Dec. 2, 1980). This act and subsequent lawsuits had far-reaching consequences for Alaska Natives. It codified their access, along with that of all other Alaskans, to hunt and fish for subsistence purposes on state and private lands. On federal lands only rural residents of the state, including Alaska Natives, have these privileges. But more important on a grander scale was the area protected at one level or another by the act. It set aside about 80 million acres of refuge land amounting to 22% of the state, of which about 27 million acres were designated as Wilderness. See http://www.mapcruzin.com/arctic_refuge/timeline.html

The Arctic National Wildlife Refuge briefly described above was established by this act. But while much of the 19 million-acre Refuge is protected as Wilderness, a portion called the 1002 area (so numbered in the act), containing about 1.5 million acres, was given marginal protection at best. It was understood to have some potentially commercially significant quantities of oil and gas, and the act stipulated that the Interior Department conduct a study of the petroleum potential as well as of the ecological importance of the land.

This area, also called the coastal plain of the Arctic National Wildlife Refuge, or by a depersonalizing abbreviation, ANWR, has long been the area preferred by the Porcupine Caribou Herd for birthing purposes. It provides the ideal conditions of highly nutritious foods, good vision of predators such as bears and wolves on the flat tundra, and ocean breezes that provide some relief for the caribou, especially the calves, from mosquitoes and other debilitating insects. The Interior Department study of the Refuge coastal plain found that up to a 40% reduction in herd size could be expected if oil exploitation were carried out (http://library.fws.gov/pubs7/ANWR_coastal_LEIS.pdf) This obviously could be devastating to the Native people who depend so much on these caribou.

The Canadian side of the border has a somewhat similar history. In the 1970's, Thomas R. Berger, a well-known and respected Canadian judge from British Columbia who wrote the

Foreword for *Arctic Gardens*, was commissioned by the federal government to study the potential for a pipeline to be built across the northern part of Alaska, the Yukon and Northwest Territories and down the Mackenzie River as a means of getting petroleum resources to southern Canada. He conducted the study and published it as a government book, *Northern Frontier, Northern Homeland: The Report of the Mackenzie Valley Pipeline Inquiry* (1977). It has sold more copies than any other Canadian government book.

Peter Jossie's caribou camp, Porcupine River, Yukon

The results of Berger's study have had many far-reaching and lasting consequences. Berger concluded that the coastal route was not feasible, and that any pipeline project should not be pursued until land settlement agreements had been concluded with the Inuvialuit and the Gwich'in. Those agreements have since been concluded, an example being the Vuntut Gwich'in First Nation Final Agreement of 1995. http://www.oldcrow.ca/vgfnfa/index.htm

The Vuntut Gwich'in are centered on the Yukon community of Old Crow, one of the communities we researched. The result was a favorable one for the Vuntut Gwich'in. They received title to about 60% of their vast original territory, and a say in managing the remainder. They received a substantial cash settlement as well, which has allowed them to invest in an airline (Air North) and in stocks as well as housing and other infrastructure improvements for the community. In addition, a national park, the afore-mentioned Vuntut National Park, as well as the Old Crow Flats Special Use Area, were also established by the agreement. Many in Canada and beyond see this agreement as a model of government and First Nation cooperation. The Ivvavik National Park was another Berger recommendation, as was the 1987 agreement between the United States and Canada to protect the calving grounds of the Porcupine Caribou Herd.

In Alaska, there is talk of more controversial petroleum extraction activity. Besides the ever-present proposal in Congress to drill in the coastal plain of the Arctic Refuge, there is additional pressure to open up more areas to drilling both on and offshore. The petroleum industry is striving on land to open up segments of the National Petroleum Reserve Alaska, an area stretching west from the existing Prudhoe Bay and Alpine fields. This will involve crossing the Coleville River, the largest on the North Slope. Attempts by the George W. Bush administration to open up an environmentally sensitive part of the NPRA around Teshekpuk Lake were recently thwarted by a legal case brought by local Alaskan Native people. Pressure was also brought by ex-Governor Sarah Palin to build a natural gas pipeline parallel to the oil pipeline to take gas to southern Alaska.

In April of 2009, a federal appeals court, at the urging of Native Alaskan and environmental groups, ordered a full environmental review of a Bush administration plan to lease more than 78 million acres in the Chukchi, Bering, and Beaufort Seas to Shell Oil. As we go to press in late May, 2010, with the book, one of the most immediate threats of expanding offshore drilling in the U. S. in light of BP's April 20, 2010, disastrous oil spill in the Gulf of Mexico is Shell's plan for exploratory drilling in the Chukchi Sea off Barrow, Alaska. Despite the spill and a supposed moratorium on new permits announced by President Obama himself, which has already been broken numerous times since the spill, the Shell contract will apparently be allowed to proceed as planned in the dangerous, icy waters of the Chukchi as early July. No doubt, a spill in these waters-- not as deep as the Gulf spill but in even colder conditions-- would itself be a disaster in so many ways.

Further, Native Alaskan groups, for example the Inupiat at Anaktuvuk Pass, have strongly opposed the opening of coal mines on the North Slope to the west of their community, as the Western Alaska Caribou Herd on which they depend migrates through the proposed mine area.

For Canada, the Mackenzie River corridor is again being considered for a major pipeline to the south. In this case, natural gas could be provided by the 1,220-kilometer (758-mile) Mackenzie Gas Project pipeline for general use in the South and potentially in the Lower 48. In addition, the pipeline may feed the prodigious appetite of the Alberta tar sands project at Fort McMurray, Alberta, for energy to convert the viscous tar to usable petroleum. The project feasibility study was completed in 2001, and the federal Joint Review Panel approved the project in early January, 2010. Only one hurdle remains, the National Energy Board, which is expected to make a decision as early as September, 2010. If approved by the National Energy Board, project supporters will make the call or not depending on factors such as construction cost, demand, and natural gas prices. The latest oil industry estimate of the total cost of the project is $16.2 billion, but that was done in 2007, and is probably too low now. Nature Canada claims that the project will trigger the transformation of the Mackenzie Valley from largely intact wilderness to an industrial landscape. Fish, large mammals and migratory waterfowl will be impacted.   http://www.naturecanada.ca/ newsroom_feb_11_10_MGPcomments.asp

So there you have it: the *Arctic Gardens* appetizer. Hopefully it will give you some basic tools to put the main course of this meal in a useful context. May the Voices be heard!

Our future is what we are fighting for, for the right to be alive. I want to look my great grandkids in the eye and know that I have done a good job, know that they will continue to be Gwich'in, that the calving grounds are protected, and that our life as a people continues for thousands of years more.
Darius Elias, 2007

Chapter Two
Caribou Nation

The Gwich'in people, some 8,000 of them, who spread out over thousands of square miles on either side of the U.S. and Canadian border, are literally the "People of the Caribou." Their 15 villages are strategically placed along the migratory routes of the 120,000-strong Porcupine Caribou Herd. The bulk of this chapter will be the story of the Caribou Nation as told by the Gwich'in, themselves. We have visited villages as far west as Arctic Village, Alaska, and the eastern-most Gwich'in village of Inuvic, Northwest Territories. We recorded the voices of the Gwich'in people from these two villages, and also from Tsiigehtchic and Fort McPherson in the Northwest Territories, Old Crow in the Yukon Territory (www.oldcrow.org), and Fort Yukon and Venetie in Alaska.

Above–Porcupine Caribou near Old Crow, Yukon

At right–A bull caribou in the Arctic Refuge

–courtesy of www.oldcrow.ca

Our Home: Yesterday and Today

Agnes Mitchell (left) and **Alestine Andre** grew up in and around Tsiigehtchic, North-west Territories, with their parents before going off to residential school. Alestine works for the Gwich'in Cultural and Social Institute in Tsiigehtchic and hosted our visit to the village. Agnes discusses their earlier lives with Alestine while vacationing from southern Canada. The two women were preparing to go downriver to their fish camp for their annual getaway. http://www.maplandia.com/canada/northwest-territories/inuvik-region/tsiigehtchic/

Alestine: I was born January the 11,th 1951, in Aklavik, Northwest Territories, Canada. Tsiigehtchic is mostly Gwich'in that is situated on the Mackenzie River at the confluence situated right where the Arctic Red River flows into the Mackenzie River, and there is about 100 people living here. We have a school with maybe 30 or 40 children, we have a Northern store, we have a band office, charter digital community government which consists of the charter that provides service to everyone in the community.

It is a nice little picturesque community with a lot of history to it that we are trying to document. There is the Roman Catholic Church, which is the faith that is in the community, but not very many show up at church; maybe one to five people show up. We have a health center and the Gwich'in Social and Cultural Institute is situated here in the community.

My family is from the land in this area, and my parents, Hiacinth and Eliza, lived on the land year-round during the times that they were both alive. They traveled in the winter months to areas where there was good places to hunt and also good places to fish, but also good places to trap. They would be on the move every part of the season so that in the spring season, they were out trapping for muskrats and wherever places those could be gotten.

In the summertime, we spent all our summer months fishing along the Mackenzie

River. Fishing took place in preparation for the winter months and for dog food or dry fish and our consumption. In the springtime, they could hunt ducks, and that was always a good change in diet. People look forward to having geese and ducks back then, as well as today. In the fall time, they would find a place where they could fish under the ice for food for the dogs. They spent a great deal of their time on the land.

Kids on the step of the Northern store in Tsiigehtchic, Northwest Territories

I had three brothers and two sisters. Noel is the oldest in the family, and there was Cecil and my brother Robert, but he passed away. My older sister Addy and she recently passed away as well and then my younger sister, Agnes. We had other brothers and sisters too, but they all passed away before I knew them.

I remember being wrapped up in a blanket and traveling by dog team. I can't remember being cold; I think Agnes was there too so there was two of us in the sled. We were not faced forward; we were always faced backwards because when you are traveling along the trails, there was always willows that could slap you in the face.

We were very well protected and made to sit in the sled and wrapped in a blanket. I was faced backwards looking at the person handling the sled, and there were always two or three dog team sleds. Being out on the land in a tent when I was smaller, maybe six years old, is as far back as I can remember.

Agnes: We traveled from camp to camp with dog teams up around the Traviar Lake area from our camp at Tree River and going to Traviar Creek by boat. I know that there was excitement in the boat. You know how you can feel it? I always recall that we had to be quiet, we couldn't be fooling around and playing around in the boat. We always had to be sitting still, so I know that there was excitement on the boat because you can feel it and you can hear it. I don't think I was old enough to look over the sides to see what was going on.

Alestine: We were always having to somehow work with wood, not big pieces because we were only five or six years old. We were sent out one time to collect, and if we came back with an arm full, that was good. I used those pieces today to help start the fire, so I remember.

We also helped pack water; in those days they had the large pails that we packed water in. Everything was down to our size, and then we would be gathering dry willows in the springtime because those were the best willows to use when you were stitching ducks and all. We were always helping. When we went out with my grandmother or mother, we collected dunk-shaw which is rotten wood that is used for the smoking and tanning process to

The ferry crosses the Mackenzie River at Tsiigehtchic, Northwest Territories

color the hides. We had our own pack-sacks to carry, too.

At camp, we were there with my mother. Sometimes I was in my brother Cecil's sled and also my mother or grandmother. We were always with my mother or brother or dad. When we were out in the winter, we had our regular muckluks or canvas shoes. I think we all had our own snowshoes, and for blankets, we had rabbit, woven blankets and maybe a duvet of some sort of flannel which was very warm.

Agnes: We were always working, always busy, always something to do out on the land for survival. You need water constantly; so in the summer time, it's pails of water, and wintertime, there is ice that you melt to have water. I think the only time that I don't see my parents doing anything is in the evening when you settle down after supper. They have their free time. My mother is either playing cards, or my dad is making some snowshoes or skinning some kind of fur in the wintertime. I never see them laying around in the day time. They might take their nap, but that is only half an hour in the daytime.

Alestine: At five or six you do not begin cutting fish, but you spend a lot of time watching. My parents knew when we were old enough to handle an ax or a knife.

Agnes: I was mostly at home before residential school doing work with my mom. I would leave school part of the year to go out on the land with my parents, and I think I started when I was about 13 or 14 years old. I would stay home after Easter so I could go out on the land and hunt and trap beaver, hunting with my dad for ducks too. I started about that age, but I never really did go out on a trap line with him to see how he set traps or even go moose hunting with him. I don't think they thought that was a woman's work; maybe they thought she should be at home, so we did a lot of sewing at home with my mom.

Even when my dad brought home his furs, I knew how to skin a beaver and muskrat. At a young age, you learn how to skin a rabbit. I guess it is a process that you slowly catch on, but handling fur just seemed to be my dad's doing. My dad would be on the floor skinning his lynx or marten or anything like that that he would be selling. I think I caught onto that by watching. I would know what to do today if I needed to do it. In those days, you didn't see that book up there that says, "trapper's manual." We had nothing like that, and if we were going to go out setting traps, me and my mom would do that, and I would watch her. It was something that I enjoyed very much, and I guess that is why every school year, I would cut off half of the year and go on the land with parents.

Alestine: Dad was always up early so he was always gone by six. I think I would wake up around eight myself, those who woke up early were maybe allowed to go with him. By the time he got back, we would be awake, and we had to be down at the shore waiting for him to help pack the tubs of fish up. We would be helping too with scaling. The older boys or maybe one girl would go out, and he would go across the river on a calm day to get the wood. We were always packing water, scaling fish, or packing the wood.

Agnes: My dad would come back after all the fish were brought to the table, and he would start scaling. He would take all the scales off the fish. He would do that till all the fish were done, and then my mom would start cutting it from the head. So you sort of cut towards the belly on one side, and then you flip it over and do the same thing on the other side.

You can't make it too thick because it will spoil, so she is very careful about not cutting bones into the side that is going to be food. Most of the backbone bones are left on the backbone. It took practice to do that without having a dry fish that you bite into and there is bones in there. From there, you have to clean out all the guts and the eggs that is on the backbone. My mom used to dry the whole thing like that, but she would remove all the guts and eggs, and then that is attached to the meaty part and is where it is hung.

After all that is done, she would hang it on the outside stage on the skin side. You have to keep moving it and make sure it is dry. It maybe stays outside for a day or morning to night and the skin would be dry. In the evening, whatever is not dry enough is put into the smokehouse while they leave overnight.

Once they are ready to put in smoke house, it's smoked from the fire that you have in there. You are looking at about five days for one dry fish. For a good dry fish to dry, you have to look after it. You can store a whole year if you look after it.

Agnes: When we would first get there, there would be a run of herring which are small fish and those ones, we could cut up because all they used it for was dog food for winter. I guess that is where we started practicing. We would try to make it really neat to cut it, and after that, my mom would take over and look after it to smoke and dry it. Little did we know that they used it for dog food, we would get lots in just one net. I recall checking the net with my dad and we would all be sitting on the side of the boat taking out those little fish, so we had fun seeing who would get more out.

The next run would probably be white fish, and that is when my dad really went out fishing because he would have four nets. Every morning he would make his rounds checking those nets and bringing all the white fish, and my mom would be cutting them up. I always recall sitting there watching her, no matter what time of day it was, I would watch. As I got older, I tried to make dry fish out of cookitbacks which are made to be dry fish, but it is for dogs. She only cuts the good white fish. I see how good she is making hers, so I try to make mine same as hers, and there is no mess on her side of the table. I would be so careful, yet there would be fish eggs all over the place. My fish would be full of eggs and hers were just neat. That is how I got to making dry fish today, and it is not that messy.

Alestine: On Sundays after our Sunday prayers and stuff like that, we would go look for berries if the weather was nice. We would paddle up the creek, a whole bunch of us would get in these canoes. It used to be so much fun because it was getting away from the camp and get away from the work and heading up the steep hill and over to check the berries. My mother and grandmother would be with us, and my dad would stay back at camp watching smoke houses. Us kids would each have a cup and my grandmother, aunt, and mother would have these big pails. So we would have to fill these cups with blueberries and empty them into my mom's pail.

Agnes: I don't know how my parents managed, but they kept me until I was eight when I had to go off to school. I was sort of excited but being with my parents -- I sort of got used to not leaving them so it was difficult for me.

Alestine: I went off to school in 1959, and to this day, when I smell cigar, I get sick. In those days, children really respected and obeyed their parents and we just went because they said we had to go. I was really, really young. On the plane, because of the motion, I always made sure I didn't eat. I didn't even drink anything because I would be throwing it up. The co-pilot would always be smoking this big cigar that smelt and oh my God. It is also the fuel smell from the plane. I was sick all the way and always threw up because of the smell.

I always remember the different smells of the place or the people or the food because it was very different and strange. There were a lot of other kids as well, and over the years, the ones that I went to school with the first year were all together with me for the next 12 years.

It was a very regimental lifestyle, and when I talk about residential school, it's the resident part and the school part that are two separate things there. I think of the school part being more of a positive experience for me than going back to the residence, where we had the supervisors, the food, the area where we slept and all that. When we went, it was a sad time for the first few weeks, but after that, it was the same routine.

We were lucky to come back to Tsiigehtchic in June and then up river to our fish camp for the summer. Sometimes at Christmas and at Easter we would have two weeks off.

There were a lot of things happening in the residential aspect for the kids. I remember them having a swimming pool. We would always have a skating rink and things like cross country skiing.

There were two residential schools in Inuvik. I went to the one for the Roman Catholics. It had senior boys and girls, and we also had a shack out in the bush where we could go for the weekend and when it was nice, we went out in the early spring. I remember eating toast cooked on the fire, so today I like toast. Because it was Roman Catholics, there were so many religious ceremonies.

I always enjoyed learning and enjoyed reading. I always enjoyed things about the universe and outer space. Because we grew up on the land, the radio was always on, so sometimes in the summer, we heard really nice information. This one program, this kid was talking about India and their life and describing their village, and I found it so interesting. Later on, I picked up a distance-learning course, and every opportunity I got, I would pick up a course here and there. I'd go to Fairbanks and do a summer course on languages.

It was at that point that I met Julie Krookshank, a fairly established anthropologist in BC. I took a course from her. When I came back, I enrolled in some distance courses and started taking my courses. I always enjoyed math, as challenging as it was. I wasn't very good in math.

A few decades later, I was going to college and enrolled in a math class because I was doing a diploma in Business Administration and needed a math, and had to up my grades. I came face-to-face with having to smarten up and do my math.

That was the turning point, and the next thing it was a breeze. I was at top of my class and had to bring my math grade up to continue with my classes. Today I have a diploma in Business Administration and Bachelor of Arts in Anthropology and Women's Studies and an interdisciplinary Masters in Ethnobotany. I am mostly doing research work with the Gwich'in culture and language.

We are writing proposals at this time of year, so we are still doing that work. But our main focus is cultural research with language, things like place names, and stories that go along with it. Whether the places are trails, hills, campsites, cabin sites, or burial sites, we record all of that with our elders and other people that use the land.

We have been involved with this work since 1993 when the GIS was established, and that is pretty well the foundation of our work. From that we have ethno-archeology projects. This last week, I went on a river trip, and again it was related to the work that we are doing with nominating and designating either national or territorial historical sites. Those historical sites are culturally important places for the Gwich'in people, and we have places like that in Fort McPherson as well as Aklavik and Tsiigehtchic.

We had an opportunity with these archeologists who had an interest and surplus of money and wanted to make a river trip. They wanted to go to Travier Creek and it happened to be one of the two places that we were going to be working over the winter to help nominate Traviar Creek as one of two places as a historical site. We took GPS readings and lots of photographs, and we traveled with an elder who gave us maybe an hour and a half interview right on the site. It's a government program and is quite involved.

Agnes: My life today is laid back. I moved to Edmonton about three years ago and three years previous to that, I went down for college. Just one year of going back and forth, I landed a job there, so I am staying there with my family. I just don't want to do anything stressful. I have been through that, and I just want to do what I want to do. Coming back here is one of them.

It is so quiet out there [on the land], and I find that I have no worries. I don't think about anything else except what I have to do right now. I might have to check the net; I'll go check the net. After that, I know I have to make dry fish so I make dry fish, and whatnot and gather wood.

You don't have to concentrate on these things, they just naturally come to me. I might make a snack out of fish guts and eggs and throw that on the fire, and you have a snack in about three minutes. Those are the things that I really miss when I am out in Edmonton. I miss just being out on the land because you have no worries. You have the Mackenzie right there, and if you need to drink it, you drink it.

Alestine: It was always a good feeling to go out there, and we were always like one big family. For me, the weather was always nice when we were out there. The sun is always shining and the wind is always from the south. Blue skies, just an ideal place, and all the stress from the town is not there.

The Dempster Highway has brought a lot of change because the road makes it easier to travel on to go south to Whitehorse or north to Inuvik. A lot of things come on freight trucks like television and building materials and everything to do with modern homes like septic and water tanks. People get paid better wages here, so they have more, and a lot of people have trucks. Heaven knows how they are able to finance them, because some of the trucks are quite expensive. A lot of people have four wheelers and brand new skidoos.

More social challenges face us in Tsiigehtchic. Addictions come in various drugs, not only alcohol, but also other addictions like gambling and being angry and worried, or even feeling guilty. People need to really have a good look at how individuals deal with things in relation to their surroundings. It's really difficult to work on yourself, and I think that the only turnaround is internal.

Agnes: I would still like to see the buildings there in 50 years, the log buildings and maybe the creek would still be running, but I would still like for it to be used the way that it is being used today and how it was used in the past. My children were brought here to Tsiigehtchic a few times when they were smaller, and today they talk about going back. I don't know what is holding them back, but maybe they will pass it on to their children and maybe 50 years from now, it could still be the same.

A River, A Lake, and a Road

Daniel Andre is originally from Tsiigehtchic but spent much of his life at the Travaillant Lake and Tree River areas on the Mackenzie River. He currently lives in Tsiigehtchic and plans on returning to the University of Victoria to complete his bachelor's degree.

From the time I was born, I spent most of my time out at Travaillant Lake with my other siblings. I remember sledding and the lake was still open, but there was snow on the ground. Some of us slid right into the lake on our sleds. It was in October, which is very cold, and the cabin was right up on the hill. Later on, we commuted to Inuvik for residential school for eight years. Holidays were spent at the cabin on the river or lake. So, all of my upbringing besides going to residential school was out on the land hunting, fishing, and trapping, and gathering.

I am now able to go set snares for animals and go hunting for caribou and moose and bears, and butcher and skin them. I also can do wolverines, lynx, mink, fox, wolf, black bear, martin, and muskrat and beaver. Our education was concentrated mainly on surviving and using the wildlife, forestry, fishery resources, plants, and berries on the land to be comfortable and well-fed and have a good life. It was a really good life.

The mighty Mackenzie near Daniel's cabin

I just started my degree in Geography at the University of Victoria. I have been involved in a number of fishery projects and forestry and wildlife plans, land use plans, and I have been involved in some of the political bodies that are in the area such as the Gwich'in Tribal Council.

I was on the board of directors, and I was the counselor with the Gwich'in Council, the main governing council for the community of Tsiigehtchic. I return to the cabin on the Mackenzie every summer for June, July, August, September and sometimes well into October just before the weather is really cold to hunt moose and fish. I think the people in the family used the education that we got from the land and incorporated the same values, principles, and disciplines to our formal education in the Western world.

My brother Donald has almost completed his degree in Natural Resource Management at Prince George, and my sister Julie got a certificate in Business Administration Assistance and then her Business Administration diploma. I have been involved in so many projects with her and made a contribution to each because I grew up out on the bush and know of migration patterns etc. If we didn't have that initial training out on the land, I do not think we would be as productive as we are today.

Not only helping to manage the land and the wildlife as it relates to our culture and history, but just the ability to be independent and to voice would have somehow been lost if we didn't have education out on the land. My father, Gabe Andre, and my mother, Rosa Andre, were the ones that brought us up in the bush and taught us everything that we know. It was mainly a style of watching and doing as opposed to a classroom where you are sitting and listening.

I was always concentrated on being there and doing it and not reading about it. It was a lot of trial and error because our history is an oral history. It is so complex that a lot of times stories and legends as well as general practices were always repeated over and over until there came a time where we no longer needed to be told because we were doing it.

Our history is based largely on place names. There are names of a number of places on the land, around rivers, lakes, and all named for either a specific harvest spot or event that took place or different resources to be had in that area. Some places are gathering places and reproduction area for animals. Everything in our oral history is based on place names, and that holds our history.

My father learned everything that he learned from his mother and his father and before them, their mother and their father. There was no book learning. It was all practical experience out on the land: listening, doing, and watching and being told over and over.

It was so different when I was a child. My mother would make Duffle parkas; we had mukluks made out of moose skins. The bottom part of the shoe is made out of moose hide and the upper part is made out of canvas. My mother would make us beaver skin or duffle mitts trimmed with beaver fur. Our duffle parkas had wolverine fur on the bottom portion and around the hood to shield our face. She sewed the shoes and mitts by hand and she sewed the parka with a sewing machine, but she put all the fur trimming on by hand.

It used to take us three days to the cabin from Tree River to Travaillant Lake which is 35 miles northeast of Tree River. We would leave early in the morning and we would camp out the first night, take camp down early the next morning, and set another camp early that evening. The next morning we would leave again, and we would get to our destination by the third day. Now it takes us three hours to get there by skidoo.

Before, all the wood was chopped by ax; now we do it all by chainsaw. Long ago people had to track along the river to get to their destination up river because they had to go against the current. Now we have outboard motors. Where it used to take them days, it takes us hours once again. There are grass cutters, and willow cutters, and people that live in town have electricity, running water, and power.

Out in the bush there is no running water, no power, no heat, and you have to cut the wood and start the fire to heat up the cabin or even cook outside. For lights, they had kerosene lamps and candles. Now we have generators and gas lamps so the transition from being a child to now was experience in the fullest way possible. We had nothing when we were kids, and it shows today because we go out in the bush by ourselves and are gone for a week or sometimes longer. We come back every time. Whereas, a lot of other people, it's difficult for them to go out because they want the comforts of home that are in town and the easy life.

To us, since we grew up with that life, it's not a hard life; it is just normal. We know what to expect and know what is expected of us. It's a part of our daily routine. A lot of other people would be annoyed to the fact that they have to carry water for their cooking, cleaning, and washing. And same with wood because you have to heat water to do the dishes, to wash hair or whatever. In town, you can just turn on the hot water tap and it's there.

Gabe was a very good and patient teacher. He hardly scolded us, and I think the tradition in our culture is trying not to beat the child's spirit down too much so that they would lose the interest and motivation to learn. We were allowed to make mistakes, and we would learn from them and just keep going.

I went up to Inuvik from the time that I was six until I was 14. We all left at the same time, and we all came back at the same time. We left on the same plane and came back on the same plane, so when we were leaving the first time, it was kind of interesting to me because I was only six. I missed my parents terribly, and it was a really hard adjustment to go through.

They came and picked us up at the lake. My parents knew that they were coming but we didn't. I learned how to read and write. By the time I got into grade three and four, I noticed that people were paying more attention to the marks and stuff. I started getting really good marks. I was usually in the top five in my class.

I figured that a degree in Geography would be best because it is a broader-based discipline. It is not just centered on fish or caribou or the weather. It is all the environment and the people and the wildlife. It is a holistic approach to managing the environment, which is exactly what the Gwich'in people would teach. I want to complete my degree at the University of Victoria because it has one of the best geography departments in the country.

I know that it will help me communicate what I know about traditional and environmental knowledge as well as traditional historical knowledge. I want to incorporate what I know into management systems using the Western way of explaining it. A lot of holders of traditional knowledge are not able to communicate what they know as effectively as if they had a better knowledge of a Western way.

I hope to make more contributions to more projects to help us essentially manage our wildlife, land, air, and environment so it will be cleaner. My goal is to teach the youth about what is available on the land and how much enjoyment, nutrition and exercise they can get by just going out there and harvesting all the wildlife and plants.

Tsiigehtchic is still one of the communities that utilize the resources of the land to a great extent. They harvest caribou, which is our main source of meat throughout the winter. People always go moose hunting every September and harvest moose. I think we get about five to 10 moose per fall for the community. We must harvest at least 150 to 200

Daniel along the Mackenzie River—staying warm and contemplating supper

caribou a year for the whole village.

In an average year, I would harvest at least four to five hundred fish and make dry fish out of 300 of those fish -- that is just me. There is then my mother and my sister who also harvest fish, not as much as myself, but there are other members of the community who do make dry fish, and they harvest at least 200-300 each. If you look in the results of the harvest study, there are numbers in there indicating how much fish was harvested each year in this community, and it is in the thousands per year.

We start fishing in June, July, August, September, and then we are still fishing in October. Then after the ice freezes, there is a fishery that happens on the Mackenzie. We harvest fish with nets under the ice in November when there is another run. Each family harvests at least 100 fish. It depends on their needs, like if they have dogs or relatives they need to feed.

And it appears to be sustainable because they have been harvesting to that extent for years and the populations don't seem to be affected. We also have lake-bound populations that live in the Travaillant Lake area. There are a whole bunch of lakes connected to Travaillant Lake that are habitats for various species of fish that are within that system, so they do not come to the river; they stay in that system.

In the wintertime when we are hunting and trapping, with the caribou populations we always take just what we need and not over harvest, as well as the moose populations. We only get one moose in the fall and that is enough until winter, and then if we are lucky enough to get another one in February or March, we get one then as well. When we harvest fish, we make sure we just harvest enough for our dogs, so the fish populations reproduce at a fairly successful rate.

In the winter when we are trapping, it is common practice for one family that is using a certain area on the land to move around on that area from year to year. From year to year, we would move our trap line around a bit so we wouldn't over-harvest in a certain area. We have done that before management plans ever came to be.

Today, I like the fact that we do have access to all those resources because we drive two hours on the Dempster, and you can hunt caribou, or you can drive five hours to the Travaillant Lake area and you can hunt caribou, or you can go across river to the Cardinal Lake area and you can hunt caribou there. You can hunt moose and you can set up fish camp and catch fish. There are berries that people pick if they choose and medicines that can be harvested and a bush tea that is a favorite around here. And, we have clean water.

The children, as of today, have passed from a living and doing culture to a reading, writing, and listening in a classroom culture. They're not spending as much time on the land as we did; therefore, when they do go out there, they do not have as much of an appreciation of their environment and what it could provide for them because everything is just so easy in town, and they can go to the store for everything.

The Gwich'in have survived in such a harsh environment, and it gives you a sense of pride and identity to be able to say that this is who I am, this is where I come from. Going to the university is very different because a lot of the people there can't do half of the things that I can do. It is frustrating when you have to make a transition just to prove to the Western world that you know something about the environment and that you can make a significant contribution to managing it.

But, if I go off to school, I will come back to harvest like I have done now. I went to the University of Victoria, and I am back for the summer to go fishing and then I will go back to school. **But once I complete my degree, I am not sure what I will be doing. I will** always be involved in the management plans and so forth, because I grew up on the land and I care for it so much. I will always be in touch with the people that are making the decisions for that land.

The Fisherman

Noel Andre is a 77-year-old Gwich'in fisherman who has lived in Tsiigehtchic all his life. We caught up with Noel on the banks of the Mackenzie River near Tsiigehtchic beside a plywood smokehouse filled with dry fish. We discussed commercial fishing today and fishing for his family and his dogs in the past. http://www.maplandia.com/canada/northwest-territories/inuvik-region/tsiigehtchic/

I was raised up working in the bush and on the river. I was trained by my parents so that I could work for myself later on, and that is what I am doing now. I fish and go trapping but now it's so hard for me to walk around. I have my own children that work for me to get my meat.

Every summer, I have been going fishing and making dry fish. I lost my wife a year and a half ago, and since then, my daughter took over and is helping me. We make dry fish, and we sell those; we have a commercial license and sell our dry fish. It's pretty hard to have dry fish year round when a big company buys you out. We already had a contract to trap 150 fish and we got that in five days. They pay us $10 a fish.

This is not the best time to fish, but what we got was white fish, which we get from a lake. It is about 20 miles up Mackenzie River and it doesn't really run like it used to. The most we got was thirty-something white fish. You have to be up early in the morning because it costs if you sleep too long. Best thing to do is get up way early in the morning. You get a lot of dead fish that you have to throw away because their skin gets kind of soft. If you just leave them on the shore, the eagles, ravens, and foxes will get them.

You don't really waste the fish, so you bring a lot of the fish that you catch to the camp and start working on them. You split it open and away you go. You hang it up on the outside stage on poles for a day. Well not a whole day, it depends on wind and sun. You bring it into the smokehouse, which nowadays we use tarp and plywood and nails to make a smokehouse. You bring the dry fish into the smokehouse, and then in three days, it should be good to eat. Coney fishing starts early in June, and then it's pretty hard to make dry fish. What we do is make strips out of it and people like that, too. In July, white fish starts coming but August is when we have a lot. If you are a good dry fish maker, you can make close to 100 fish a day and then you sell for 15 bucks each. If you do not sell it, just use it.

In the olden days, before fish nets came around, people made them out of some kind of bark. You didn't have the net in the water all of the time. So after that, nets came around, and then they made their own nets with cotton. That is the way they used to get their fish and now we have plastic nets, and they last for years. When they used to use bark to make net, in the fall time, they had to throw it away.

There used to be people all around the shore, somebody staying there because their fish camp was there. You can set net any place and get a fish because there are lots of fish all along the Mackenzie and right through the delta. Some people went long ways to get fish if they were on the Delta. It is a good fishing spot, and people used to go there just to fish and they would come back with 50 barrels of dry fish. They would use that for themselves and dogs in winter.

I got married in 1954. I had my own dogs; about five dogs is good until later on when my wife and I would go trapping in the bush. We needed some more dogs, so we raised up more. We had nine dogs, I had five and my wife had four. We used two teams for trapping and hunting. Until skidoos came around in 1970's, people still had their dogs.

Nowadays, there is no more dogs, just pet dogs. We fish and hunt moose. Back then, we would leave the house and just start walking. We would walk all day; sometimes you would come back 10 o'clock at night, and you have been walking for 14 or 15 hours. The next morning, you would do the same thing. You were lucky if you got a moose. If there was a lot of moose around, then it was good, but that is if you are lucky.

We traveled 40 miles a day easy, and that is with dogs. You would have an empty load going into town. You would have a bag of clothes, dog food and a blanket. On the way back home, you have bags of groceries and then you have a load. Sometimes, you had to walk ahead of your dogs.

Lots of times we would travel in cold weather and when I say cold, I mean about 60

Mackenzie River where Noel Andre catches many of his fish

below. There were people always living here and there. Seems like people always used the same roads all of the time. They would contact each other when they left, and figure out where they were going to stay.

There is some stories of hard times, sad stories, but that was the way it was before I was born. People would die of starvation because there was just nothing. When I was born, they were already lots of canned meat.

I eat everything, and that is the way I was raised. You eat whatever is put on the table, and it is usually everything like rabbit, moose, caribou, and fish.

Nowadays, everything is in the store, and kids are just raised up on chips and pops. Two years back, I heard about cows being shot up with things that would make them grow up big and fat because they wanted more fat. They eat too much junk food.

There is lots of things that people used to do long time ago, and people don't even realize it. The language is dying off slowly, but the bush is still being taught. Some of them go to school, pass grade 12 and go to university, and then they finish and get a good job.

I like Tsiigehtchic because it is free and it costs me nothing to stay here. I am used to it and I enjoy it. It is not a real hard project nowadays because you got truck, and boat, and fish table.

The Leader

Darius Elias, a Gwich'in Native, was born and raised in Old Crow, Yukon. He spent much of his youth hunting, fishing and learning traditional ways on the land with his grandmother. At 13, he moved to Whitehorse for school. After earning Renewable Resources and Aboriginal Businesses Management diplomas, he spent nine years as a warden for Vuntut National Park. Today, he is a Member of the Yukon Legislative Assembly and raises four children with his wife Tina. He is pictured here with his son, Johnny. http://www.maplandia.com/canada/yukon-territory/yukon/old-crow/ http://www.maplandia.com/canada/yukon-territory/yukon/whitehorse/

I have tried to be articulate in so many different ways to so many different crowds at so many different levels, from elementary school to the Parliament of Canada. So I'm just gonna start by telling a story. I'm in Crow Flats in the spring when the snow is melting. I'm with my Grandmother Mary Kassi, she's passed on now, and I've been here since March. It's June now and we've harvested our caribou. She is explaining to me how important the caribou are to us Gwich'in. As I'm playing around in our traditional area she says, "Sonny, you gotta go to school. You can't come here next year."

I remember the pain I was going through when she told me that. I thought about it all year until March of the next year. I couldn't go because I had to go to school. She sat down and told to me that I will lead someday, and that I have to learn the Western society. "You have to learn the other way," she said, "so you can talk like they talk and so you can write like they write."

I know now why she did that. I know how important it is now that she made the decision to stop me from going to Crow Flats. It was for the caribou. It's for our culture. It's for our very survival. So we were packing up dry meat getting ready to go, and I didn't see Crow Flats again for 10 years.

That's when the journey began for me. I grew up in a very traditional way. I spent the first years of school from September to February with my mother in Old Crow and Whitehorse because she traveled around a lot. Come March, I came to Old Crow to live with my grandmother and my uncles.

Even today, there is no road access to Old Crow. The closest road is the Dempster Highway, 170 kilometers to the south of us. We are a fly-in community of about 301 people on a hot day in June. A jug of milk cost $12, a loaf of bread costs five bucks, and a pound of butter costs about $6.75. We all live in small log cabins and live off the land.

At our winter camp, my grandmother and I trapped muskrats that lived under the snow. We lived in an eight-by-ten wall tent. We gathered firewood, and we slept on the ground when it was 40 below outside. I didn't think of it as hardship, it was just the way it was.

When I was raised, I was on the tail end of the use of dog teams. I still remember going to Crow Flats by dog team before snow machines were in heavy use. I was taught land-based skills by my uncles. They taught me how to read and talk to the wildlife, the water and the weather.

My grandmother lived out on the land the majority of her life. I moved around with her in the springtime from Happy Lake to Zelma Lake. She had so much trust in her dog team. I was six or seven years old and she would talk to the dog in Gwich'in, and the dog would take off and take me over five frozen lakes and stop at the spring camp. She would come behind. I remember sitting in the middle of a big white lake with a bunch of clanging pots and pans with no one in sight. I look back on it now, and it is quite an incredible life I have.

When I was 11 or 12 years old, I was allowed to hunt because I always wanted to, but my family had strict rules for young guys. Finally one fall -- my birthday is in March -- I came up to Old Crow and my grandmother took me aside while cooking bannock in late August. She said, "You can go caribou hunting now." I remember not being able to sleep all night.

The next morning, my uncles got ready, we had something to eat and drink, and we started walking. That walk was so hard because there was no road to Crow Mountain. I couldn't wait to get to the mountain. Just before we got to the fireplace, my uncle Harvey said, "Look, right there, in the trees!" There was a bull caribou standing there. My heart was pounding and I was shaking, and I remember trying to load that .30-.30. He must have seen the look on my face because he said, "Calm, calm," as he was trying to calm me down. And that caribou gave himself to me. He stopped, looked at me and he turned sideways. He gave himself to me.

I was about 50 yards away. I was so proud. You couldn't wipe the smile off my face. My uncle said, "Well, you cut it up." So I cut it up the way I watched him do it a thousand times. I made a few wrong cuts. It took me a little longer. I was so proud coming down the mountain packing it. When I got down, my grandmother said, "You gotta give it all away." I had to go around and give a piece to everyone and tell them it was my first one. Everyone was so happy and my grandmother had a big supper at the house. People were coming by at all hours eating soup and meat.

In terms of formal education, I went to college for four years for a Business diploma. Then I went to get my pilot's license and I came home for the spring, and my grandmother got wind of this; I will never forget that tongue-lashing. She said, "What are you doing? Don't you remember what I told you? What are you doing trying to go around flying planes? You get back to school and learn something about looking after the land."

In 1995, I finished a Business degree and then a Natural Resources program in Whitehorse in 1998. When I came back to Old Crow, I came back with a family.

As a warden, I got to walk a lot of places and see things that haven't been seen for a long time, like caribou fences. I took elders up there that haven't been there in years, and they broke down emotionally. They told us everything. Like flowers in the springtime, they just bloomed.

There are seven known fences, and I have been to all of them. Even through the years

Darius (far right) talks to Appalachian State class members in Old Crow

of archeology focusing on two or three fences, we found a lot of interesting data there. I listened to a tape of Lazarus Charlie saying that he heard through his great-grandfather that the Thomas Creek fence went all the way to the Firth River. I looked for evidence for this every time. I went there and one day, I found it. Lance Nukon, my young apprentice, and I got chills up our backs.

I followed the wing of the fence, and you could barely see cut stumps under a foot of moss and between the tussocks. I think I walked 17 kilometers that day. The fences were made of all natural materials: trees, willows, and rocks. Lots of the trees were cut and lots were built tripod style. They used a lot of the natural slope. It was a pretty labor-intensive harvesting technology that ended just before the repeater rifle came out which began being traded up on Herschel Island.

There were strict rules when the caribou fence was used. It was taken down in the spring migration and used during the fall migrations unless there were times of hunger. Basically it looked like an airplane if you look at one from the top. That was the outline of it. Families would harvest the caribou there until they had enough. There were caches of meat on the sides, and they were impenetrable to grizzly bears or wolverines. At the corral, right at the tip, the harvesting took place. Once the harvesting happened, every bit of blood was removed because it was disrespectful for the next caribou to smell their own blood.

I tried to strike a balance between our traditional lifestyles and how it is out in the world. So now I'm a politician. We are the richest people because we are still able to live off the land, and there can be no monetary value put on that. I fight for that. I have always said that all our greatest resource is our land, water, wildlife, language, and our culture. But I know it is very important to have a balance between the traditional lifestyle and the knowledge of a vast number of things.

In the same fashion that I have learned, I will pass on the lessons to Johnny and Bohdi, my sons; and Rachael and Heather, my daughters. I explain the importance of the caribou. Many of our people have said that our hearts and chests are half caribou and half Gwich'in. We are part of one another. Our blood flows through each other. I started eating caribou when I was in my mother's womb. That's where it starts. It's a part of our structure. It's a part of our biology.

I explain to the rest of our country the importance of community. We are one big family really. Everyone looks after each other; everybody lends a helping hand. We come together, we eat together, work together and try to make the community a better place to live. The community is very close-knit. So when babies are born, we celebrate together. When people die, we mourn together.

Using a traditional education in a manner that is complementary to Western society is especially important today. I find myself addressing global warming and how these changes affect traditional living. I find myself talking about this steadily.

Some elders have told me that mother earth is trying to cleanse herself from the destruction that humans have caused. It is like the immune system has kicked in. I have seen it around here, and it is just as simple as walking on the clear ice. About 12 years ago, I was walking with an elder, Irwin Linklater. He stuck a stick down a muskrat house (a hole in the ice) and pushed it down once, then pushed it down again and said, "Hmm." As he pulled it back up, he said that he had done that since he was a kid and he could maybe push it within 2 inches at the bottom of the lake. Now there was a foot and a half of mud on that pole.

The wood frogs that used to be very plentiful in the lakes behind Old Crow are not so plentiful. The caribou migrations have changed, the caribou patterns have changed, and we are seeing a lot more parasites on the caribou, and we are seeing insects we have not seen before. Also, there are pelicans arriving. The vegetation is growing up the side of the mountains. On the coastal plain, the dwarf birches are just invading from the mountains at a very rapid rate which is also alarming. The weather patterns are especially noticeable.

We see summer clouds in December, the fluffy clouds. It rains in December and causes havoc amongst the animal population. The cycles are not as consistent as they used to be. It doesn't get 50-60 below anymore; it's to the point where it is costing people their lives. My grandmother and an elder were walking across a stretch of river that they have walked across the same weekend their entire lives to go fish. She fell through and drowned. We had to find her underneath the ice; luckily we found her. That same stretch of ice for 70 years, they trusted it, and now we can't do that anymore. When we go out in the bush, we don't know if we are going to encounter an overflow or an open lake, so people are hesitant to go out. If so, they have to go with a group of people to make sure they are safe. Things are changing, everything.

[At this point, the interviewer reminds Darius that he hasn't talked about the lake of his boyhood draining out, part of a previous conversation. With obvious emotion, Darius responds.]

I have tried to avoid the topic of permafrost melting because I get emotional. But, I just went up to Crow Flats two weeks ago to a lake at the center of my family's traditional

Crow Flats area where Darius grew up on the late Zelma Lake
–courtesy of www.oldcrow.ca

area I spoke of earlier, Zelma Lake. My grandmother protected it like I will never forget. This lake is very central to our family. Recently the permafrost melted on the south end of the lake. It drained catastrophically to the point where it emptied. It's gone. I paddled around that lake with my grandmother in a little canoe many memorable times. She taught me so much on that lake, our whole family from generation to generation lived on that lake. And now it's gone.

I will end with another story about my grandmother. When I was a little kid, she talked to the land and the animals and to the weather sometimes. A raven was flying by one day and she was a hard teacher. She stopped me and didn't say anything, and she put her hand up in the air and talked to the raven in Gwich'in. Translated, she said, "Raven, tell us when the caribou are coming and we will give you the caribou's eye." She watched the raven and nothing happened. The raven just flew away.

Later on that day, she did it again. Much to her delight, the raven circled us and flipped over three times in the air and flew off. Immediately, she looked at me and told my uncles, "Get ready, the caribou are coming soon." That night, at about two in the morning, the caribou arrived. So they did what she said they were going to do. She put a caribou's head on the ice for the crow to eat its eyes. That relationship is thousands of years old. That belongs to the land, to the water, to the wildlife, and to your natural environment. It is thousands of years old.

I went to Crow Flats the other day just to fill my tanks, I tell people. It replenishes us in a way I can't explain. Sometimes it still feels a part of my soul, because you get vulnerable if you don't join your mind and body with the land. And even that short three days that I went up there to smell the earth and listen to the birds and touch the water and drink the water and walk the land, I refilled my tanks again enough to be strong and finish my job. You can't explain that.

You have to come live with us for a year and live through one cycle of the caribou to just get a glimpse of what it is to be Gwich'in. Those kinds of things we continue to battle for. Ironically, man's burning of fossil fuels is affecting our lives a lot, and more quickly. It is a bit ironic that the 200 years that fossil fuels have been burned [elsewhere] is a double whammy here. So the battles are increasing, but we will fight on. We will always battle on.

The loss of our sense of belonging to land, if it should perish, would impoverish mankind to no end. If big oil succeeds and gets in the calving grounds, the caribou die, and the Gwich'in culture is gone.

Another indigenous people on this planet will cease to exist. Over what? Over what? Over 200 years of man's hunger for fossil fuels versus the existence of another aboriginal people. We have a living language. We have a living culture. Thank goodness we have our isolation and we are able to pass this down.

That is what we are fighting for, the right to be alive. I want to look my great-grandkids in the eye and know that I have done a good job, that they will continue to be Gwich'in, that the calving grounds are protected, and that our life as a people continues for thousands of years more.

Porcupine Caribou near Old Crow, Yukon
–courtesy of www.oldcrow.ca

The 27 Caribou Story

Donald Frost is a resident of Old Crow, Yukon, where he has lived all of his life. He is 80 years old and is known as one of the real hunters of the community. He has five children, one of whom is Glenna Tetlichi, whose interview is printed herein. http://www.maplandia. com/canada/yukon-territory/yukon/old-crow/

I remember one winter when I was older. We had no dog food. My wife was here in town with some little kids; everyone had nothing to eat. I went down on my trapping line and I was alone. I saw a bunch of caribou in the afternoon before dark.

I went after that bunch the way they tell me to do it. Now when I saw a caribou going over a hill, I ran to that caribou with big snowshoes on. But when I hit that caribou trail, I had to look to make sure it was caribou, and not 50 wolves! But I looked to make sure, and I see that they followed each other and I was happy.

But you don't step on that track; you step back and go all the way around. The caribou know when something is on their track. Then I saw them and they were looking for food in the snow. I rubbed several sticks together like I had been taught, and they didn't even see me. I started shooting. I was hoping for one or two, just to get something. I used all my shells. But I ended up with 27 caribou! Wow!

About those sticks, when they hear you rubbing those sticks, it sounds like more caribou. That's what they told me. It makes them sleepy. Isn't that something? I was really happy to get all of them. Sometimes you are so happy you want to cry. I don't know how you say that, but I was all alone and that's how I felt. But I couldn't cry even though I felt like it. I said to myself to forget it and to think about your wife and family. Twenty-seven caribou. I was busy!

It was dark, but when you are in a hard time like that, you don't waste anything. You don't even waste the blood. You leave it in the cage. Tomorrow I took a cup and put it in with the guts – but save all that blood because we just got through starving! You don't throw anything away!

After several days of butchering, I was really worn out, but I needed to get the meat back to Old Crow. I was getting ready to leave and I heard a noise. All I had in my head was "wolves!" I thought they were after the dogs so I got up, but the dogs were looking back toward Old Crow. I knew somebody was coming and I smiled at my brother Gordon. Now I had his gun and shells and he was happy I had gotten all those caribou. So he helped me get it back.

Faith Goes to Copenhagen

Faith Gemmill is a Gwich'in Indian from Arctic Village, Alaska, a small village of 150 people. She spent her childhood learning from elders and depending predominately on caribou for subsistence. From a young age, she was exposed to the challenges her village faced being situated just south of the energy rich Arctic National Wildlife Refuge. With development on their doorstep, she fights to retain their traditional way of life. She is currently employed by REDOIL (Resisting Environmental Destruction on Indigenous Land). http://www.maplandia.com/united-states/alaska/yukon-koyukuk-census-area/christian/

My name is Faith Gemmill. I am 34 and was born in Fairbanks, Alaska, and raised in Arctic Village and Venetie, Alaska. I went to school here in Venetie and in Fairbanks. When I was young, I had thought that Arctic Village was the entire universe. Our whole life was based on the caribou. My earliest memories were around this time of year, end of July and early August, walking to the mountain. Even when I was a little baby, they carried me up the mountain. I remember camp on the mountain and hunting caribou with my mom and family. All I knew was caribou meat, moose meat, rabbits, ducks, fish, muskrats and that was our food. To have something from the store was a luxury.

Here in Arctic Village, we didn't even have electricity. We didn't have TV's until I was about nine years old. We had one TV in the town and everyone would go over there and watch movies. Our elders taught us everything about our culture that you need to know when you live out here. You have to be quiet, be still, and don't make noise when they're hunting. The only Western influence for us back then was the school where everything was English, and that's where our language started getting broken. I remember playing our own Indian games like Mejore, Gitzy or hide-and-seek through the whole village because we didn't have television, computers, and Playstations.

My grandpa, Isaac Tritt, taught us our songs and traditional dances. Having all our elders here was great and I used to go and hang out at their houses. I remember all of them.

The grandmas would always be sewing or tanning skin, and all our grandpas would have caribou meat boiling on the stove. Grandma Alice, I remember her smile and the smell of tanned skin. As soon as we walked in the door, she would say, "Give them something sweet," because we didn't have sweets around.

I remember Grandma Rena taking care of us and I drove her crazy. I remember visiting Grampa Issac every night. We would play Vitsit and he would tell us how to be shrewd, how to win, and how to use your mind. We learned about the mountains, our history, and the importance of sitting with the really old ones. I look back, and I feel that it is an honor to be from here.

When I was three years old I visited Los Angeles because my father is from the Pit River Tribe. My grandmother said that she took me to a butcher shop to buy meat; I got up on the counter, and I slammed my hands and said, "I want caribou meat"! She tried to explain that they didn't have it, but I didn't know any better. Like I said, I thought Arctic Village was the world. I thought everyone lived just like us.

One year when I was 11, all the guys were getting ready to hunt because the caribou were coming. Everyone was just getting excited. Me and my cousin wanted to go up, but they didn't let young girls go because of tradition. We begged them to let us go and they finally gave in. With about 20 men, we camped on this side of the mountain, and we sat up all night listening to the men tell old stories. Every few hours they would go up and look for caribou. There was this elder, James, who was always watching the caribou for the village because he had a telescope. "Where are they?" I would ask. He would say, "four days."

There were about 50,000 caribou coming. It was as far as you could see. They just looked like little ants marching very far away but we waited and watched them as they came up the tall mountain right to us. The men got 40 caribou that fall, enough to feed the whole village for the winter.

I remember hunting and no matter how cold we were, we had to wait until they butchered all of the caribou and packed it on our back to camp. The dogs even had dog packs and they even carried meat. At night, we would wrap in the caribou fur to keep warm, and they give us the milk from the caribou. When my brother was a baby, my mom gave him caribou milk and I asked, "Why are you giving him that?" She said, "You drank it too, that's why you're healthy."

In 1988, I was 15 and first realized there was potential for oil and gas development in this region. Our people found out that oil companies were trying to drill in the Arctic Refuge with the help of an environmentalist. Myra Kyikavichik, an elder in Canada, insisted on having a traditional gathering like we did a long time ago. We would discuss important things that affected all of our communities and have traditional games, competitions, feastings and dancing. I was at that meeting. It was here in Arctic Village and was very powerful.

We hadn't seen our people from the other side of the border for ages. The elders were just crying because they were so happy to see everyone. There were only certain rules for the meeting: anyone could speak, speak from their heart, and hold their talking stick while talking. They opened the floor to everyone. People spoke of the importance of our way of life, and a lot of the elders prophesied what was coming in the future. Many elders from the Canadian side talked about their experience with oil companies coming in, taking what they wanted, and leaving. People were devastated, left with nothing. No more jobs, pollution, broken families, and all these social ills that are left behind after the companies leave.

That's how the Gwich'in Steering Committee was created. They created it at that meet-

A sunset in Arctic Village, Alaska

ing and allowed one document to come out of it: the Gwich'in Resolution. The village chiefs realized the need for a special body whose sole purpose is to protect the calving grounds and fight for our people. They hand-picked each board member, selecting two people from each region based on how they were raised. Do you know our way of life? Do you know our language? Are you a strong spokesperson? Once selected, the elders gave them direction on how to represent us. One of the main things they told us was to go out there and tell our story not only for us but for all people. Just imagine coming from tiny Arctic Village and going straight to Washington D.C. But they did it. And they did a good job.

I got mentored by all of those people and started working with the Gwich'in Steering Committee in 1995. I started speaking out publicly when I was 17, and I spoke out because I went to Oregon and experienced the situation there. That's when I realized that nobody really had what we have up here. I always thought that Native people always have their rights to their lands and their way of life. I spoke to the youth in Oregon where a lot of them weren't allowed to hunt, had to get permits, and they didn't have their language. They just lived like everyone else. In Alaska, we have our language, our subsistence, our traditional foods, and our own government.

Later that year, I moved to Venetie and started working with the youth, trying to increase interest in learning from elders. About that time, at a Youth and Elders Conference, I gave my first speech on the caribou. Our state representative at that time was Irene Nicklay, and she came to me and asked me to write a resolution about something that is important but needed support. I didn't know what a resolution was, but I eventually brought it to the floor of the Denacnock meeting. I had a chaperone with me; I told her, "I can't go up there and speak by myself. I can speak but I want you up there with me, and I want you to hold my hand." Because there were 500 elders from all over, she went on stage and held my hand while I spoke. I got a standing ovation, however, and I was only 17.

My dream was to become a teacher. When I graduated from high school in Fairbanks, I was working at a day care provider there. It wasn't like being an advocate was my vision. I wanted to work with kids because they deserve everything that I had growing up, and I want them to experience it. I want them to know what it's like to live out in the bush because it's peaceful, it's very spiritual, and it's very powerful. Where we walk is where our ancestors walked, and we follow in their footsteps with what they gave to us. They had a hard life where they struggled to just survive. It's amazing that we are here. It's amazing that we still have so much of our culture and our way of life intact in North America in the year 2007.

When I think back, I have had a lot of experiences on our land and our rivers that make me strong and make me do what I do. My grandfather, Abel Tritt, always wanted me to learn how to live out on the land for a winter with my uncle Raymond in Christian Village. Finally, I decided to do it and started gathering everything that I needed. I was 19. I quit my job even though I was up for a promotion; I would have been the top level supervisor 'cause I worked a few years there and moved all the way up. When it was time to go out, we found out that my grandfather's brother, Christian Tritt, Sr., the traditional chief of Venetie, had gotten cancer. Our whole family went to Venetie and we started helping their family, because everyone comes and helps when someone gets sick. Me and my uncle decided to put everything off until he passed. There I was in Venetie without a job, with everything packed and ready to go out on the land and we couldn't.

All the while, Sarah James kept calling me the whole year trying to get me to Washington D.C. to speak and work down there with the caribou issue. I kept telling her, "No, I am working or no, I've got to go to Christian Village" but finally there was nothing so I called her up and told her that I wasn't doing anything and I would go. She said, "Yeah, there is an internship right now and I want you to do it!" Next thing you know, I flew to D.C. and started working.

I stayed in D.C. for two months to lobby. I went on the hill to educate Congress, and I talked about our way of life and why we want that area protected. I was good at it, and it felt natural to me. I went there with t-shirts and jeans, the way we dress up here. I had no formal clothes to go to offices and I stayed with three women. They taught me how to wear clothes and how to go to government offices. I learned quickly that people were busy workaholics that work from seven in the morning until 10 at night. They have so many issues coming into their office that my issue was not a priority, and my people are definitely not. They don't know anything about us, they will probably never come up here, and to them we don't matter unless I make them see that we should matter.

While I was in D.C., I craved our traditional food. I called Sarah because she was coming down for a conference and I said, "Go to my mom's house and get caribou meat for me." So she brought me normal food.

With the meat in hand, I told my roommates that I needed a saw so I can cut that meat up and they said, "What is that?" and I said, "It's a saw that you cut meat with." They said, "Oh, you can just take it to the butcher shop and they will cut it for you." I spent all day calling all these butcher shops in D.C. asking, "I have a piece of caribou meat and I need it cut up for fry meat." They didn't know what fry meat was, and they didn't know what a caribou was. They were like, "What the heck is that?" I was on the phone trying to explain caribou, "Its like a deer." The butchers wouldn't do it for me so I ended up having to do it myself.

When I first got down there, the first day I went to the office where there was a meeting with all the staff with a big environmentalist group. They said, "Okay, we can all go on the hill and do a drop." I didn't know what a hill was, a drop was, and the guy that was supposed to be training me said, "Just follow the group and here is your list of offices to take this letter." So, we went to the hill, to the Rayburn House building. My trainer said, "Okay, when you are done with your floor, we will meet by the statue."

So we split up, I did the drop, and I started looking for the statue. I walked down stairs and there was no statue. I went outside and there were lots of statues, all kinds of statues. I couldn't see "The Statue." I had to ask a passing lady, "Do you know where the statue is?" She goes, "Oh, the statue is inside." I found my friend inside so red from running all over

**Reconstructed church in
Arctic Village, Alaska**

inside the building. He thought he lost me. That was one of my first experiences in D.C.

I got to meet Senator Daschel in person, take a tour of the White House, and the opportunity to organize a trip to the White House for Gwich'in elders and young people. Every time our leaders came down, I organized all their meetings and took them around D.C. I got to know Washington D.C; it was like I lived there all my life. I got to know all the Native organizations that worked on behalf of Native people in Washington D.C., and I learned a lot in two months. It wasn't when I was there, but the vote for the Refuge was coming, and it was going to be in the Budget Bill, as a two-line item, to balance it out. A two-line item in the national budget bill was how it appeared and nobody knew it, so we educated all over the U.S.

After the internship, I eventually came back home and started working at the school with the kids. I was just on call for the Steering Committee and I lived up here in Arctic Village. There was never a plan, it just happened. I started working with the media, the tribes, and I started going to all the national tribal conferences and working for our people. Now I work for REDOIL, an organization we created in 2003 when the national energy bill was moving forward, which streamlined development in Indian country. It actually gave the Native corporations more rights than the tribes and recognized Native corporations as tribes.

We fought it hard and we killed that energy bill. What I mean is there was three of us that were with grassroots organizations who attended the National Congress of American Indians (NCAI), and we debated the council's energy research committees. We won the debate on the floor, we fought it out with all of those pro-development forces of NCAI at their annual meeting, and we won! We got a resolution passed, and faxed it straight to Senators Inoue and Akaka. They voted against the energy bill and filibustered it.

People don't know the political power of Native people, and I have seen a lot of things in years working on these issues. I have seen miracles happen while speaking for our people. The elders say to not worry about anything and don't be afraid because it will be taken care of. They said for me to take care of myself, of my spirit, and of my health; and so I did it for all these years.

I give my energy to change people's opinions and have nothing left by the time I am done. I come home to replenish myself and this land is where I get replenished. My spirit gets strong again. Every single time that I get a chance, I come home to get renewed.

It is a very spiritual relationship we have for our land that we have always had. We cannot live without it, we won't be who we are without it, and that's the bottom line. I don't want to see my own people trying to live and be someone they are not. I can walk in the cities and live in the cities and live our people's way of life; I can balance it in my life and some people cannot. They just need to be Gwich'in.

If I didn't have to do this work, I would be living up here. I would pick blackberries, and go hunting and fishing. Now it's time for me to pass what I know to my kids. I want them to learn from our people like I did. This village raised me and it gave me a lot. I brought my son up when he was a baby. My daughter was only three and had already been on the mountain hunting with us.

I work on behalf of Native people throughout the whole state including the people that live on the North Slope, the people that live in Bristol Bay, the people that live in Cook Inlet, and people in the Yukon Flats. We face issues like the land swap Doyon (a Native Corporation) has arranged with the U.S. Fish and Wildlife Service to facilitate oil and gas development on oil rich lands. The Fish and Wildlife Service ought to be doing what they were created for: protecting habitats for the animals instead of in this case facilitating development within the habitat and threatening the subsistence lifestyle of all southern Alaskan Gwich'in villages including Fort Yukon, Beaver, Venetie, and Birch Creek.

This is a classic example of our relationship with big companies and the Western way. They say this oil field is three times the size of Alpine, the oil field that is by Nuiqsut. Nuiqsut is one community where oil and gas development is right next to the community, and they have massive health impacts in that village. They go into the community and make all these promises about the best jobs, better schools, healthcare and indoor plumbing while not interrupting the subsistence life. They promise that there will only be two flights a day, and so on. Once the community agrees, all of the promises were broken.

They have had very few numbers of their community actually work there. All of that income is going to the Lower 48, it ain't going to the Inupiat. Now 80 percent of the community has asthma and upper respiratory illnesses. That community is highly impacted by that development and they have been speaking up and fighting to raise awareness about what is happening to them.

Nuiqsut actually joined forces with Alaska Intertribal Council, and a doctor initiated a study to track human health effects and oil development. We are hoping from that study we will get legislation in Congress passed to prevent development near communities. They are just running all over the people.

America's dependence on fossil fuels is what is causing our people up here to suffer and that's why we are advocating for better energy use and better energy policy. We want the United States to pass policy where they use sustainable forms of energy that won't harm people or the land especially up here. We could have wind energy, solar energy.

They did a pilot project here in Arctic Village two years ago that showed that we could run this community three-fourths of the year on solar. The only thing that is stopping us from having it is the federal dollars that could be put into an energy bill and released to tribes, but we don't have it. If this community could run three-fourths of the year on solar, imagine what an example that would be to the Lower 48. There are cities over in Europe that are running their communities on good clean energy, so why can't we do it? And why do native people suffer? It's not right.

We have to replace the jobs that are given from the industry with jobs that are sustainable; there has to be a transition like that. People shouldn't have to destroy their own land for jobs. Opportunities are few. So when we're told that we can have jobs if they allow this development, people are stuck, and they don't really have much of a choice.

Instead of prospering, we have the highest rates of incarceration, domestic violence, alcoholism, suicide, and all other social ills that happen when people are forced to be something they are not. It's like post-traumatic stress disorder when soldiers go to war. It's a shock from one way of life to another way of life just like that, to change who you are, and people are still climbing out of it.

People are still trying to figure out how to deal with the transition and the jobs that are not helping us. Our land makes us rich; it is a different value system and Western society does not understand that and maybe they never will, but they should.

A Lifelong Voice for the Calving Grounds

Sarah James is a 66-year-old Gwich'in woman from Arctic Village, Alaska. She was a 2002 winner of the coveted Goldman Environmental Prize for environmental activism in her campaign to protect her tribe by ensuring the health of the Porcupine Caribou Herd. She is one of four Gwich'in in Alaska appointed by her tribe in 1988 to the Gwich'in Steering Committee. As such, she has worked tirelessly for 20 years to gain Congressional approval of Wilderness status for the Arctic National Wildlife Refuge coastal plain, where the Porcupine Caribou Herd calves. She has spoken to the United Nations about the Porcupine Caribou, was part of the Earth Summit in Rio de Janeiro, and was a part of a Pan-American Indigenous Conference in Quito, Ecuador. She has also traveled extensively in the United States. http://www.maplandia.com/united-states/alaska/yukon-koyukuk-census-area/christian/

Beautiful multiple rainbow near Arctic Village, Alaska

I'm from Arctic Village, Alaska, about 110 miles north of the Arctic Circle. It's very isolated and there's no roads. The only places that has running water is the school and the washeteria. We do have school that teaches K-12. Gwich'in children from other villages like to go to school in Arctic Village, because the country is very beautiful, we talk our language, and we get to go out [on the land].

I grew up mainly on the land with my mom and my dad. I remember two of my older sisters do the same things my father does. They had their own trap line, and they got their own dog team. They became trappers, because that's one way to make a living and still live out there.

But my dad doesn't trap out everything. He looks at the varmint, depends on how healthy the varmint is. If the varmint is hurting for life, then he is very careful about how much he takes. He keeps his limit, and that is how we paid our grocery bill mainly in the trading post. We go out with our traditional food which we combine with white flour, white rice, white macaroni and stuff like that.

First time I can remember, about 1950, we were living here in Arctic Village. My mom said we have to go to Fort Yukon, because that's where the school is at. So my mom said we had to move to Fort Yukon, and we moved there for about three years or so. There we also go out on the land, like during the fish run, salmon and other clear water fish along the Yukon. My father used a net and also fish wheel. We snared rabbits and trapped muskrats. Even when we were living in Fort Yukon, my dad still went out. Sometimes he got these local jobs, because he's a good carpenter.

Then one of my brothers got in trouble, so my mom said "This is not a place for my family either." So we had to go back out on the land. She thinks that people can make it better on Salmon River, because there used to be a village there. She thought that would be a better place for us, so we moved out on the land, just our family.

Then Arctic Village people want us back up here, because

The Goldman Environmental Prize

Grassroots environmental heroes too often go unrecognized. Yet their efforts to protect the world's natural resources are increasingly critical to the well-being of the planet we all share. Thus, in 1990, San Francisco civic leaders and philanthropists Richard N. Goldman and his late wife, Rhoda H. Goldman (1924-1996) created the Goldman Environmental Prize. The Goldman Prize continues today with its original mission to annually honor grassroots environmental heroes from the six inhabited continental regions: Africa, Asia, Europe, Islands and Island Nations, North America, and South and Central America. The Prize recognizes individuals for sustained and significant efforts to protect and enhance the natural environment, often at great personal risk. Each winner receives an award of $150,000, the largest award in the world for grassroots environmentalists. The Goldman Prize views "grassroots" leaders as those involved in local efforts, where positive change is created through community or citizen participation in the issues that affect them. Through recognizing these individual leaders, the Prize seeks to inspire other ordinary people to take extraordinary actions to protect the natural world.

Sarah James at Arctic Refuge Day with Bishop Mark McDonald

they think that they have enough students, and they think they might get something going. If they have enough students, then there's a chance we might start a school so we came back over here. Then in 1955, the first volunteer teacher came. We had to get enough wood for her, then provide housing for her and everything like that. She was just a volunteer, just a first-aid person, but she was very good, and that was our first teacher and our first school year.

All along I tried to go to school, but I hardly could. In 1959, I had to go to boarding school in Chemawa, Oregon, and that was culture shock, because I didn't know how to speak English. I went to three summer schools and one summer job, because my parents they don't make money, so I don't get money from home.

Anyhow, it is pretty far from here. That's another thing. My parents wouldn't let us come back, because they think getting an education is good for us. I ask over and over. I wanted to come home, but they wrote back and say that you have to stay, stay, stay. One of the things that really helped me in my education is that when we were out on the land, we learned how to persevere, share and we learn about life out there. And if we don't, then we can get ourselves stuck. We have to be part of the family to make it out there.

My mom taught us to take care of everything in order for it to take care of us, like the environment. That was how I grew up. I got my high school diploma in six years. I jump from K to 12 within six years, and that's really helped me. But when I first got there, I felt like there was a lot of greed and waste, and I couldn't understand, and I still have a problem understanding. I grew up taking care of the environment, and from the time I can remember that's our way of life and still is. Ill probably die doing that, because that's who we are.

Back in 1988, it was alarming to hear that they were going to get into the coastal plain of the Arctic National Wildlife Refuge because we were caribou people. Caribou help us survive between the first contact with Western culture and later when a disease came through. So we went through hard times.

Then the trappers trapped out everything too, because that's all they came for. They was our first visitor. Our first visitor was not Russian, it was French trappers. They came up the coastal plain, from those Inupiat people. Outside whalers came in first, then trappers came, and we got caught in between. Our people went through hard times.

If it wasn't for the caribou migrating through our country, then we would starve. So that connection is very strong with our people. Anytime anything saves the tribe, we take that as sacred to our life. That's how it is with caribou to us.

Before contact, we used to live in caribou skin huts. The caribou skin hut works like a portable tent. They carry it on the back, the poles and all that. That was our shelter then and our food. Even today, our protein is 75 percent wild meat, which is made up of caribou, fish, Dall sheep, moose, small animals, birds, and ducks.

Now, we have to live in a cabin; we have to live in the two worlds. I walk through the worlds all my life because I have to. So I had to try and choose between each culture the tools I could better live with. We all need to do that. It's the only way we can look into the future for our children. My mom taught us that you guys go get your high school education but respect the environment and respect your elders. You know we still teach that, and it's very hard to walk in the two worlds and walk in a good way.

In 1988, we called our Gwich'in nation back together after 150 years to meet in Arctic Village. The Canadian and U.S. border separates us. All 15 village chiefs came in, and each brought an elder and a youth. It was like a rebirth of the nation.

The group of chiefs were saying, "This is good, this is really good what's happening, but the world needs to know about it." But the 15 elders put their foot down and said "We're going to run this meeting like we always did before." So they even threw away their regular agenda and presented a talking stick. So we talked with a talking stick. We had to talk our language and all that.

But all the chiefs that came from Canada and U.S. talked about it around the campfire away from the elders meeting uptown, and

A lake near Arctic Village, Alaska

they wrote a resolution to protect the coastal plain of the Arctic National Wildlife Refuge, the birthplace of the Porcupine Caribou and the Gwich'in way of life. It was the only resolution on that subject and still is today.

They brought it back to the elders' meeting. They had to convince elders that the only way the world will know about it is if it's in black and white. They finally passed it, and they said we need people to make this resolution work.

So they choose four from Canada and four from the U.S., and I was one of them that got chosen from U.S. That's how they formed the Gwich'in Steering Committee. The other three from the U.S. were Jonathan Solomon, Kay Wallace, Ernest Eric. And at the same time, they said that this is your way of life, so you're in for all your life.

Then there were four from Canada. We lost three; so we only have one left, Norma Kassi. It's up to the chiefs over there, and the chiefs think it's working fine the way it is. So when they decide that they're going to choose three more, then they will do that, but it's up to them.

Then they give us direction to do this in a good way and no compromise and to state your mind. That was the decision the elders made. Then they said the Gwich'in nation was going to have to meet every two years. So the Gwich'in people have been meeting every two years ever since.

It just happened this (2008) July 13-17 in Old Crow, and we reaffirmed the resolution. We were still united and the directions still the same; nothing change. The reason they said we had to do it in a good way is that it was really hard for the elders to make that decision, because we can't do it by ourselves. Oil companies are multimillion dollar corporations and that's too huge. And they said we have to make friends; we have to do this in a good way and teach the world why we say no to oil.

So that was our mission. We went out, and the first thing we ever did was educate the media. Just like L.A Times and New York Times and People Magazine. It was hard to do, but that was our first mission, to educate, because nobody knows about us. And if they know about us, then they tell the correct story.

It's human rights to us, because we always been here as a Gwich'in people. We believe the creator put us here to take care of this part of the world, and that's our responsibility, and we have to live up to it. We didn't come from anywhere, and we're not going anywhere, we're here to stay.

So at that time the elders they said another thing. They said, we're going to have to bring in people and show them and tell them why we say no to oil development. That means we're going to bring the traffic in. So at that time they said if we educate them in a good way on why we say no to oil development, maybe they might not be a threat, and maybe they might become our friend.

And that's been happening since 1988. We made a lot of friends with the environmentalists, with mainly Democrats and a few good Republicans. This whole thing is up to Congress, because the Arctic National Wildlife Refuge is a public interest land. It's up to the American government. We fought battle after battle, all of us, some big ones, some not. It's been a long battle since 1988 for the Gwich'in. It's been 20 years now, and we just celebrated it at the "Gathering" in Old Crow.

So it's been a long haul, and right now it seems that we're keeping all our friends that we made. But it looks like the pressure from the price of gas being high, we need to make more friends. And that's what we ask our friends to do, because we haven't yet made a lot of difference; we stopped the drilling, but it's not permanent protection. So hopefully if we get a good Administration and Congress in Washington D.C., maybe we'll get Wilderness; that would make it a permanent protection so we can go on with other life, I can go on with my life, and many people that's committed to it as well.

Many, many people have been committed to it for many, many years. On behalf of the Gwich'in nation, I just want to thank these people that came forward that helped and made their voice heard and call their Congress people. We need to do that some more. We need it now. What we're looking at is it's not going to raise the price of gas. In fact, by not developing the Arctic National Wildlife Refuge, we're going to help to bring the gas price back down, because we are going to get away from fossil fuel and go to alternative energy.

Right now here in Arctic Village, we don't use the solar energy in the summertime near enough. Come April to August, it's 24-hour daylight. That's a lot of energy not being used. Up in coastal plain where they wanted to develop, it's windy there all the time year-around. That's alternative energy we need to look into, and then we need to change our life.

We need to change our way of thinking, and we need to change our way of doing business and everything like that toward getting away from fossil fuels. And that means recycle, reuse, and reduce and refuse. Yeah, we just have to plain refuse, just say no. And using less oil and eventually not using oil at all.

Out there on the land, to survive you had to ration. You know, what little sugar we have, we had to ration, or what little flour we have, we had to ration it and eat natural food and all that. We need to go back to our natural food because during the time of the caribou skin hut, you know the air was clean, the water was clean, the land was clean, life was clean. Our people used to die only of old age and now are dying of drug and alcohol-related problems. There used to be TB, you know, other diseases, and now it's drug- and alcohol-related.

Finally, let me say to the folks in the Lower 48: there's not many of us, and we need friends, and we make many, many friends throughout the world. And that's why we still keep the oil at bay, because American people spoke loud and clear repeatedly battling since 1988, and they help us overcome these battles. Mainly environmentalist and grassroots people out there help us, and the churches sign on with us. Also, the tribes sign on with us on human rights. This is human rights to us, because it makes us who we are, the caribou people.

Education

Roger Kyikavichik was born and raised in Old Crow. He has lived there except for two years of high school and working in various places for short periods. He is in his 50's and has a wife and four children. The oldest boy is 16. He goes hunting with his dad. Roger works for the Vuntut Gwich'in band, and enjoys his lifestyle. He has been Chief of the band and is now Vice-Chief. http://www.maplandia.com/canada/yukon-territory/yukon/old-crow/

In the early days when I was going to school in grades one to five, our culture was not part of our school. Whatever was supposed to be taught in school, like math, reading, and writing, that's all there was. But nowadays it's different. Through discussion with the government, we are letting them know our culture is dying. The only way we can save it is through teaching our young people traditional things. So now they develop programs within the school with the language class, and they bring elderly people in. They allow students to go out on the land during the spring-time.

Both boys and girls go out there. They established a program here, and it's basically teaching them how to set up a camp, how to get things ready, how to figure how much food you need. All this is part of it. When they get their camp set up, now they got to decide some things. Are they going to set rabbit traps, muskrat snares, or look around for caribou? If you can't get caribou now, you must look for moose. So all this is part of the teaching.

This bush-teaching happens every year. A child starting kindergarten, he's got nine good seasons to get these teachings. And then there are other programs. Families take their kids out hunting, take them out to Crow Flats. Also, within the community at public meetings, they talk about how to keep the land clean.

Of course, there is more to it than just caribou and maybe moose. The kids learn to fish and hunt ducks too. And then there is berries and stuff like that. And you know, cooking is a skill that each of us have to learn, both men and women. But women are the best cooks.

Girls go out in the bush to learn, because they may be a widow someday. During my lifetime, I have seen a lot of them out there hunting. They go out to Crow Flats. Really they are the mom and dad of their family and they do a good job. Sometimes the community will help out, but only if the help is really required. They are not going to take the responsibilities away from them, because if they do that, they will not be able to survive out on the land. My own wife enjoys hunting. She can shoot, but I do all of that.

The Caribou and Me

Concerning the Arctic National Wildlife Refuge, every Gwich'in is involved trying to protect it. We've got to stand behind it and support it. The fight is on. We were taught from childhood that part of the Porcupine Caribou Herd's land, especially the area where they have their calves, is not to be touched. Very few Gwich'in people have ever seen that area. I have never seen it.

The caribou is sacred to us. We must stay away from their calving grounds. We were not even allowed to hurt birds. Our parents were really strict about that. You cannot even touch an egg because a bird will never go back there again. So that's like what they taught us about the calving grounds.

When a person from Old Crow goes down to Washington to lobby, you support them. Give them some more tools and encouragement as you shake their hand. You tell them to have a safe trip and tell them that you will be praying for them. I've never been, but I might go someday.

When a new chief comes in, that's his mandate: protect the caribou. The chief has to do it. He can't tell his people that he won't support this. He has no choice.

You know, you've got to have caribou. There's lots of meat down there in our Northern store, but you can't live off that; you can actually get sick on the beef by not having caribou meat. My youngest children love it. Sometimes we talk about what kind of life we would have if we didn't have caribou meat. We can't imagine it. You feel really sad when you think about it. That's why we continue to fight.

The fight is really for our survival and our way of life. If you don't have caribou meat for supper, you will be sad. If you can't go out to your freezer and pull out caribou meat, you will be sad and sick, spiritually, mentally, and physically sick. If we run out, we let others know that we don't have caribou, so they give us some. We bring it home, and the kids are excited. But that's our way of life.

In our house, we have it for breakfast and for supper, seven days a week. At least once a day, every day. Sometime we have meat in the morning and have something with beef in the evening, like a hamburger or chili.

Caribou swim the Porcupine River near Old Crow, Yukon
-courtesy www.oldcrow.ca

As far back as I can remember, it has been this way. I remember when I was about 10 or 12, one time nobody had caribou. We were hungry all the time. We had pancakes, oats, rice, beans. That's all we had. We didn't know where the herd went that fall.

One February day, we heard through a two-way radio that there was a plane coming in. I remember that it landed at 10 am. The federal government had chartered a plane and was bringing in domesticated reindeer, which tastes a little like caribou.

They landed down on the ice. People went out and loaded the meat. I remember that when it was time to go home for lunch, kids were running home. When I got home, my mother had fried meat and boy, we ate it right off the stove. We were so happy to have meat.

What Change Looks Like To Me

John Norbert is from Tsi-igehtchic and was born in 1938. John was the sixth in line of seven children, and spent all his life in and around the area. Although he grew up on the land, his father worked for the RCMP, and he held modern jobs where he didn't have to depend completely on subsistence like others. John supports development in northern Canada and explains why in our conversation.

As a child, you do almost everything with your parents. You never left your parents. You go somewhere only with their permission. You didn't have any freedom at all, you had to listen, and it is all of the time. You do

whatever the parents do. It could be fishing, snaring, trapping, mostly around the camp.

Long ago when people used the land, they took care of the land. They didn't usually trap the same place for years and years. They trapped one place for a couple of years, and then they moved to a different place. It was the same thing with the fishing, so they don't clean the place out. I like to say that in those days, they used everything. If it was in the old days, I would not be in town. I would be out at the fish camp already, or I would be getting ready for the next winter's dry fish.

They would never throw anything away but the fish scales. Even the guts were boiled, and the grease was taken out of it. They would use that for martin bait. They dried the heads and used that for bait. When they killed moose, same thing. They never wasted anything, and caribou was the same thing. That is what I learned from my parents and the old people.

I associated a lot with the old people when I was young and that is why I could speak the language fluently. In my young days, I learned to respect the elders, and my parents always told me not to speak English to the elders. Since I was a little kid, I always did that, and that is why today, I still speak my language even though I was in the private school for five to six years. I was the translator in the private school, too. There was an old lady that did the sewing, and I had to translate to her for the sisters, and that is how I kept my language.

In the old days, by now [August] you were already getting ready for the next winter, dealing with next year's trapping or where you were going to go. If you were going to go up to Bernard's Creek, then we would be dry fishing all summer. In the fall time, they moved to Bernard's Creek or wherever and trap.

In February, we moved to the mountains and that is where we got all of the meat. It was a long way, but in those days, it was nothing for the people. We were fit for whatever.

So, if there was nothing we could keep going farther looking. That was about 300 miles from here. They were well prepared for everything. They may stage way up high and put sugar and stuff like that in the cache just in case they ran out.

After making a kill, the next day we'd go with dogs to pick the meat up. They only get what they need. You can't carry and haul but so much. So you carry ahead, and then next day you do same thing. At that time, I was too small to go with my dad, so I stayed home most of the time.

I stayed home and helped my mother keep camp and get wood. Those days, when you were out in the bush, you were taught everything. The mothers are really busy because she has to work with that meat all the time, cook for us, and wash our clothes. My mom was a hard-working person. When Dad was away, she was the boss. She was very strict with us, and today I am happy that she was strict. My dad was away most of the time because he worked for the RCMP. They go on long patrols using the dogs, so we had to pull wood.

In the summer, we used to pick berries. The whole family used to go. I enjoyed that. We used to make fish and fish guts. In the fall-time, we fished on top of the ice.

I went to school pretty young, maybe seven years old. I spent quite a few years in school in Aklavik. While we were in school my mother had tuberculosis, so she had to stay in the hospital there. I had to stay for quite a few years even in the summertime because my dad, working for RCMP, couldn't keep us. Only thing I regret about school is that I was too young to be away.

To me, I am of a different generation. I went to school not only here, but in Yellowknife also. I did trapping, but I wasn't dependent on it. Sometimes you work for three days and you might not get anything. If I work, I know I've got eight hours' pay coming. Before, if you worked for two or three days trapping, it didn't mean nothing to you because you were fit. It wasn't hard.

I worked most of my life anywhere there was a job. I worked in Pine Point. I worked in Yellowknife in an auto body shop for about three years seasonally. For the young guys [today], we can't blame them for what they are. They want to be in a warm place working with the computer. Time changes, and everything flows with it. People say we are losing our language, which is true. We are losing our elders too. I hardly have anybody to talk to. It wouldn't be right for me to talk English to an elder. I hate to say this, I can't see the young people out on the land. Maybe some of them. First of all, they don't eat the food. They have chips and pop. It comes with the change.

What if we had to go back to that way of living, how would we make out? I'd make out. Those guys out there, I don't think so. I have my doubts. We cannot change the people too much. It's just about impossible. That's the way I look at, but I can't blame them. To bring back language is pretty hard.

But, I would like to see more employment here in the North. More employment for people will help with a proper living and get what they want. That

Tsiigehtchic on a cloudy summer day

will make their life worthwhile. I think of other people. You want to make a happy life and bring up your family; you've got to have a job. What affects me most is what is happening around Yellowknife. North of Good Hope, we hardly have anything going for us, except the pipeline if it comes.

South of here, they don't care because they have got diamond mines and everything going for them. They are blocking everything, so that the people here cannot work. They have lots of work. That's why they don't care. I speak at the hearings for my people. I would like to see more development in the North so people around here could work. If they can't get the pipeline, maybe they can make the highway or make it together. As long as they don't have work, you will have unhappy people.

There was a boom here at one time. I don't think it will be much different. It wouldn't hurt the land, because we have modern technology now and we have monitors. It's controlled. It's not going to be like years ago where they tore all the ground up. That's not going to happen anymore. I don't see where it's going to hurt anything.

People who are against the pipeline are the guys who are employed, who have a steady job, who make about $60-70,000 a year. These guys are against it. I think these kids may change their ways if they have jobs. One of the main things is education. You have to be educated no matter which way you look at it, or have skills.

I would like to see a bridge across that river, too. I would like to see this place develop so that everybody could earn a decent living instead of standing in line in front of the welfare office. I am 69 years old and still have a full-time job as a custodian. I tease the young kids all the time about it, and they tease me back, "Go back to your work!"

The Lady Legislator

Lorraine Peter is from Old Crow, Yukon. She was born May 24, 1956. Her mother's name was Mary Vetro. She has five sisters, and her mom was a single parent who brought them up mostly out on the land while they were young, strong women. She was raised and surrounded by a lot of strong women. She served two terms in the Yukon Legislative Assembly, the governing body of the territory. She speaks the Gwich'in language and understands it fully. http://www.maplandia.com/canada/yukon-erritory/yukon/old-crow/

I will share a story with you from when I was born. I was born in Old Crow and at those times, there were not many buildings or houses anywhere around. We lived in a tent frame and that was our home and where I was born.

Some of my earliest memories were always about the caribou. We have always had caribou to eat. My mom was both a hunter and a trapper. There was no economic base for Old Crow at that time except with her trapping, so that is how she kept food on our table and raised us, a family of six girls. We mostly lived off of caribou and rabbits, and muskrats, whatever was available in whichever season. We lived off food from the land that my mother was able to get for us.

I had many friends as a child; most of them were my relatives. You knew everyone in the community. In the springtime we would spend a few months out on the land with my mom. There she would do muskrat trapping and we would stay out in a tent. We were so free, and it was the happiest times of my life with my family. I would go out with my mom and we all had our different responsibilities. Some of mine were to take care of my youngest sister because my older sisters were more experienced on the land. They would go hunting, and she was teaching them how to become hunters.

After that I went off to school. We had a good school system in Old Crow at those times. They adjusted the school system to our way of life. In the spring, everybody went out to their spring camps because they had to trap muskrats as the income for the year. We started school at different times of the year. I think it was in August, and then we finished in early March, so it just worked really well for us. We didn't have to miss out on too much schoolwork.

We had to go to school until grade nine. From early years, my mom always stressed how important education was because she never went to school. Not only her, but my grandmothers used to come visit every night at seven o'clock and they would visit for about two hours. We would sit and tell stories and talk about long time ago and they told stories. I would half listen to them and then also try to concentrate on my homework. My grandmothers used to tell us how important that education was because times were changing fast.

When it was my turn to learn how to become a hunter and trapper at age 16, I had to go home and attend high school in Whitehorse, so that was a really big loss for me today compared to my older sisters. I tried to tell her that I did not want to go. I wanted to stay. She wouldn't have it.

I had never left Old Crow, and going to Whitehorse was like going to Vancouver. It was amazing. After the first week and the excitement of the city, I was ready to go back home. It was really challenging to try to fit into that society. It was so very different than the life we were used to in Old Crow. They changed classes every hour, and here we just sat in one class most of the day.

Change started to take place when we had to leave home to attend high school in Whitehorse. This education system was important to us, and for our parents to ensure we got an education. In order for them to show their support to us, they walked that path with us. A lot of times it meant staying.

The school system changed again. We needed to keep up with the rest of the Yukon. They had to make that adjustment, and

Lorraine at the Old Crow General Assembly

then they're not out on the land as much. They're not trapping so they needed an income to replace that. I think many of the families had to start looking for work in order to take care of their family as best as they could. I think that was the turning point for our community.

I graduated from high school and that was a huge accomplishment for me because I struggled the last year, and I remembered the words from my mom and grandma and that is what drove me. There were a lot of times where I just wanted to give up, rebel, and go home. How did they know that? I pushed on and I graduated.

My last year of high school, I stayed at Yukon Hall. There was an administrator there who encouraged me to think about going to college and I said, "No, I am taking a year off, enough of this learning business." He really challenged me, and I really challenged him right back.

He helped me see that if you take a year off, then your interest is not going to be there as fully as it would be coming out of high school. I listened to him and thought maybe he was right. He came from Victoria, B.C., and he knew that city. That was where his wife and him called home. They took me under their wing and really shared a lot of information with me about opening my eyes to the outside world beyond Whitehorse. I thought that maybe I could do this and so I did it. I went to college in Victoria and I thought Whitehorse was big until we flew over Vancouver.

When I got to Victoria, I thought that I made a huge mistake. It was strange to be by myself. I managed with their help to get room and board close to the college, and it was walking distance. The first semester, I kept thinking, "What did I get myself into?"

It was 1975 and at that time, they didn't have many services for First Nations people like they do today. I was taking the business administration course and by the end of my first year, I told myself that I could not do it anymore. I was not a business-minded person.

The only business I knew was how to dry a muskrat pouch and take it to my grandpa's store to exchange it for whatever it was worth. I wasn't business-minded in that way, and some of the subjects you had to take to prepare you for the business world, like statistics, was just beyond me. I spent a few years there.

I was home for Christmas and summer holidays and worked, and being away from home was so hard as my mom didn't have a phone. Just being away, from age 16 was just brutal -- no internet, no phone. The only way I could communicate with my family was through writing, and my mom who never went to school could read my letters. She educated herself by reading the Bible.

It was hard enough to try to make the adjustment, but keeping that connection with home and family was so important to me. I couldn't survive otherwise. My family would send me dry meat, dry fish, and berries and that was like gold when I was away. They would send me care packages with pictures of family. That connection was the key.

During the summer, I worked at our First Nation office and started to gain the experience on how an office works and how to work with people. It's those summer jobs that were really helpful in building that confidence.

So after I finished college, I came straight back to Old Crow and low and behold, there was a job available. I was young and ready for a good challenge, and I got that job. I did that job for eight years. It definitely made some differences for me and for people in my community.

I moved away afterwards because I needed a break. My son was nine years old when we left Old Crow, and I was a single parent. I moved to Edmonton, Alberta, and lived there for four years as a customer service representative at the Royal Bank and then moved back to Whitehorse with Royal Bank there for three years. My son wanted to go to high school in Whitehorse so we moved there. It was closer to home and family. All that time, no matter where I was, I had that strong connection with home.

Since very early, I remember Norma Kassi, Gladdis Netro and Lenny Kohm doing the slideshow presentations and talking about what was happening with the caribou issue. In 1988, they had the Gathering in Arctic Village. I was not here because by then I had moved away.

Always in my heart and soul, I've wanted to help and make a difference, but I had my responsibilities like raising my son, and that is where I kept my focus. I always kept myself informed on what was going on and who was doing what, and used to hear about people traveling down to the United States on tours to Washington. I always yearned in my heart to do that.

After my son graduated from high school, I took on another challenge with the Royal Bank. There was an opening on a First Nations reserve in Chilliwack, British Columbia, so I applied for the job and got it. I was hesitant to apply for that job because my mom was getting older, and my auntie Sarah Able was getting older.

I went to my mom and my auntie and told them what was going on, but they supported me. "Get as much experience as you can now," they said, "because later on, we are going to need you." Auntie said, "There is some hard work that needs to be done, and you'll know when it's time to come home."

Sure enough, I went to the Gathering in 1998 in Fort Yukon and knew it was time to come home. It was just good to be sitting there among my people. I felt it in the very core of my being, so I went back to Chilliwack and told the bank manager that I wanted to be home by Christmas. I came home in '98 at Christmas time and have been home since. A lot has happened since that time.

While I was away, they had these gatherings in Arctic Village and different communities, and I would hear about it from my family and friends. I always wished I could go. When I got back, there was an elder that passed away in Arctic Village, and I went and spent time with my relative, because she was grieving and they had seats available on the chartered flight. I got to meet my relatives there and fell in love with that village. It was just so beautiful. After two years, I came back to Old Crow, and I had worked my whole life. I decided to take some time off from the workforce, and I saw a sign up at the store asking for interested people to travel to lobby on behalf of the Porcupine Caribou. I thought about it and decided that it was my chance.

Lorraine (right) and sister Alice

I put my name forward, and they wanted us to write an essay of our interests. It was about 30 days. During that time, I got involved and did a lot of volunteer work. I started sewing in case I was selected to go on this trip, so I started making my outfit. I was really thinking while I was sewing about what it would mean for me. I was selected to go, and I flew, and ended up in Washington, and it was an eye opener.

To travel out there and share my story about where I came from, telling the story of how I was born and where we used to spend our time out on the land with my mom. It was such a powerful time for me. They knew nothing about us as a people, yet they were interested in helping us to make it different for the caribou and giving them a safe place to come to and give birth to their young every year.

That first trip was so powerful, it just grounded me. I remember all the stories my mother used to tell me, and I remember all the times we used to spend out in our camp. It was such a learning and emotional time.

I just cried, and it helped me to understand what my mom and the elders in my life were talking about. How very important what we do, how we live, how we treat people, how we go about being part of this community and world to take care of what we have and to be grateful and respect our environment. The rules and the teachings that my mom taught us while we were growing up just made more sense.

The first time I ever gave a talk, I was out on the road with Lenny. He did his slideshow presentation. There were about three to five hundred people there, and I did not know what to expect. Lenny did his slideshow presentation, and here I am trying to be so brave, strong, and thinking in my head how I was going to go about it. I decided that I was just going to tell my story, and then I saw a picture of my son and his two friends when they were six years old, sitting on the banks of the Porcupine River. They were happy and had their arms all around each other. They had teeth missing, and just were smiling. I saw that picture and other pictures of people who have done this work before. I saw family members in that slideshow presentation, and by the time it was my time to speak, I just felt that there was a reason I was there.

I needed to share my story; I needed to help people know who we are and what is important to us. I told that story about being born in a wall tent. I tried to describe it to the best ability so that they could just imagine in their mind of what it would be like, and even though it was such a simple beginning, to me that was rich. I am a rich person. And then I shared with them how my mom took us out on the land, and how she was a hunter and trapper. One of the roles was taking care of my younger sister.

One time, my sister was taking her afternoon nap. She was just about three or four years old, and it was just quiet and peaceful while I cleaned the dishes and kept things tidy in the tent.

It was springtime, just sunny, and I heard this noise outside. I went to the door, which was just a blanket covering the tent, and I opened it real slow because I could hear other noises. I figured it was probably caribou, and I peeked out the doorway, and there were about 200 caribou going past my mom's tent because that was one of their old trails. I just lay there watching, and they were just taking their time and walking. I just lay there and watched them because that moment was just natural.

I didn't get excited because it was just a beautiful sight to see. We knew where the caribou were going. We knew they had a special place to give birth to their young. The way we believe, when the animals are in their time at birth, we have great respect for that. It is like a silent rule or law that is just there. I just watched it go by and then just went about my business of what I was supposed to be doing. I didn't realize that it would be one of the most important moments in my life to help people understand what it means for us to be one and live in harmony with nature and with the animals.

That moment gave me an understanding of how much we are one with the land. I told that story so many times, and it just helps people to see where we come from and why the caribou is so important to our life and how much we are taught to respect animals. When we eat the caribou for food, it gives us life.

I shared that story when I did my very first talk traveling with Lenny. I don't think there was a dry eye in that whole place. Afterwards, it just really overwhelmed me because all these people that I didn't know just had tears in their eyes, and they came to help us and do whatever they can to help save the Arctic National Wildlife Refuge in this sacred area where the caribou give birth to their young.

They thanked me for being there, and I told them that they had it all wrong. I thanked them, because without that kind of support at the grassroots level, we couldn't do it alone.

When they had that 1988 gathering at Arctic Village, the elders asked the young people in our nation to take that journey and start educating people out there to let them know that this is very important to us. I always wanted to be a part of that, and that was the beginning for me. It has never stopped since that first time I went to Washington. It was incredible and scary.

I remember walking into an office, and they said that we had 10 minutes with the person there. I couldn't believe that we had 10 minutes to ask for their support, yet our whole life was on the line. After I walked out of my first visit with a Senator, I remember just crying because I felt the responsibility, and it was so great. It was like it was my responsibility to be here, and I had no problem with that. But the responsibility that I was beginning to understand fully was that it was not about me.

I didn't have grandchildren at that time, my son was 18 years old, and it wasn't even about him anymore. It was about my grandchildren who are not yet born. I felt that very deep, and again I thought about my mom, aunties, grandmothers who taught me in their simple ways. It gave me strength to be in Washington doing what I needed to do.

Moose antlers displayed in Old Crow, Yukon

After I moved back to Old Crow, I worked in the chief executive's office as assistant to chief and counsel. There was a territorial election, and I knew one day that that would be my path. I knew it was time and put my name forward. I was elected as a member of Legislative Assembly for the Gwich'in. I won and soon began that journey. I ran for two terms, and served for six years.

To work in that political environment and try to make a difference for your people, I was very new to that whole scene. It was another huge learning curve for me. Again, it was an incredible experience and yet, it was a place to voice our concerns and issues. One of them was about Porcupine Caribou and the Arctic National Wildlife Refuge.

The first Gwich'in gathering was in Arctic Village, and the elders at that time gave us the responsibility for the caribou issue. They said, "Go out and educate people out there." They told us to do that in a good way and to make contact with people. So the bottom line is to have that respect. Our only concern is with the Porcupine Caribou birthing grounds. That is a sacred place that has to be protected, and then there are all these other challenges that come up along the way

That Mackenzie project is going to impact us for sure, but we didn't take as strong of a stand on the pipeline project. We have strong feelings about projects happening all around us, but we have to remember what the elders said about our [first] responsibilities. We have to stay strong and united for one reason and if we start picking apart every project that is happening out there, then we will all be fighting.

That is why they warned us, and believe you me, it's been really hard. It's a painful journey because everyone needs oil and gas. Everybody just wants to develop. There are some very hard decisions to be made. We need to stay united through all those challenges we face. We can't lose sight of what is important to us as a people. We can't lose sight of what our grandparents protected since ancient times.

A Guide and Teacher

Charlie Swaney is a 48-year-old Native person living in Arctic Village, Alaska. He has lived in Arctic Village for 20 years and in Alaska all his life. He guides visitors to the village on trips into the Arctic National Wildlife Refuge, which borders Arctic Village on the north. http://www.maplandia. com/united-states/alaska/yukon-koyukuk-census-area/christian/

A Moose Story

I've got a moose story for you. One time, some friends told me that we should go up river to look for a moose. We took a boy with us named Jordan. We went way up there to a mountain called Medicine Man Mountain. We got halfway up there and I saw cow and calf tracks quite a bit. During that time of year, prior to rutting, is when the bulls are looking for cows. As we walked up, almost to the top, I looked down to see if there might be a big bull moose with them.

Well, Edward and the others went up to the top and whistled. Right at the top there was about a three-year-old bull moose. There was a cow with him. He decided to go down there and get it, but while they were going down, they heard him and took off to another creek. He went over and wounded the bull when they came down to the river. Right there at the river, we got it. At that time, I ran toward it. Another moose then came out, and the guys still on the mountain got that one.

Well, it got dark and they couldn't find it. We waited until the next morning and made camp and cut up the bull moose that we had got. The campfire was going and we ate ribs and slept good after a good night's meal.

Early next morning, we went up and found the moose right away. We packed that one down. We decided to take the moose back to the village and come back to get the other one. So Gideon stayed there by himself while me, Edward, and that little boy loaded up the moose and started back.

It was getting to evening time, and then it started to get cold. It was going to snow soon and when we went around this corner, we saw a horn go by really fast, back into the brush. Farther down, there was another bull moose that was only 700 yards from us. It was big! There was a cow and calf there too, and another medium bull moose. The big one jumped a couple of times, because it didn't want the other bull moose to get to the cow. He was right out in the middle of the open and I wasn't sure of what to do. I looked into the scope, and I told Edward, "Let me try it from here."

He told me it was a long way, but I lay down and loaded the gun and got the moose in the scope, well I put the scope above him so that I couldn't see him. That's how far I raised it. I pulled the trigger and you could hear the bullet going.

When the moose went down, you could hear the noise when the bullet hit. It hit and it took a while for the sound to get back. I hit it right in the back of the neck – a 62 inch rack! It weighed about 2,500 pounds before it was skinned.

We started working on it, and it started snowing like crazy. We got it all done and covered it with brush and put the skin over it with more brush, and went back to the boat and continued going down. We had to stay at the first tower that night, because it was too cold and wet in the boat, and we didn't want the boy to get sick. We made a big fire that burned until daylight, and then we came back down.

Later on that afternoon, we went back up to where Gideon was. We didn't tell him about that big bull. We loaded up everything and came around the corner where the big bull was covered up, and we stopped. When we got out of the boat, he grabbed his gun because he thought we had seen a moose. We went out to the opening, and he said, "Huh." He always says that when he is satisfied. That night, that was a slow ride due to the heavy load. We had gotten three moose in three days.

One thing that makes getting a bull moose easier is during rutting season, they kind of have a one track mind. If you clean a shoulder blade, you rake it up against a branch and they think it is another horn. They think it is another bull moose around there. If they think that another bull is around, they think that they can fight off the moose and steal his cow. Then they come right up to you.

When a moose is in full rut, he isn't eatable. The smell is too bad. They will still drink water, but will stop eating. Their liver will change and will let off different hormones for rutting. The same thing happens with caribou. So just before the rut, they are the fattest they can get. Prior to them stopping eating, that is when people try to go out and get moose as we did with these three.

Arctic Village Kids

When I was really young, I lost my parents and my one brother and one sister. My grandparents were from Cantwell, which is near Denali National Park, and they adopted me. They were the ones who raised me. The Cantwell area is similar to this area here. The elevation and the weather are similar to here, and we are both surrounded by mountains. So a lot of this country I related to right away.

As I was growing up, things were a lot different with me because all of my classmates went home to moms and dads and brothers and sisters, but I was different. I think my grandparents noticed that it got to me as I got older. One thing that they wanted was to keep me totally focused on our way of life, how to live off the land and use things that the land provides for you.

I started learning all of that when I was five years old. After school was out and on weekends, we would always be going out. We spent about half the summer in the woods. They wanted to take my mind away from what was affecting me, and focus on what was going on out there.

I remember 20 years ago, right at this time of year, we were always on the mountain with a camp. I remember that our camp was always full of kids. We'd go up there and then come down, and the kids would see us in the village getting supplies. They would run home and ask their parents if they could go up the mountain with us. During those times, my wife and I were the ones who stayed up there the longest. The kids, they couldn't wait. They would ask during the summertime, "When are you guys going up the mountain?"

Now, with so many things changing, that has really changed. Satellite TV and computers and Nintendo games, all that is what has really got these kids focused now. It was nowhere near like that 20 years ago.

What I try to teach the kids is staying focused out there. One of them, he wanted a new bike. I bought it for him, and I told him that since I bought the bike, he had to go out with me and grandma this fall hunting. His brother, the oldest, wanted a couple of Xbox games. I got them for him because I want him to come out hunting with me and grandma this fall. Even if they don't want to, their mother makes them go with us.

Even though they may not know it beforehand, they enjoy being out there. One thing I noticed two years ago was how it helped getting them to finish their whole meal. Before going out, they are not eating good because they want to go back to their game. Those four days when they were out in the woods with us, they ate more than me! They ate more than ME!

We caught fish the first night. When my wife cooked the fish, they ate it all! That's what I like to see. I told their parents that too. They ate so much because they were out there. The oldest one, Duran, walked with me up that hill. Even though they lose patience, I tell them to not lose patience because it can take a while to spot things. That first full day, we sat there for eight hours. We had food with us, but we sat there and he would say, "Come on moose. Where are you?" About five minutes later, he said, "Grandpa, I see something!" Sure enough, a moose had come out. It was almost like he didn't know how to react because he had never seen anything like that before. We got the moose.

One thing that really makes me feel good, those two boys enjoy school. That was in the beginning of September, and we were supposed to come back on Sunday because the next Monday school was about to start. The weather was bad and it rained, so we had to stay another day. The youngest one, he couldn't care less, but the oldest one even cried because he wanted to come back so that he could go back to school. Coyote, he wouldn't care if we stayed up there a month. He likes it out there. That's one thing I notice when you do get those kids out there, how they change when they are in the woods.

A few weeks ago we went up river, Danny and Coyote and Gerald. We went up and put a fishing net up at the first tower. The water was high on the river but it started receding, so the creek water cleared up.

We gave Coyote a fishing can and put the hook on. On the fourth cast, he caught a pretty big pike, and it made me laugh. His dad was standing next to him as he was reeling it in, and the pike opened its mouth really wide. He got scared and just gave the can to his dad.

Coyote had the time of his life then, catching those fish. Prior to us leaving, I had asked him if he wanted to go up river with us and he didn't want to, but it turned out that he had fun. That's what I'm trying to do. Even though the kids get lost in TV, I try to make sure they focus on what is out there, because that's what I was taught by my grandparents.

How the Two Worlds Work for Us

Glenna Tetlichi, 53, is from Old Crow, Yukon. She was born here, raised here, and moved away at age 15. She moved back to Old Crow with her husband Joe in 1996. Glenna, Joe and their two sons moved to Whitehorse in 2008, where their two boys are attending school. http://www.map-landia.com/canada/yukon-territory/yukon/old-crow/ http://www.map-landia.com/canada/yukon-territory/yukon/whitehorse/

Sometimes I think about the past here in Old Crow. Times have changed a lot, eh? There have been so many changes with the lifestyle and our diet and the climate and the environment. We had a very simple lifestyle. We lived mostly on what we harvested from the land and the water. There was not a lot of store-bought food and it was a basic traditional diet.

The community was a lot closer. I remember hearing the language every day, all day. Our elderly people didn't die off from all the diseases that are around today like cancer. I don't think our people even had diabetes. There was no concern about health issues because we lived and ate healthy. Elders lived to be very old. But today we lose a lot of people at a young age and that is scary.

Our children today eat more sugar than we would hope, and there is junk food around that never used to be. The brighter side is we do get a lot more fresh fruits and vegetables. I remember getting that once a year in the summertime when the barge used to come up the Porcupine from Dawson. Other than that, we had the very basic food like caribou, moose, fish, and if were lucky, rice and macaroni.

I can remember when TV first came out. We never had video games. A lot of kids' time today is spent in front of the TV and playing video games. In that sense it is very challenging for parents. Some food today contributes to bad health of children and even adults.

Concerning cancer, it is the change in the lifestyle. Our people at one time were very, very healthy. There was a lot of physical activity. Today, people don't go out on the land as much, because it's moved from a caribou and trapping economy to a wage economy. People have to stay in town to work. For a lot of the work, you're stationary all day, so we don't get the physical exercise that our parents and grandparents did.

When it was a caribou economy or a trapping economy, they had to be out on the land from morning to night. As a result, it was stress-free. For their mental well-being it was very healthy to be out there.

Way back, we didn't have all the toxins and poisons in foods that we have nowadays. I think what's in the air goes into the vegetation. We eat that, and our caribou eat that. Likewise, we don't know what the fish eat. We don't know what all the game that flies up from down south like geese and ducks eat.

When I traveled down to the states, I saw lots of geese just sitting in contaminated ponds. Then they come north. How much of that contributes to our bad health? Also, it is a lot more stressful lifestyle today, and that contributes to not just cancer, but other diseases.

The stress level has definitely increased. For one thing, it is a wage economy now. Everything costs money. We are at a crossroads where we want our children to learn the culture. On the other hand, they have to get their education, so that's stressful. I have been in it and I know how stressful that is. You want them to have these two, but to find a balance is very challenging. Addictions can be stressful, very stressful. There is a lot more addiction around today. There are many different kinds of drugs that never used to be around, and it is scary.

Another subject I'd like to talk about is growing up in my family with my dad, a very accomplished hunter. One thing that really sticks out in my memory is that I didn't see him a lot, because in those days, the men were out all the time providing for their family. *I can hear even to this day my dad telling stories about what he had to do to get food, not just for his family, but for the community when they were near starvation. You know, my dad had to be a skilled hunter and have good instincts, because it was based on survival.*

When I started school, my dad got offered a job at the local school as the custodian. He took the job and switched to a wage economy in a very short time. The reason he chose to do that was because he never got an education. When I started school, I can remember my dad getting up and going to school for the night shift.

The role of the women is another interesting story. Before my husband and boys go out, I get their food ready. In our culture, we don't touch their hunting gear like the gun or the knife, because we say it brings bad luck. Mostly what I focus on is making sure they have enough food. If I have time, I will bake bannock bread. It is always good to have home baked meals because it stays in the body longer, especially when you are out on the land.

So then off they go. Most of the time I won't go with them because it is better in our culture for the women not be around the hunting because that can also bring bad luck. I will just leave it at that. So when they come back, I prepare our meat cache. I make sure it is cleaned out, the poles are ready to hang the meat, and there is enough fire wood to smoke the meat. Sometimes I would put fresh spruce boughs out, because it smells nice and doesn't affect the taste of the meat.

When they come back, we would get all the meat to the meat cache, hang it up, and smoke it for two days. When they come off the river or off the land in the winter, it is pretty cold and really important to have a meal ready. And of course hot tea and hot bread. So we would smoke it for a couple of days, and then I would start cutting the dried meat and putting it in the freezer. It is like beef jerky, but it is better.

My sons learn something every time they go out with their dad. Joe grew up as a very traditional man. He knows a lot about hunting, and he teaches them about how to respect

Boats at the ready, Porcupine River, Old Crow, Yukon

the animal. When they do go out, he teaches them to only take what they need, not just go and shoot because they see an animal. That is lesson number one.

Actually, they enjoy it all very, very much. When the caribou migrate through Old Crow in the spring and fall, it is very challenging to keep my sons inside or focused on school-work. If they go out hunting, then they are OK.

Sometimes we will have to take him out of the classroom for a day or so to get that out of our 12-year-old's system. It is very hard to strike a balance between school and bush, especially during caribou season. I don't mind his missing a little school at all because I think that it is a wonderful learning experience. How can you replace that?

You know I have a different understanding than the mainstream education system. Education is not just taught in the classroom. Someday I hope that the education system will understand that land-based learning can be so valuable.

Actually, the school gives them some opportunity to write or speak about the bush life. But, I think that could be improved on. Maybe it is hard because a lot of the teachers who establish the curriculum come from outside.

As for the formal education, they are learning reading and writing. But there is always room for improvement. As a matter a fact, the meeting I'm going to tonight is exactly about that. They are consulting with community members to look at what is working and what isn't. What can we do better? The challenge is how are we going to implement what the members are asking for.

There does seem to be a consensus. We are asking for balance. I think that children can learn better outside the classroom. They can learn by hands-on experiential learning. That is how our people were taught way, way back, by doing. If our children do a science project, then how can we integrate into it something from the land? We are not doing that yet. It is still really controlled by the bureaucracy of the Yukon government. It's sometimes a slow process for people outside the community to understand.

You might be interested to know that I killed a caribou myself when I was young. I shot it myself. I was maybe 14. I was proud of myself. We had to carry it back from Crow Mountain. I put great effort into it, I gave it away, and it felt good. It was a good cause and not for the sake of killing it. I shot it to provide food for my family and others.

I was especially proud because we carried it all the way down on our backs. My Dad wasn't with me, just some boys and girls my age. Nowadays, kids would drive a four-wheeler up to hunt and to bring the meat back.

When my dad would kill one, he would usually skin the caribou out where he killed it and bring it back in pieces. We would cut it into smaller pieces and put them away in the freezer. If he didn't, we'd skin it together. I feel really comfortable doing this, because I learn from him. He spent 20 years on the land, and I did not. There is a lot to learn. I could skin a caribou if I had to do it, but I have the luxury of getting help.

So much for my "bush" education. I had a good formal education as well. I started in grade one. I spent all the elementary years here in Old Crow. When I was 15, grade nine, I got transferred to Whitehorse to attend high school.

I can remember when I went to Whitehorse, it wasn't by choice. We had to go. To this day, our students still have to leave the community at grade 10. It is actually very sad that it is still like that today. That needs to change.

So anyways, leaving family and leaving the community and going into a totally different environment, culture, and diet was very, very challenging. I would say it was even somewhat traumatizing, because you are at the age when you need your parents the most. *I am like 15 years old and here I am, going away staying with another family. A day later, I am going into a school of 800 kids. Here I am used to going to a school of 30 students. That is really scary*.

The other thing that is very difficult is that our level of education is lower here in Old Crow, and there are lots of reasons for that. One is that we have multi-grade classrooms. We have three grades to one teacher. So the instructional time is a lot less compared to Whitehorse.

As a result of that, there are huge gaps. We start falling through the cracks. We are behind. Not only are we in culture shock, moving to a city, our grades are way below average. Part of it is multi-grade and the other part of that is the quality of education. It is not up to par in the Yukon let alone Old Crow. That is the purpose of this meeting tonight, to talk about that.

How can we improve the education system in the Yukon, not just Old Crow? When I was going to elementary school, I always got good grades. I had no problems. As soon as I got to Whitehorse, it is not a very good feeling to be at the bottom of the scale. Imagine what that does to a child's self-esteem. So there are a lot of odds against a child from Old Crow.

**The Northern general store
in Old Crow, Yukon**

Joe Tetlichi

Sadly, it was hard for the teachers to do much about this problem. They recognized it, but they didn't have the resources to help me. They didn't have tutoring, they didn't have the time, and they didn't have funding.

Today, Gwich'in First Nation has a community education liaison coordinator based in Whitehorse. Because of that, more of our young people graduate. However, they are still at a lower grade level. There is a lot of work to be done to improve that.

Nowadays, Old Crow kids get to come back home at Christmas, Easter, and Spring Break, and of course, for summer. When I went to school, I came back at Christmas and summer only.

I lived with a family when I was in Whitehorse, because I was into competitive cross-country skiing. Arrangements were made for my older sister Shirley and I to live with a family. They were living near the ski trails and their children were in the ski program. When I was in school, there were times I was very, very homesick.

While I learned a lot in my 20 years away, I knew that some day there was going to be that call to come home to your roots. For me, one day there was a strong call to come home and I just did it. I don't regret it to this day. The good thing about that is learning to live in two worlds.

If young people don't have an interest at first, some day they will. And as long as they have a strong foundation and they know where they come from and know their identity, they will. There is a whole world out there and I would never try to stop it. I would encourage them because there is so much to learn. I just want them to be confident in the choices they make and confident in themselves. The most important thing is how to bring the two worlds together.

Joe and I talk to them about that. Recently our little guy sat there and interviewed his dad. He wanted to know about all these different careers. What is a pilot? How much money do they make? He is already in his mind going to the university and getting a trade.

If it means going to Whitehorse because they have to get their grades, then as parents, we are going to have to work with them to understand this priority. If they want to camp with their friend tonight, but they have homework to do, what is the priority? As we go, we always have to guide them and talk it through. Again, it's a matter of balance.

[At this point, Glenna's husband Joe comes into the room and Glenna addresses him.]

Glenna: So what do you think about our kids' having balance, Joe?

Joe: In regards to protecting the land and the wildlife, yes. This morning my nephews were here and pretty soon I am getting a boat.

I said wow, you know, I am going to be teaching the little lads. Three years from now, I won't have to go with them, because they will have the skills to operate a gun, to skin a caribou, dress it, and pack it out.

So the tradition continues. There are going to be some to go away and not be interested in coming back, but the majority of kids are going to have that balance.

Glenna: Even if one wanted to become a medical doctor and move to Toronto, I would be ok.

Joe: I would be comfortable with that knowing that they are doing something that they want to do. It is still engrained at an early age that they know where to get caribou and be proud of it.

Glenna: They have obviously contributed to society in a healthy way. That's fine by us.

Joe: You know, everybody has a choice which road to go on. Some people will be more fortunate than others. And that is just part of life.

Glenna: If Joe and I choose to spend our earnings on drugs and alcohol, we are not going to have a hell of a lot; we are not going to have a truck, that's for sure, or a four- wheeler, or a healthy family. It's the choice of an individual regardless of whether you're in Old Crow or in Boone, North Carolina. It's a choice. That is what we are trying to teach our children regardless of whether you're here or in the States or Australia.

Joe: You know the interesting thing about that, too, is that people here are rich in the way they live, because they have land and the wildlife. I mean you can get up tomorrow morning and you can go down and pitch a tent, get your fish.

Glenna: And you know, compared to people in the states, we are more laid back. We don't get too excited about anything. We have all this land, we're not going to get harassed, and it's less stressful. We are pretty lucky.

Bush Lady Turns Teacher

Alice Vitrekwa is a 59-year-old Gwich'in Indian from Fort McPherson, Northwest Territories, Canada. She spent most of her early years on the land with her siblings and parents, learning all the skills necessary to live in the wilds. While her schooling was all too brief, she learned to read and write. Hers is the story of a Native person who has a foot in both camps, and whose life has become a triumph of the human spirit as she navigates the tumultuous waters of a rapidly changing cultural landscape.

I was born here in Fort McPherson in the late 1940's, and back then people made their living by hunting, fishing, and trapping. Maybe only one or two people had jobs in the community. The rest had to make their living hunting, trapping, and fishing. In the summertime, the month of June-July is when we go up to fish camp, where you have to make dry fish during those days, because there were hardly any freezers. We help our mom make dry fish not only for us to eat, but also we make this dry fish because we have dog teams. Helping our mom was what we did.

We used every bit of the fish, whether we ate it or the dogs ate it. The fish guts we would eat, the herring was the one we would cut for the dogs and even the guts of the herring we would hang up on the porch. After it dried real good, some we would cook, and then we would put it in pails and into the ground. It was a lot of work back then, but it was what you did in July and August.

When there was no school in those summer months, we didn't want to leave town, we had to go. We went with our parents; we never came back into town until it was time for the kids to come to school. When I first started school in 1959, I was nine years old. My older sisters went to residential school outside our community. When I was of age to go to school at age six, there was no room. I didn't go to school until they opened the hostel here in McPherson.

The hostel was a place where you stayed as well as went to school. Everyone in the community made their money out on the land, and they decided they should build a hostel. We were put in a hostel because my parents couldn't stay in town, because they made their living out there.

When we were at camp, my mom and dad and grandmother and uncle were there, so both my parents talked a lot of Gwich'in. They both understand English, my mom mostly spoke Gwich'in and my dad and my grandmother spoke straight Gwich'in. I was in that environment and when they put me in the hostel, I couldn't understand English. When I went to school, I had to learn English. I don't know how I ever learned, but I learned.

I'll tell you, it was hard working when you made your living out on the land. But towards the end, it got to be something that was normal to me. You got up and had a lot of water to pack, you had wood to cut, we had to get the dry weeds to have smoke under our fish camp and then we had to do our laundry by hand.

I look back and it was hard work, but then it was part of our living. If we sat back and did nothing, what's going to happen? It was something we had to do every day, and we did it.

Back in those days, we had large families. There were 12 of us kids in the family: four brothers, and eight of us girls plus my dad and my mom. My dad would take care of the nets, and when he was coming back to shore, we would all go down together at about 7-8 in the morning, and hike the fish up. We never really said, "Oh, you do it".

After we brought the fish up, we would start working with fish, and about 11, mom would say, "Well two of you are going to have to cook lunch" and we don't argue, two of us volunteer to do lunch. If we didn't volunteer, she would say, "Oh, it's Sarah and Alice that do lunch today," so we prepared lunch.

Fish were important to us but so were the caribou. In the fall time, we move to our cabin. In the month of September and October is the month that it freezes up. Right where we stay is a trail to the mountain. I remember when it was safe to go on the ice, my dad would say, "Well, we have enough fish now, we need to work towards trying to get caribou because when you are out there, you do not want to eat fish three times a day."

There wasn't much stuff in the store, except the basics like tea, sugar, flour and rice. No junk food. So when we were at our fish camp, the only way we were going to get dessert was to work for it. If we wanted to be lazy, then we got no dessert. We really looked forward to berry-picking because in camp, they didn't have powdered juice or anything like that.

In mid-October is when it freezes up and it starts snowing. When the ice is safe to walk on, we go hunting. Nowadays, we have caribou in August because of the Dempster Highway. It is easier to go up with a truck and get the caribou whereas before the Dempster Highway, nobody really got their caribou in August. You would have to wait until there was enough snow so that you could travel down the mountain to haul them back.

I always like to compare then to now. Now you go on the Dempster Highway and you get your caribou on the back of the truck, and it's gutted but not skinned or butchered. Whereas my dad used to go with a dog team like all the other people that would go hunting. You never see them bring a whole caribou back; it's all prepared when my dad comes back. When he does, I usually go out and tie up the dogs and unload his sled including the caribou.

My mom and grandmother sometimes talked about how they would use dogs with little packs to haul caribou. They would have a pack on each side of the dog so it would be balanced.

Of course, we didn't have skidoos in those days, so everybody had dogs. I had a dog team but I didn't own the dogs, they all belonged to my dad. But I was always there to look after and help my dad with them. In the fall time, like in October when it starts snowing, he would start cutting wood in the bush and I would start hauling the wood. Sometimes, we used to put the pups in the little harness and start training them. When you first put a harness on them, they want to get out and they get tangled.

Lots of times, I helped my dad train pups. It is a lot of fun because you travel by yourself, sometimes just to break trail. If there is another family staying above us or below, they might come.

When we didn't really have much work to do, my mom would say, "You should go on the river and break trail." So I'd hitch up five-six dogs and away I'd go. And when I am traveling with dogs, I am feeling that I am not alone because the dogs are there.

In 1964 when they took me out of school, I had to learn a lot of things like how it was to make your living out there. My mom taught me how to dry meat. With my mom, whatever she did, she always told me, "watch how I do this." I even watched if she didn't tell me. She showed me how to prepare a whole caribou or how to prepare a whole moose. She told me many times that I had to know how to do this when I was out on the land, because she wasn't going to be here with me forever, and who would carry on?

I remember though, that we did get to play some. If we wanted to sew or if we wanted to play hide and go seek, my parents would say, "Get your work done, and once you get all your work done, then you will have your free time." While we understood that the work had to be done, we always looked forward to playing.

But don't get me wrong, my parents were strict. It is not like today where kids talk back to their parents. Nowadays is really different compared to my growing up because you can't spank kids. That's where the problem is because the kids can do what they want. We got a strapping in the school if we didn't listen. When I first got a strapping, I thought I would never talk back again because I learned something from that strapping.

When we got spankings from my dad, I never forgot it and we were really disciplined. If my mom spanked me, my dad is not going to get mad at her; they both supported each

other and made decisions together. I'll never forget, mom
always used a skinny willow.
It wrapped around your leg,
and that's why I never forgot
it. I told myself that I was not
going to do anything that my
parents would spank me for.
We learned that if we had
disagreements, we had to re-
solve them among ourselves.
We kids were seen and not
heard. Nowadays, you can't
spank, even your own kids.

In 1964 I was out on
the land most of the time
and then I started working,

**Anglican Church in Fort McPherson,
Northwest Territories**

I think in 1976. In 1980, I worked in the community and by then my little boy was old
enough to go to school. In 1977, I got married to my husband, Ernest. Anyhow, when my
oldest son was six years old, and we were out on the land most of the time, I decided that
it was either that I took him out on the land to teach him the skills out there, or he had to
go to school.

It was a big decision that I had to make, but it wasn't that hard. When my dad took me
out of school it was because of my mom's illness. My dad wanted me home so that I could
help my mom. At that time I was really upset at my dad as to why he chose me out of 12 of
us. Why did he choose me to go out on the land, because there goes my teenage years to
be spent out there. Sure, it's good to be good to my mom and dad and to my grandparents
because they had taught me lots. But the way I looked at it at the time was, why did they
choose me?

At the same time, I don't think I was doing really good in school. Although my dad
valued an education, and it was priority that his children get their education, when you are
young and foolish, you don't really listen. I didn't realize that education was so important,
that I was going to be the one that was going to benefit from it. When he chose me, I was
really upset but we never talked about it ever again. But, by the time my dad pulled me out,
I could read and write and I didn't go back to school. I blamed my dad for taking me out.

Now, for my son to go to school, and there is no hostel by that time, we had to stay in
town. It was the hardest thing for me to leave the land and come into the community. I had
to find a job in order for my boy to go to school. As much as I love the land and wanted to
be out there, I came into town. I wanted so badly for my son to have an education, because
I didn't have that education and my self-esteem was pretty low. If the RCMP came to my
door, I would say, "Oh I can't talk to these people because my English is too poor." That's
how low my self-esteem was.

Today, it's different because my self-esteem is up. Anyways, looking at my son, I don't
want him to have those feelings that I had; I want him to get his education. If I keep him
away from school because I love the land, down the road, that will be held against me. I really stressed to my children that I wanted them to get their education, and so that's when I

started slowly staying more in town. Right now, I am here and do have foster children. If I didn't have the foster children, I would be up at my camp.

You know, while education is really important to a person's confidence, in 1974 we lost our mom and that was bad. She died of cancer. I'll have to say that I turned to drinking to make me feel a little better, but it didn't help, it just made matters worse. I slowly sobered up and then I started talking with people. I realized that talking was a good medicine because it helped me to release pain when things were bothering me. When I started talking, I didn't realize how much was bothering me. I didn't realize I was carrying a load.

I talked to people that I felt comfortable with. Once I started doing that, I found that it was the lack of education that got my self-esteem so low. I regret not having that education, because there was so much I wanted to do that I couldn't do, because I didn't have it.

I would start thinking, "Well, I don't have that education but my parents taught me something out there". They taught me the land skills. My mom taught me how to sew and all those things. I had pushed it aside and decided to bring it out and do something with it, and so I started doing that. Now, I don't put myself down as much. Back then if my brother would have said that a professor was going to want to interview me, I would have said that there was no way. But today it is different.

While I struggled till I figured out that my land skills were important to my self-esteem, I still wanted to make sure my kids got their formal education. My two oldest got their education. They graduated in the same year.

My adopted son went as far as grade 10 and he couldn't continue because he was having a lot of problems. I pushed him, but he was at the point where I finally talked to my older sister and told her that I didn't know where I was going wrong. She said, "I think you need to leave him alone. You said what you could and did what you could for him and now it's all up to him. Maybe down the road he will decide to finish his education." So I told him that.

But I still know that the land skills are important. This winter, Ernest and my boys went hunting, and they brought the caribou back. My oldest son wanted to skin the caribou. I had to show him how to cut it up. He would skin about three caribou and I told him, "Skin it and I am going to cut it up, you watch me." So he skinned it with my help at a little place behind our house. I asked him to watch me because my mom and dad told me to watch them if I wanted to learn in order to survive out on the land. He watched very carefully. He was willing to learn because I told him that anything he wanted to hunt for, he will also have to cut up.

I had the opportunity to work as an alcohol counselor for 10 years and then I got into cooking. There is a camp about 20 kilometers up river and I work there cooking whenever they need me. Then I got into the school and they wanted me to sub so I got into subbing. I was able to work with the teachers and kids who were having problems with reading. I had had all the experience on the land.

Last year I was practically living in the school where I was subbing. I would just follow the instructions left from the teachers and I would tell the students, "This is what you have to do. If you choose not to do it, just go down to the principal. So you have a choice that you either do your work or not."

Arctic Refuge Day

I really noticed that the kids were good with me, and I found out that I have a lot of patience. But that's because of my education on the land. Sometimes I say to myself, I didn't even finish grade seven, and here I am in grade 12.
-- Alice Vitrekwa, Bush Lady turned teacher

The Tetlit Co-op store in Fort McPherson, Northwest Territories

You see, the animals come to us. We always believed that the animals give themselves to us. We have never hunted them. That's why we're here today…. This is our garden. This is who we are. This is it.
    Point Hope, Alaska, resident Steve Oomituk

Chapter Three
The Gardens of the Inupiat and the Inuvialuit

While most of the Inupiats and the Inuvialuit (the Alaskan Eskimos and Canadian Inuit) also count on caribou for subsistence, theirs is a vastly different relationship with the natural environment. They are a people of the sea as well as of the land, traditionally taking a living from the bowhead and beluga whale, seal, walrus, and fish, as well as caribou, moose, Dall sheep, and other terrestrial wildlife. The Inupiat settlements stretch all across the length of Alaska's northern coastal plain from Point Hope on the Chukchi Sea to Kaktovik. The Inuvialuit are centered around the Mackenzie Delta of the Northwest Territories. One exception to this sea-oriented subsistence practice is the Inupiat village of Anaktuvuk Pass,

Alaska, located in the largest pass through the Brooks Range. These people are 200 miles from the ocean and hunt primarily the caribou that migrate through the pass. For most of these Native people, then, their gardens are in the sea and on the land. Our interviews emphasize their whaling, fishing and hunting pursuits.

Kaktovik Whale Hunt—Isaac Akootchook and James Lampe offering a prayer—Inupiat and The Whales, Kaktovik, Alaska —Photograph Subhankar Banerjee, 2001

The Ex-Roughneck Movie-Maker

Dennis Allen is a 48-year-old Native person from Inuvik, Northwest Territories. He is shown here with son, Hayden. His mother is a Gwich'in Indian from Old Crow, Yukon, and his late father is an Inuvialuit person from the Mackenzie Delta. He came from a large family and now has a wife and two children of his own. He worked for 13 years as a roughneck in the Beaufort Sea oil-fields then went to college and began writing films and TV scripts. He and his family now live in Whitehorse, Yukon.

http://www.maplandia.com/canada/ northwest-territories/inuvik-region/inuvik/

http://www.maplandia.com/canada/ yukon-territory/yukon/whitehorse/

My history is that I never finished high school. I worked in the "Oil Patch" from age 17 until I was 30. I worked for the oil and gas industry on drilling rigs up in the Beaufort Sea and Norman Wells and wherever I could get a job as a roughneck. It's not a great job. It's bad on the back and hard on the liver, because roughnecks all drink a lot.

We had a big boom in the Beaufort Delta for many years. They were exploring offshore. The federal government was sponsoring the exploration for oil and gas. They were giving people tax breaks and incentives for oil companies to go up to the Beaufort Sea to explore. That happened for over 10 years.

It was crazy. Money was cheap and everyone had cash. We made a lot of money but we drank away a lot of it. So that was it. Lots of drinking, partying, and doing drugs. People were buying boats and skidoos and stuff like that, but we Native people had had no experience with having money. That came later on in life.

That was a huge industry with lots of drilling rigs in the sea and delta. You need a lot of crews. There was lots of people from Fort McPherson and Aklavik. People were moving around a lot because they would get lazy, have a hangover, and get fired. They would just go and get another job the next day making just as much money. Money was just crazy – everyone had money.

It's a hell of a lifestyle. You work for two weeks and then you come into town for a week and piss away all your money each week. Then go back to the rig and come back to town.

I did that for years and years. It was crazy. I'm a recovering alcoholic. It was fun when we were younger because we had a lot of money and we did a lot of traveling, we bought trucks and skidoos, you know. We had money! We were young and crazy! We just didn't give a shit.

Some of the workers were from down South. Some of them were drinkers and partiers, but a good part of them were banking their money and going to school. They were just

**Downtown Inuvik, Northwest Territories, the heart of the
Mackenzie Delta "Oil Patch"**

working to make enough money to go to school. That went on and on and on for 13 years. For them, it was more for the money. They were smart with the money. They would pay off houses or land. They would invest their money. They went back and enjoyed the fruits of their labor. But unfortunately, we didn't have that philosophy. We were too interested in having a good time.

The industry was pretty careful about the environment. If you spilled diesel in the snow, you had to scoop it up and dump it. There was also a lot of ignorance as well. I think the prior boom cycle, the 1960's, that's where you find oil drums up at Caribou River. All of those toxic things and sludge and oil, they just dumped it. They just left the barrels there. No one was policing them and they didn't have to clean it up. That was up in Caribou River and the delta was the same thing. By the time that our boom came around, the early '80s, it was more stringent. There was more control from the federal government. It's even tighter now.

My whole youth was spent doing that. After I turned 30, I didn't want to do that anymore. I knew there was more to life. At that time, I was writing songs and I was expressing myself artistically. The more I did that, the more I wanted to make my living doing that. So I went back to school. I knew I had to get educated. When I was 31 or 32, I had to upgrade myself.

Then I took one year of Native communications, where I took photography and graphics and cameras and learning how to do interviews and stuff like that. It was called *Introduction to Communications*. That piqued my interest.

To be more specific, I wanted to be a filmmaker. I want to make films. I had to go and get a university education. I had to get all my intro courses, education like math and English that you need to get into a university. I had to do another year of that.

Once that was done, I did a two-year college diploma where I studied filmmaking in Calgary at the Southern Alberta Institute of Technology. I really enjoyed it down there. I did really well in my classes. After I graduated, I worked on a TV show. The CBC drama show hit "North of 60" was what I worked on. Then I came home and bought a used beta cam which is a huge broadcast- quality camera, and I started making films with that. Now, I could really see me spending 20 years or more in the film and TV industry.

The first film I did on my own was a half-hour drama that I wrote, produced, directed, and edited. It was called "Someplace Better." It was based on things that I had seen and what had happened in my life. The storyline is of this elderly widower who kills his abusive grandson in self-defense, and he wants to leave the physical world and join the spiritual world with his wife and family and friends. He wants to leave this world. In between, there is a Native cop who is torn in between two worlds, and that's where my brother was – in RCMP, being caught in two worlds trying to enforce federal law and yet to live as a Native person with our own laws. Even further was my dad's uncle who shot his son in self-defense one time. There was a big court case.

It did really well – it went to the Sundance Film Festival. People really enjoyed it, because it dealt with two worlds. The slug line was "When two worlds collide, there is nowhere else to go." It aired on APTN, the Aboriginal People's Television Network in Canada, and then it got licensed in New Zealand as well. Yeah, it did well.

It went to two big festivals here in Canada that are sponsored by the National Screen Institute. The festivals are called Local Heroes and Local Heroes International. The international festival is the best of the short films from around the world. It played there and did really well.

People were telling me to do bigger things. That was the last drama I did. I started doing documentaries. I was living in Yellowknife, and there is this little town called Colville Lake just between here and Yellowknife. It's a traditional Dene community. They called me up and told me that they were doing a traditional walk between Colville Lake and Fort Good Hope, because they used to walk between communities years ago before they had plane service. The last people to walk on that trail did so in 1964. The guy was still alive – Paul Kotchily – and there was another elderly couple who knew the trail. So they wanted to take some young people on the trail before they forgot it, so the young ones would know where the trail is.

They called me and this other guy up and asked if we wanted to come along and film it. So we went on this 80-mile trek through the bush on a trail that hadn't been walked on in 34 years at that time. We went on this big walk. There were some real interesting stories on that trip. There were two young boys who were ordered to go on the trip because they were delinquents. They had an interesting story too – they went and learned something about themselves. Well, that one was called *Walk a Path to Healing*.

The second one was about a community caribou hunt. Each fall they go out to the barren lands and they work for 10 days. They work with skins and make dry meat, pretty much like Old Crow. Like a traditional community.

The third film I did was a documentary about my dad called* My Father, My Teacher. *It was about my relationship with my 80-year-old dad and the generational gap between us. He grew up in the traditional lifestyle and I grew up with electricity and TV. His world was probably 1,000 square miles. My world is almost the globe.

Now I think I have paid my dues. And people like it. I'm starting to play with some of the big players now like the Discovery Channel with a guy who won an Emmy. I'm associate-producing his film. I'm moving past the starving artist phase. I'm raising a family now

– our second child is coming in August. We are going to move to the Yukon. We are hoping to buy some property outside of town.

My wife and I would like to send our kids to school in Whitehorse. What I would really like to do is spend winters there and come home to a cabin in the delta for the summer. I might build 16 x 16 foot cabins and use it as a retreat, either for people who are recovering or living off the street. Maybe social services could pay for their room and board there. Or maybe it could be for people who want a retreat like a corporate group or tourism.

Also I want to do more with my music. I'm going to record original songs for the first time in November. I hope to make a little bit of money everywhere, maybe selling CD's, films, and having a camp on the land. It's fun. That's kind of the plan.

Traditional Subsistence and Modern Technology

Larry Burris is a 39-year-old man living in Anaktuvuk Pass, Alaska, who has an Inupiat mother and a white father. He has a wife, three children, two dogs and one cat. He is the Village Liaison for the North Slope Borough of Anaktuvuk. He is President of the Nunamiut Corporation.

http://www.maplandia.com/united-states/alaska/north-slope-borough/anaktuvuk-pass/

There was a lot of traveling in the 80's with ATV's, when they first came out. For us, that was the best thing since sliced bread, because you could get to more places that were further away in less time. If you knew of caribou that were a long distance away, you were limited on foot, especially if you have a family. It makes it almost impossible to get there quickly. You would have to go yourself or with a partner, and you would have to be swift, not lose any time. Now, with ATV's, you can get from place to place so much easier. You can haul all your gear out there, and haul the meat back.

Now life is full of concerns about money, jobs, and bills. That's part of our new life for all Alaska Natives, but at the same time, we need to keep our subsistence going. One way to bridge the gap is using the ATV's.

For the most part, we struggle just like the person in a city would struggle, but in a different way. We have our garden right here on our traditional land; we just have to be able to get out there to harvest it.

We are not completely without other modern amenities. Besides the ATV's, we have

The beauty of the peaks overlooking Anaktuvuk Pass, Alaska

been able to acquire phone services, cable and satellite TV, and internet services. In that sense, we in rural Alaska have become more like people in the cities and small towns in terms of staying in contact with modern society. We are not oblivious to what goes on outside of the village when, in years past, we would have been.

In that sense, we are just like a person living in a city. We have a pull in that direction, but we need to keep our subsistence lifestyle. We can't do that without having these modern amenities, like motorized vehicles. You could say that it was not the people's choice to use these things. Actually, the Nunamiut had no choice, because a choice had to be made to give up our traditional nomadic life for another lifestyle. It became mandated by federal law to have all children in the United States and its territories schooled under federal standards established by the U.S. Government. That was part of the reasoning for the settlement of the village of Anaktuvuk Pass. The Nunamiut had to make a settlement so that children would have a place to go to school.

Without modern amenities, we would have to go back to the bows and arrows and dog teams. If we did that, our jobs would go. Good-paying jobs are not going to be here waiting for us if we go chasing caribou on a week-long or month-long hunt.

We have faced some challenges to maintaining our use of modern amenities. Years back, we wanted to have ATV access to our traditional hunting areas that had been put in the Gates of the Arctic National Park. For the most part, we were trying to select lands for ATV access that would allow us to go where we felt like we needed to go, where usually you could find caribou or sheep. I don't remember the exact number of acres that changed hands, but it was a good agreement. The Park Service was able to gain more land than they gave up, while we were able to gain land that we needed and give up land that we really didn't need in the first place.

With Gates of the Arctic, Anaktuvuk Pass is the only community in North America, or at least the United States, that is completely surrounded by a national park. And we do not have a road leading to our community, and consequently we must fly in. These factors give us good protection from having too much outside influence.

It's pretty hard to get a road built into a park; it would take an act of Congress to do that. If you remember, there was the Hickle Highway that they wanted to put through Anaktuvuk Pass, but there were concerns from our elders, and that was that. They ended up going through Cold Foot and Atigun Pass to Deadhorse and Prudhoe Bay.

There are some places on our land where a four-wheeler can't make it. In those places, an Argo can allow you to climb up really steep hills without worrying too much about falling over. With a four-wheeler, you would be walking it up or you won't do it at all. With Argos and four-wheelers, we are always staying on the established trails. The only time you go off the trail is when there is a caribou or some type of animal that you want to catch. Then again, when you go off trail, you get into a rough ride, sometimes increasing the chances of getting stuck.

Caroline Cannon was born in Point Hope, Alaska, in the old village. She has five brothers, two of which are whaling captains, and a sister. She is married to a man from the Lower 48. http://www.maplandia.com/united-states/alaska/north-slope-borough/point-hope/ http://en.wikipedia.org/wiki/Point_Hope_Alaska

When we were young, we were not growing up with too much. We grew up with practically the bed and stove, and little dishes. But you know, we were happy with the little we had. When marbles and jack stones came, those were really valuable to us.

We don't have trees, as you can tell, so we relied on seals to keep the fire going, and today we still practice that out on the ice. When we are out whaling, we use that to heat up the tent. When you think of family values, that was it. We grew up in a one-bedroom house, and there was seven children and two adults in there.

Again, I want to say that we didn't have much. My father was blessed that he was working for the school district as a maintenance man. We had more than what others had. There were only a few jobs in the village. I think we were happy because we had to work for everything. We had no running water, and it was only 10 or 15 years ago that we got it. We had to haul ice or snow in order to wash clothes. We had to get the snow melted, and it was a lot of physical work, but all good.

We always had parkas and once a year, my mom made us new parkas with fur inside. Everyone in the village had mukluks; we didn't have any Converse or Nike at all. The fur inside was caribou skin, and it kept us warm. A lot of us had traditional clothing.

I went to school here in Point Hope. By the time we were in eighth grade, we were shipped out, meaning I went to Rangle Institute for a year. From there, I went to Montagium and did a couple of years in Anchorage and graduated here. This was going back into the 1970's so we didn't really have any TV. All we had was the radio; that was our way of communication. When I was in eighth grade, we found out that we could write letters and mail them out. With what little money we had, even though a stamp costs nine cents or something at that time, it was still a lot of money.

I never knew anything about prejudice until I went out. The North Slope Borough and oil industry had a lot of money coming in at that time. So, there was a group of high school students they picked for a cultural exchange down South. They chartered a bus from Seattle all the way to the top. There were six from Point Hope, and I think 10 from Barrow and there was at least 30-40 students on that charter bus. We were going to get educated by the outside world and hopefully come back to help our people.

Whale bones ceremonial site at Point Hope, Alaska

I think there was a plus to that, and I learned prejudice during that trip. We came from a whaling community where we were exchanging our culture and tradition on a slide show. They saw the whale, the cutting, and then called us all kind of names. My heart really hurt at that time and didn't realize they could be so cruel. That was something that I'll never forget, and I hope that my children and grandchildren won't have to go through. It was so mean.

Here we come from a small school, and we are proud of who we are and excited to show the world. That was one thing that took me a long time to pray and forget about it. There was some good about it, too, because they educated us in a lot of areas, in things we would never have seen. I know there are some people my age who have never even left Alaska, so I was blessed to see the other side of the world. It also made me who I am, and I am not afraid to say anything.

I believed in myself, and I was determined that nobody was going to hurt me. I know my parents used to talk about how they were treated. I guess if I were to walk in their shoes, I can't say it was that bad. I looked up to my aunt and uncle, Patrick and his wife, Eva. But, it was mainly the whaling captains because they were the main providers. They are hard workers and provide to others that are in need, so I have always admired these people.

Whale was our source of our food, and we were taught at a very young age to help. I think it was common to have a little kid around the age of seven to come out there and learn and observe. The young men chopped the wood, while the little boys observed and carried the wood into the tent. They learned how to dry the wood and separate the wet wood from the dry. During the summer, there are drift trees. I can't say that there are tree trunks, but there are logs that wash up in the summertime. We put those aside, but our main source is seal or whale blubber that keeps the fire burning.

I was about 10 years old when I went out whaling. I just watched and helped whenever I could with the snow or the dishes. That is how you pick it up. You train at that very young age and start learning your responsibilities. My parents were very traditional and have always believed that whales were not ours, but a gift from God. The Bible speaks of "cheerful giver." So when you give cheerfully, it will always come back. My parents have always believed that and relied on that. We are responsible for the widows, orphanages, and the homeless. When we catch, it is tradition that we go share with people.

The people that don't have transportation or the handicapped are blessed with whatever we have. Growing up, my mother's parents were Lenny and Dacy and were well-respected whaling captains. From family to family, that has been passed down. I got my first share when I was 10, and it made you feel good. Right now, I hear some people are soaking

A Point Hope feast: muktuk, seal, and fish

their skin. This is the time they sew the boats and as you can see, in that boat right there, it is covered with seal.

This time of year [March] makes you anxious and you start preparing: you clean out your meat cache; you clean your equipment; the ladies make sure they sew the skins; and they start making their parkas and mukluks. We always use our traditional clothing. When you are out there, it gets very, very cold, but the boots, the mukluks, and parkas keep you warm.

We get the boat and the whole crew. It is not a one-day process, it is probably a week-long process where you prepare and get all your equipment together. You get your tent, the stove, and cooking equipment together. We, the ladies, are out there cooking for the men. I am going to stress again, it is very cold.

My mother was very strict that we fed the men at least four or five times a day, a hot meal to keep them warm. The stove is constantly going because they need that warm coffee and tea.

There is a big sled for the whole crew covering the hole in the boat where they keep their equipment. We have about three or four different sleds, and the men actually sleep down there so we have caribou and polar bear skin to keep warm. My parents always had us bless the boat before we went anywhere.

The crew usually consists of six to eight men and the cooks vary. I know that we like to keep it around six to ten men total. We get together and pray around the boat and ask for safety. It can be real harsh, and the ocean itself can be real unpredictable. Communication is vital; the paddles were used too as a way to say stop the noise because there is activity. Everybody knew that except today, kids don't know about it. When you hear three gun shots, there is a crack in the ocean ice. You go out there when there is an opening. Only when there is an opening will you see activity. They put the boat on edge and wait patiently. It could be weeks or a day, it just varies. And you'll know when they catch a whale. Sometimes, it is so calm and real quiet and all of a sudden, you hear communication. They make noises to let other crews know that they caught a whale. It ends up about 30 men making the same noise, or at least the 12 guys on the boat. If the other crews hear you caught a whale, they are going to go put their equipment on that whale so they get a share. You have to give your first whale away as a captain.

Once you harpoon it, we cut a little hole near the flipper and start paddling it in. There are no motors so it is the only way. You have to go out two or three miles but I think the last time was 12 or 14 miles out. The previous year, it was really bad. It might have been because of the weather and global warming. We had no whales and it was disturbing to us.

When you get it on the ice, you then have to divide it through that pattern right there (as she points to a drawing on the wall). It says, "captain's share, captains crew share, first two crews," which is a very vital part right there.

We still use that from our ancestors and traditionally that is how it's always been. Some parts are more tender than others. You will see that we save some for Thanksgiving, Christmas, the whaling feast, the first ice, and year-round festivity.

It is a lot of work, when you get a whale. It's a three-day process. You cut it up and share with everybody. You haul it to the village and put it in the meat cache and divide to each household. It is at least a 72-hour process when you land a whale. It gets very tiring.

I am worried about the future of whaling because of offshore drilling. It is a national thing that everybody knows about. I am worried about it because I feel that scientifically they have not proven anything if there is a spill out there. We feel the impacts of the Exxon Valdese spill. I am hearing our brothers and sisters that live in that area, the land is still being impacted. They are

Downtown Point Hope in March

not doing their traditional things that they used to do 30 years ago. It is a slow process of how nature takes its course, if it heals. I am worried not only because of the bowhead and beluga, but also the seals, polar bears and everything that has provided for us.

My father was a good provider; I have always looked forward to this time of the year. Dad normally gets polar bear, and since my dad has been gone, it's been awhile. Sometimes, we will get a treat from someone, but it was an annual thing and when you don't have it, you just feel like you are lost. I worry about that, and if there were some oil spill, I wonder how it could impact us.

There were times when my brothers and father were out hunting, so I had to literally put five gallons [of fuel oil] into the tank to heat up our house. When I spill, I see it go down there, red in color. I know what it does to the snow, it evaporates and makes it like it melts and that is the scary part. Scientifically, I do not know the impacts. Visually, I saw what it did to the snow. Can you imagine if it's in the ocean?

It's very touchy for me. I have been involved in the political arena and a voice for our community for 30 years. I have heard elders at public meetings since I was a youngster. In the village while we were growing up, the whole town didn't have electricity, so there was some parts that had electricity and could afford to have heat going out. If there were a community gathering or meeting, us kids would go in there to warm up.

We had to sit and listen. A lot of them were stressing how important it was to protect our livestock. Remember, we were impacted by Project Chariot, and these were the leaders that were speaking up at this time. They were speaking on behalf of our people and telling us to never give in. They would tell us to be very alert when outsiders came. When I first heard about it, it brought tears to my eyes. I have always respected the whaling captains, who after five whales become a higher priority and an honored citizen. You have to prove yourself because those whales are big.

You had a voice, but back then there were the few people that had earned their time in a public meeting. As a child, I would come listen, but I didn't realize I was soaking in a lot of information. Everyone spoke in Inupiat.

When I hear about the offshore drilling, my first reaction was by all means, we can't let this happen. When they first came in 1971, they established the North Slope Borough, and they came to our village. They had a community meeting, and one of the elders said, "We can't give our land, our ocean away because it doesn't belong to us."

I remember him also saying, "If we rely on and respect our land and our ocean, Mother

Nature will never ever quit providing."

I have always known that the oil industry are the giants and have all the big money versus us little people. I'll never give up hope, and historically we have always been here and we will always be here. The constitution says we have a voice, and we need to be heard. We need to protect out way of life; we have seen many places on Discovery Channel where there is genocide and there are people that no longer exist because they mess with Mother Nature. Whether it be for coal or oil, when you take something out of the land, there is a price that you will pay. It is going to impact the structure, the land, and there is a cost to it. It's a scary thing for me.

I have always said that God didn't make a mistake when he put us in the Arctic. He knew we could handle the harsh environment, the cold, and what have you. Our lifestyle is free, and here I can still go and be as free as I want to be.

Inupiat Caribou Hunter

Andrew Hopson is a 33- year- old Inupiat hunter who lives in Anaktuvuk Pass, the largest pass in the Brooks Range. This village has been occupied for hundreds of years because it is on the migratory route of several caribou herds. The people of Anaktuvuk are the only Inupiat that are not whalers, as they are about 200 miles inland. Andrew provides caribou and sheep meat for many people in the village every year. He has a family with four children, which he wants to have educational opportunities he never had. http://www. maplandia.com/united-states/alaska/ north-slope-borough/anaktuvuk-pass/

My earliest memory here in Anaktuvuk is just living in the sod house when I was about two years old. I remember them building our house where I now live. The sod house was down in the village, very near where we are. As with most of these older houses, it got torn down. My grandpa sold his land and it went to the Park Service.

I have always loved hunting. When I was a kid first learning, the first thing is you need to know your country, your weapons, got to have all your gear, got to be prepared. Basically, you got to have everything pretty much ready to go out hunting. The most important thing is to know your land because the weather here is unpredictable.

One of the most important things my dad taught me is learning your country and always observing and looking around because in a matter of minutes, a storm could move in, and there are times that you can get a little bit lost. Little things like a rock or a hill, maybe even a side of a mountain that you can recognize. Then you think about where you are in the land and that can save your life.

One really important thing is knowing the land so well that you can always figure where you are in all kinds of weather. First, you take a few minutes to collect yourself and get your sense of direction. The littlest thing can be recognized, like a willow bush or a big rock, mountainside, hillside. It is really important that you learn your country as much as you can, always looking around and being observant, because just one of those things can save your life and save you from being lost. You just have to control yourself and not panic in situations like that.

Remnants of the old ways -- a sod house in Anaktuvuk Pass, Alaska

My dad was my most important teacher, but you learn from pretty much everyone, like uncles and grandparents. We are always learning and trading stories. I like to listen a lot to everyone. How I was brought up, storytelling was the best time with the hunters. It was the best time listening to their stories when you are out there. Lots of good times talking and trading hunting stories. I like to know a lot about this land and all the seasons, how to survive. Subsistence is a big part of my life and a lot of people around here in the community, because there aren't many jobs around.

The old guys are the best storytellers, because most of them were doing all of the talking, so I am a good listener. I know as I grow older, I will become a better storyteller, because it comes with age. But for now, I like to listen to all the stories. Like stories about growing up, the history of the people, learning the country, struggles and hardships, adventures, pretty much everything, but mostly struggles because you learn as you go.

My favorites are hunting stories. The chase, anticipating, waiting, and the patience that is needed because sometimes you can wait all day for a group of caribou, but it all pays off when you wait.

It is much better to wait than to rush things, because you need to plan out your hunt. Sometimes you just take it as it comes, and sometimes they will just pop out of nowhere right in front of you, and it catches you off guard. But times like that, you got to stay calm and try to think it through. Hunting stories are my favorite, listening to everyone talking about waiting for caribou or stalking the caribou, who has the

Andrew and his mother

better shot, or number of kills, and how fast you can butcher a caribou and stuff like that.

One that really stands out is about one of my dad's hunts. It was in the middle of the summer when I was 12 years old. It was hot, and in June and July. There is not much caribou around but lots of fishing to do. Everyone is really hurting for caribou around this time of year because there really isn't many. I was maybe 11-12 years old. I am the oldest out of the six in my family. I have three younger brothers than me. My dad got a caribou but he only had a couple of bullets. This one day that we were traveling along, we saw this caribou right on the glacier cooling off in the hot weather, and my dad shot it right on the front quarter so he was wounded, but we didn't have any more bullets. We were struggling for meat for a couple of months and we were hungry for caribou.

My dad told us to surround the caribou, so we got up on the glacier and we closed in on it. We were so young and didn't understand what we were doing and were really scared because it was a big bull and he was wounded. My dad was walking around us and the caribou and telling us to stay calm. He told us that if he started charging to just stand still. We always listened to our dad, and as crazy as it sounds, we just did what he told us to do.

We were closing in about 20 yards diameter between the three of us and my dad was walking around us, and we were getting closer and closer in. Pretty soon we were about 13-14 feet around it in a big circle. We were getting really close and this caribou didn't know what to think, he was looking at us and we were scared. As we were closing in, he was grunting and snorting and was watching all of us but mostly paying attention to my dad as my dad was walking around us. He was using us as distraction to close in on him, but he was always looking around at us. He told us to try to keep the caribou's attention so we were clapping, whistling, and screaming to keep the attention on us, and he wouldn't see my dad coming in from behind.

The bull was ready to run and bolt right through us from about 13 feet, but my dad just jumped and grabbed his antlers and took him down with both hands, put his nose into the ice, and was holding his antlers with one leg over, grabbed the other antler under his leg, and killed the caribou with his knife.

I know this story is pretty wild, but it is true. It is the most memorable story growing up hunting with my dad. I tell it to everyone and my brothers still remember it to this day.

I can remember when I was a teenager and mostly the young men that were in their 30's to 40's back in the 80's, everyone just went hunting. I remember this one fall not far from here, people were getting like 15-20 caribou and announcing on the CB's telling everyone to come and get caribou. That is about the most I can remember ever seeing someone catch at once.

More than half of what I know, I know from the older guys. Growing up, all of the families would hunt together. After 2001 is when I really started hunting on my own, because my parents died and I took it as a memory of my parents to keep the tradition of hunting and subsistence for my parents' sake. Actually, my dad was hunting and trapping most of his adult life until he died at age 52. My mom was about 48.

My dad would trap wolves, foxes, and lynx. He dedicated his life to trapping and the subsistence lifestyle. Trapping was a big part of his life because you can make a lot of money off of the skins. The better jobs at preparing the skin you do, the more money that you can get. Sometimes he would get $300-$500 a pelt of mostly wolves. He would sell them in Fairbanks and Anchorage, to relatives, and people he knew all over the state. He learned how to trap from all of the elders here in the village.

I was maybe 12 when I started going out trapping with my dad, driving around on a snow machine out there. We would sometimes travel 200 miles setting different trap lines. It is a lot of work, because sometimes every week you would need to go check them. My dad would have six to seven different trap lines all over the country.

Lately, I have been cooking in restaurants in Fairbanks some, but Anak-

The mountains around Anaktuvuk Pass, Alaska, where Andrew hunts

tuvuk is always home. I will go away for a couple of years, but will always come back. I always miss the subsistence lifestyle when I am gone, because we are lucky to be living here.

There is nowhere else that I can be doing this, just walk a mile or two to drop a couple of caribou and go home and start eating. But I am always here for the for spring and fall hunt. Fall time is the best time because there are thousands of caribou, and you can pick and choose which bull you want. The best time to get them is in August and September, because they have a lot of fat on them and all the bulls are competing for females so they are big and strong, lots of meat and fat. I like to smoke meat, make dry meat or eat it frozen.

Another animal I love to hunt is Dall sheep. I hunt sheep for other people because it's really good meat and it's an adventure looking for them, traveling the country. If we didn't get any sheep on the hunt, at least we had a good day traveling and looking at the country, talking, having campfires. Sheep season opened up last Sunday.

When I was 13 years old, I got my first caribou and first sheep in one day. It was probably 12 miles east from where we are. I got my first caribou, a bull, and it was around August. Just a few hours later we were traveling back, and we saw some sheep traveling on the mountainside. The wind was perfect and it was just a good time to take them. We got up high above them and started looking around. They were right below us, so we got off to the side and got almost eye level with them and got three of them right there on the mountainside. They were probably a little over 80 yards, which is really close because they can listen good, and they have a good sense of smell.

I remember I had my dad's .256 and I think he had a .270, and we both started shooting at the same time. My dad missed and I shot all three of them as they were going over the edge. We didn't know if we got any or not because they went over the edge as we were shooting. We just really hoped that we got some, so we started hiking down and up the other side until we saw all three rolling down the mountain dead. I know without my dad's help, I wouldn't have been able to find them.

Passengers load the Wright Air Service flight in Anaktuvuk Pass, Alaska

Next, we rolled them down the mountain, and then my mom was down the mountain-side with her brother watching while me and my brothers were up there with my dad. We were up there rolling them down to get them as close as we could, and then mom drove up, and we all butchered them right there. But we didn't keep it all to ourselves; we would give it away to people that needed meat. And we use all the parts of the sheep. My mom made mittens and boots and stuff. They would make drums with the skin, so they gave them to a dance group to make their skin drums.

I remember another interesting caribou hunt about four years ago. There were a bunch of us hunting in a big area right over there in this valley. It was probably late August. It was dark and there was a quite a few of us hunting back there, waiting for caribou. The caribou that we were going after were high up on the mountainside, probably about three-quarters of the way up or even higher, and there were a couple of us guys hunting those caribou.

I was probably the youngest guy, so I ran straight up the mountain while one of my buddies was running along the bottom of the mountainside. I had chance to shoot so I shot three of them right there, and it was getting dark. All of us were rolling the caribou down the mountainside because we were racing against the dark to get them down.

Two guys got their caribou down fairly quickly, but I ended up rolling my caribou down right in a big hole in the ground maybe 30-40 feet deep with nothing but boulders. Since it was getting dark, I didn't really have a sense of direction where I was rolling the caribou; I just wanted to get it down.

So I was by myself and it was getting dark. I was trying to get it out of the hole. There were huge rocks and it was really hard, so I knew I had to take the guts out to make the weight go down. I had him sitting against the hillside to drain the blood out of his belly. I was trying like heck to get that caribou on and over my shoulders so I can carry it up the hill, I just tried over and over. I had good footing and was grabbing the farthest legs away from me and using momentum to get the caribou up on my shoulders and stand up at the same time.

I took a few tries and finally got it up. But when I got to full extension standing up, my head went inside the rib cage where it was really dark!! I was kind of mad and I knew I had to sit back down and drop the caribou and try again, and by then I was really tired. It was kind of funny, I laughed for a minute and sat and took a break for myself.

By then, I was really mad, and knew I had to get it up the hill because it was dark, so I tried again and finally got up and was determined to climb the hilltop, and I did. I got up to the hilltop and spun my body around and just threw it off my shoulders and down the hill. Once it started rolling, it was easy to just roll down the mountain.

We were skinning the caribou in the dark with our headlamps. I got down there and the guys were asking me why my face was so bloody and I told them that my head was in the ribcage. We had a good laugh.

I think a lot about the future of me and my wife and children. I have two boys ages five and seven, a daughter who is two, and had another daughter but she died from complications after birth. She had a blockage in her intestines and was a couple months premature, so it just didn't work out. I have a son on the way, due in October. I see myself doing what I do, working part-time jobs and hunting, trapping, storytelling, and that's what I am doing now.

For all of us here in Anaktuvuk, we can go to Fairbanks for medical care. With my oldest daughter, we did not get an ultrasound, which was one of the most exciting things that happened with my kids, having to wait the whole nine months to see if we were having a boy or a girl.

Thinking about my future, I know I will leave but will come back. This is what I can fall back on if we are struggling elsewhere and have no work. At least I can always come back to the village and know that I can always support my family through subsistence hunting, fishing, trapping, making money from trapping and selling antlers.

As for my kids, I don't want to see them do what I do. They have their own choices when they get older, but I hope that they hunt and have subsistence in their life so that they can pass that onto their kids. But you can't force them to do anything. You can just hope that they will keep it up. I also believe that they should get all of the formal education that they can get. Go to college and better schooling in the bigger places. But I would also like for them to have subsistence to fall back on if they are struggling.

The Whaling Captain

Luke Koonuk is an 80-year-old whaling captain from Point Hope. Luke moved and worked in many trades before eventually coming back to his home to take over his father-in-law's whaling crew. Luke speaks of his own experience starting a crew in the 70's. As a hobby, Luke makes baleen baskets (pictured above) to offset the high cost of living in northern Alaska. http://www.maplandia.com/united-states/alaska/north-slope-borough/point-hope/

When I was young, I worked as a carpenter and later on I went to Chicago to school for cooking. We lived down there for about 19 months while going to school. From there we went back to Alaska when I got a job in Nome as a baker. We stayed there for about eight months until we opened our own bake shop. We stayed there another year on our own. I didn't do very good on our books, and I was supposed to go half and half on the money with our landlord, but he didn't follow his promise.

I left there and started working for an Alaskan mining company in 1961 or '62. I worked there for about two years until they closed up. The mining companies were going broke, too, at that time, and we went back to Point Hope. Ever since that time, we have lived here full-time. I started working as a carpenter again with all the new housing.

It was going on for about three years until they finished most of the it. I got another job after that when the pipeline started in the fall-time. I was working there as a cook and baker for one of the oil companies, BP, for four years. After being a cook, I didn't want to work with people that had been drinking so much. I then worked as a security guard for three years until they cut down employees, except for the work at Prudhoe Bay.

I started whaling at the old town site with people around here. I was whaling with some other crews before I got my own equipment. I worked with two different boats. One was Peter Koonuk and the other was Donald Oktuluk. From there, my father-in-law, a whaling captain, turned everything over to me. My wife is the oldest one and his health wasn't good. After he turned everything over to me, he had two or three sons who wanted the boat. It's all rotten now, but I built my own boat. We bought our own shoulder guns. From 1975 we started. They're gone now, both of my wife's parents.

We have at least eight in a crew and there are always people looking for a better crew. When some go out, they don't supply their crew members with food. Some are too tight. Every year it seems like I end up with 15-18 members working for me. We caught our first whale in 1976. Every year we have caught a whale. One year, we got two of them.

If we don't catch one, we get shares from other captains. There are 19 crews and they divide the whale among the people that help. A lot of work. One time they got 14 whales when we were at the old town site. Today we will be lucky if we get three or four, sometimes five bowheads. Big bowheads take about a day and a half to two days to butcher.

Right now we are having a little problem with the oil company. They want to do some drilling all around the Chukchi Sea and Wainwright area. We are

trying to stop that. They are still coming every three or four months to have meetings. We are supposed to have another meeting the last part of May.

All the whaling captains were just in Barrow for a meeting. Each village like Barrow is going to strike 20 whales as a limit; Wainwright, nine. All those farther up like Barter Island has seven or nine strikes. Kivalina gets two strikes. St. Lawrence Island and Gamble get 22 strikes together.

Every year the limits change. We are trying to support it as whaling captains. It's getting harder and harder because the fuel is going up. It is almost four dollars a gallon nowadays

Luke's handiwork, a baleen basket and an ivory polar bear

around here. We are not too bad around here, but from what I understand in other villages like Koetzbue who don't hunt whales, they use gas to go up river. I think they pay $190 for 55 gallons of fuel oil. We are lucky here. My wife and I pay ninety-some dollars for 35 gallons. Motor gas is about $3.59 a gallon. It goes up and down, up and down. I don't know what will happen later on.

There are some people that are having a hard time with money. They don't charge at the store anymore. Everything has to be in cash. I have been pretty lucky money-wise, though my wife and I are just barely making out with telephone bill, TV bill, and light bill. The light bill is between $350 and $400 per month.

I make a lot of baleen baskets and I sell them in different cities like Kotzebue, Barrow, Anchorage and Fairbanks. They like my work when I make baleen baskets. I got one around here.

Right now, I am out of baleen but I have a little bit of ivory. If I am really gonna make baskets, I have to buy it. Some people charge $75 for one baleen. Ivory, when I buy it, one tusk would cost $150. When it is on the skull, some people sell things like that for over $1,000. Fossil ivory is hard to get. People go up about 19 miles up the beach when the wind is coming from the northwest. Ivory gets beached. You have to be there when the current and the wind come together in the same direction. I always keep my ivory in a cool place so it doesn't crack on inside.

When I was about 19, I learned to make baskets. I made two or three before at about 13-years-old, but they weren't very good. I started making them better. When I see baskets made around here, they are all wrong. Mine are oval type. Nobody makes the oval type, because it takes a lot of baleen and ivory. I heard some people in Wainwright selling baleen for $45 dollars for eight or 10-foot baleens. They have to be clean.

Right now, we are living off our pension every month. With my baleen baskets, sometimes I sell, in the summertime, about two or three each month. The University of Alaska at Fairbanks has some of my work.

One summer, my son-in-law was working for NANA above Kivalina. He found some people that were interested in baleen baskets. They wanted big ones. He told them, a big one like that will cost you around $1500. They were five of them that wanted them. I was busy all winter. They don't want to pay that much anymore. I make different sizes: small ones and little bitty ones. They go fast. Real small ones are $250 and regular size like that one I have, $300, and the big one, $800.

One basket, this big, will take one whole baleen. It takes about three weeks for the big one. You have to soak it in water for about two weeks and strip it with a saw. Then you have to make the bottom with ivory. The top handle is a figurine of ivory like walrus, seal, polar bears. When I have enough ivory, I make eagles. A lot of work. The white pieces of baleen are hard to find. Some are jet black with no white on them. I always have my name inside. I used to finish one like that in 10 days. My eyes get bad and it takes more than that. This basket I've had for over a month now. This time of year [March], they are hard to sell.

Whaling time is coming up, so I have to get that sled ready. I still go out in the boat. I'm 80, but as long I can walk around I am ready to go.

A Teenager Tends the Gardens

Jules Lampe is an Inupiat boy who lives in Kaktovik, Alaska, which is on Barter Island about 100 yards off the Beaufort Sea coast. Jules was whaling by the time he was 15 and caribou hunting as well. He did this interview when he and his mom were visiting Washington, D.C. in 2007, when he was 16 years old. http://www.spotadventures.com/trip/view/trip_id/172853

On the Sea

When you're out there whaling, it's a lot of fun, and there are a lot of people who make it interesting. We hunt for bowhead whales. Usually there are at least six people per boat, and there is six or seven whaling crews. We usually come back with three a year, and they can sometimes get up to 50 or 60 feet long. The biggest one we caught was about 60 feet long, and that took us almost a day to bring it back, because it was out about 50 miles. We can be at least 20 or 23 hours out on the water.

To take the whale, we use a harpoon with a bomb at the tip of it, and the whole thing is about six feet long. There is a trigger which sets off the bomb once the hook goes inside the bomb, and it explodes. If that doesn't work, they have a big whaling gun which is like an elephant gun or something. We usually try to get it in the heart somewhere and after they kill it, some people might even jump on top of the whale while it's in the water.

Jumping on a whale is kind of dangerous, but one time, there was this guy named Sheldon, who is at least 30 years old. We just got done killing or what we thought was killing the whale, and it was plopped upside down. It was in the water, and he was going to go on top and start dancing on the whale. A few people noticed that it was still moving its eyeballs, but they didn't think anything of it. So Sheldon got on top of that whale, and the whale started moving around, and he jumped off. He almost didn't make it off the whale. Fortu-

nately, when he jumped, it was right next to the boat, but he got a good scare out of that one.

To take the whale, they throw the harpoon at first, and the bomb releases. Then the wooden part falls into the water. There is a rope which is tied to a buoy and is tied to another buoy so that once the harpoon goes in, and if it doesn't kill the whale, we can tell where it is and where it's going, because the buoy is at the top of the water. Sometimes the whale might go down to the bottom for a fairly long time, and we will search and search and search until we find him.

He can actually pull the buoys down. The harpoon that is in the whale is the thing that tows it. There was one year that they had it just in the skin just deep enough that it might stay in, it might come off, and we would have no idea where it was going. If it did come off, we would have lost that whale even though he would have been dead by then. He was going to die. It was just a question of whether we would get him or lose him. We were lucky to get him.

I'll tell you, when you take a whale, it's really exciting. It's heartwarming and it's, it's ecstasy! It's a very good feeling to get a whale and see everybody happy to have another year's worth of food.

When we get back to the village, everybody celebrates. First they just beach the whale. Everybody goes and parks their boat except one that has the whale tied to theirs. They keep it in the water close enough to the shore that they can get a rope around it. Once they get that rope around it, and they get it high enough up to where it can start coming up on the beach, everybody helps to tug the whale in, women, kids, everybody we can get to help.

As we pull, if it doesn't come up all the way, we just use a loader. There's a big yellow rope that has a loop and they put that around the whale's tail, and then they drag it up on the shore. Sometimes the whale might be too big, and it might break the whale's tail or the rope might break.

Once we finally get it on shore, people climb on top of the whale and stand there and take pictures so everyone can see. After that, they might wash it off so that we can go home and get ready to start cutting up the whale. Once everyone gets back, they cut it up. They start from the back end, they cut the whale, split it, and they have to "X" a mark. I really haven't figured out what the "X" is for, but somewhere you have to stop.

To divide the whale, the captain takes it, and there is one big share for every crew, and everyone that is on that crew gets a part of the captain's share. Then we go on the tundra on the island, and we divide that up and cut it in sections, put it in rows, and take a loader and bring it to people's houses so they can have their share. Almost everybody ends up getting a share, cause there is a crew for every family.

Whale meat is real good. Most people not from Kaktovik don't like it, because they think they might get sick. But whale is really good, freshly cooked. When we come back from a long, long, long hard day from being out on the water, we cut it up, and have the first piece of that whale. It just tastes really good.

Cooking it is pretty easy. You usually boil it in a shack we have at the beach. People bring a slab and they have a table, and so they cut that up. So then they bring that in, cook that, and serve it to the people that are cutting on the whale. Sometimes it might take maybe eight, nine hours to cut up the whale, maybe even more, especially if it's a big 50-footer. But if it's too big and we couldn't get it all the way up on shore, we would have to wait until we got the first half done and then try to bring the rest in.

Ducks on a small lake near Arctic Village, Alaska

Of course, you can't eat it all right away. Most people take it to an earth cellar for storage. Not everybody has a cellar anymore, because it's either caved in or melted. Of course, they want to save that for Christmas, Thanksgiving, and all that.

On the Land

Well, sometimes, we would walk over to the mainland if the water is frozen. But we are actually not allowed to take a four-wheeler all the way across the frozen river on to the mainland. I don't know how come, but we either walk or take a snow machine. We go out to the mountains and we can hunt pretty much anything from squirrels to birds to sheep to caribou. We have a lot of fun doing it, too! Not too many people this year got sheep, because I guess there wasn't enough snow for anyone to get over to the mountains, because it all melted.

To kill a caribou, you wait around for a while. You might be with a group of two or three people, or you might be alone. I usually carry a .22-270. They come in herds, and you wait, and you wait, and you wait. Once they come, we can shoot them then and there. We cut them, skin them, and gut them, and put them on the sled and go back home. There you go, dinner!

Our guns are pretty powerful. I'd say we can shoot at least 100 to 200 yards with deadly force. But most of the time, we would get up closer so that we could have a nice clean shot to kill the caribou.

We usually go after the caribou every year beginning in about December. We go to the mountains or on the ocean to get caribou from the Central Arctic Herd. Sometimes the Porcupine Herd may migrate through and they come really close to the village, which makes it easy. This is usually in the spring.

My grandma and grandpa, Lily Uperchik and Daniel Uperchik, taught me so much. He taught me since I was a little kid. For as far back as I could remember, I was hunting; I was always out there. That was probably since I was first born that they took me out to the mountains to go see what it was like out there. I don't really remember everything, but it was fun from what I can remember. I was probably not even a year old when I first went out there. I was probably eight or nine when my grandma gave me my first gun to go out and shoot ptarmigan with a little .22.

But really, there is still a lot of stuff that I haven't done. I haven't shot sheep yet. That's in my plans right now. After I got the .22, they gave me a shotgun. After that, I could not get away from duck season. Duck hunting is still my favorite part of the season. We go out either to Pukuk-- it's way out there in the ocean, probably 30 miles away. Or we go towards the mountains and go shoot. It's fun. We go for ducks and geese.

I killed my first caribou when I was 12. That was exciting right there, because after you shoot your first caribou, you have to go and skin it and gut it. I didn't like that part, but that just fell into place. But anyhow, I catch it, skin it, gut it and bring it back home.

I have to admit I had a little bit of help the first time. My grandpa showed me how to cut the caribou and what not to do and what to do. You're supposed to have a nice, sharp knife. He showed me that you can take the bones out without breaking them with the knife. I always thought it was easier to cut the whole caribou with just the knife. I'll tell you what, when I got that first caribou, I was pretty excited

Over the years, I have caught quite a few caribou. But when I hunt them, there are at least three people with guns that start shooting, and you don't know which one you hit because you're going to have to go for another one after that. After you kill one, you try to get as many as you can. I would say I have killed at least 10 or 15 caribou.

Now when we get one, we do not throw anything away except for the guts; everything else is used. The skin, the bones, the meat, the fat, everything else but ribs, we eat all that. Nothing else goes to waste. When we get back home, we usually just throw it into our freezer and wait until we want to have caribou. Everybody gets caribou. It doesn't matter whose it is.

When I was a kid, they said it was better to give your first catch to an elder. So I gave mine to my grandpa which made him happy, and that made me happy also. But I still had to cut the thing up.

It is a lot of fun to go out there, especially if you're with a whole bunch of people, and they can make it a good time. Just two months ago was the last time I caught a caribou. It was in January or February. We went out on a snow machine, and sat around and got a couple of caribou with a couple of my other friends. They brought their rifles, and we had a sled and two machines. Most of the time, I go out with kids of my own age. It's fun. But if you have an adult along with you, they make it a lot easier because they know exactly what they are doing and how they're going to do it and when it's going to be done.

Most people really like to go hunting There is this one family, Eddie Rexford and his sons, they all like camping. His sons like to go out and shoot caribou and sheep. They do it all the time. They have a cabin out on Slater Lake, and they go out there to fish, and hunt.

Other Sea Mammals

I haven't exactly caught a walrus yet, but I have shot a seal. He was on the ice, so we went over there and ran around the ice, sat down, waited for a second for him to pop up, and we shot him. But he went back into his hole and came back to the ridge line. He was still alive. I just decided to give him one more and put him out of his misery.

We were trying to get him but he went down. We had thought that the water was just a foot deep, and it turned out that when I shot him, he fell off the ridge and he went down six or seven feet. I had no idea where he was and we were looking for hours and hours. That was a big disappointment there, because I really wanted to come home with that bearded seal, but it never happened.

The seals mostly come out in the wintertime, and we shoot them. It's not like the old days when they would just bash them over the head with a stick. I don't think that I would be able to do that. Back then, they were really tough. Sometimes they would just use their bare hands to kill that seal, just hit it in the head, and bring it back home. I think I could do it with a stick, but with my bare hands, I don't think so.

The Lady Soldier

Martha Lampe is a 51-year-old Inupiat woman who grew up in Noorvik, Alaska. She spent 15 years in the Army and now resides with her husband and kids in Nuiqsut. She grew up poor and rather shy. Her years in the service and subsequent accomplishments in her life in Nuiqsut have produced a confident, assertive woman with a great sense of humor, all quite evident in this interview. http://www.maplandia.com/united-states/alaska/north-slope-borough/nuiqsut/

My name is Martha Lampe. I was born in Noorvik on the other side of the Brooks Range. I met my husband in the military; he was in for six years and I was in for 15 with an honorable discharge.

After those 15 years in the Army, this guy with a big beer belly told me, "This food is what you are going to eat if you want to stay in the Army." He had a plastic tray of the food that I was supposed to be eating in order for me to continue my military career. I told him, "I don't think so. I am breastfeeding my baby, eating for two. You can stick that plastic stuff somewhere where the sun doesn't shine."

I told him that he could just give me my papers and I would sign them and goodbye. I didn't say that nicely, because he ended my military career right then and there. I had six more years to go in the National Guard.

After I met my husband, we moved up here to Nuiqsut, and I worked with the police department for eight years because of my military background. The money ran out, so I quit and went to work as security guard for maybe four years at the oil rig.

But before my military service, I remember a lot of little things. There were always dog teams, we had to go pick berries, pluck billions of geese. That's something that I don't do anymore because we just take the skin off, and the feathers were just time consuming. I used to have to chop wood, pack water maybe two miles down a steep hill, that kind of lifestyle every day for so many years.

I finished my education in a school that they had just built where I went from 9th to 12th grade. They asked me if I wanted to go to college, and I said no that I didn't want to. They could keep all that other stuff down South. So I joined the military, because

The cemetery in Nuiqsut, Alaska

I knew that I could do better with hands-on and outdoors stuff than what the colleges had to offer.

When I was a girl, I remember my grandma used to have mukluks that went up to here which are made of caribou, really warm. I had to chop wood and turn the wood stove on every day by hand.

We couldn't afford the oil a long time ago so we would have to wake up with cold breath, be cold and have to light it with a match. I used to be the last one to go to school. My house had sawdust for insulation under the house and that wasn't good insulation; it was cold.

Every Christmas my mom used to make me mukluks, and I remember and miss those. My grandma used to buy me a dress and used to have maybe $65. She would get me a dress with her money because my mom and dad weren't working at the time. He was in the military but he didn't spend his pay wisely, is what I remember. I remember being really poor, really poor. I consider it being poor because we didn't have much to eat, it was so hard. We didn't have dogs like other people did, and we didn't have snow machines because we couldn't afford it. They were so expensive, even though it wasn't expensive then compared to today's prices. We were one of the poorest for a fact in a village of about 800.

We had an uncle that came with his dogs all the way from Buckland, which was a long ways from Noorvik . He would come and bring us a whole sled load of dried fish and dried caribou because we were a big family. My mom and dad were young and had a lot of kids; I have a lot of brothers and sisters, but we were self-sufficient.

When we got the chance in the summertime, we would go across the river, go put out nets for fish. In wintertime we would walk across the frozen river and put snares for rabbits and ptarmigans. I remember walking across with my mom checking the snares inside the willows and stuff. In summertime, I'd help my aunt go check her salmon net with a little motor with a big boat a long time ago. That's how we had extra food when we needed it. We couldn't even afford much of the store stuff, just the basics. I was raised up on tea and pancakes rolled up with caribou liver and onions for breakfast.

I remember some things about the snares. My mom showed me how to tie up the little wires with willows along the little trails that they have. In the same snares, we caught ptarmigans, but it was mainly rabbits.

A lot of this was done every day after school was over. We would get ready for winter because we know winter would be cold. My dad and brothers would go get wood from across the river as well, because there are a lot of trees out there, and then we chop them up by hand.

I remember a good bit about school. I was not too interested in many of the subjects. I can understand why my kids never liked it either. I try to explain to the teachers that they have to make it interesting or they will get bored, and boredom is the worst thing that you can do for a kid.

I didn't find that interesting what James Madison did in tights with wigs way down South somewhere, civil war and fighting against each other. I'd just say that and when I got really bored, they would make me stand up at the chalkboard, make a circle, and keep my nose there.

Algebra didn't interest me because I couldn't understand it, but I excelled in shop, carpentry, photography, and home economics. I was really good at baking, but I never liked it because we didn't have an oven to cook in. All we had was a wood stove that was made out of a drum, so I never knew much about baking. I made only one pie crust my four years of home economics, and everybody clapped in our class and everyone was congratulating me like I made a big deal, one pie crust. I didn't like science either.

One year, I remember eight people came to the school district asking the parents what they could do to make it interesting. I went over because I was always concerned what we want our kids to learn. I told them that they need drivers' ed, shop, training for oil fields because of Prudhoe Bay. They also need music.

All they had were books, books, books. Now they have computers, but still, you sit there for hours and I don't know if they find that interesting. We never heard from them again, those people that came. They asked for our opinion and they never followed through. That was really sad. I was upset over it, but I didn't want to go out and bluntly ask what ever came of it.

You know, we don't care what happened down South. They always tried to make us remember dates and I was good at dates. But if you haven't been there, who cares. I have been to New York and Gettysburg and Plymouth on a senior trip on our last year of school. That was interesting to see what we did study. I went to the grave of Kennedy.

That stuff interests me, but the books themselves have no meaning, because at first I didn't know who these people were, and didn't care. I don't mean to be mean, but they're way off somewhere. We could have gone to Hawaii for a week, but we said Hawaii can wait. We wanted to go someplace different, so we chose to go to the East Coast.

We earned our own money to go. Since we were going to be together for four years, we said we might as well start making money now, and every weekend we would have cake walks, bake sales, dances. I can't even remember, it's been so long, but we raised money every weekend.

By the end of our twelfth year, we had enough money. The companies up here liked us so much and saw that we worked so hard, so they matched the money that we made. They matched that money. We got to go see "Dracula" and "Play Bill" in New York City. We earned it and we deserved it.

My favorite part of trip was just the little things. We kids would laugh about us girls putting on pantyhose and the boys trying to work on ties. We got to eat in real fancy restaurants, and the musicians would come to us and play music while we were eating. We were laughing so hard to walk down in New York City, just the simple stuff. I wouldn't want to live there though. It was kind of sad to hear about that 9-11 thing though. All in all, it was a good trip, but we were glad to get back home.

Shortly after graduating from high school, I enlisted in the Army. After basic training in Anchorage, I got sent to Georgia for advanced training. It was harder and hotter than Anchorage, and I don't like to be hot. I didn't like that Georgia much, but there are hardly any jobs in my village, just the subsistence lifestyle. I like that, but I wanted to go to work and do something while I was young and didn't have any kids. I went to Georgia in July-August and got my training all done.

Actually, the way I left Georgia was remarkable. One day about two weeks before I was supposed to graduate, I was raking a general's yard and he looked at me and said, "Come here," and I went to him and he said, "What are you doing here?" I thought well, here is my chance. I said that I was an Alaskan Eskimo waiting to graduate. He said, "What the hell are you doing in Georgia this time of the year?" I told him that I was waiting to graduate, and he got one of his guys that worked for him to get in touch with my company to get all my paperwork done.

I was lucky and thought before I answered him. I always appreciated that, and the next morning I was doing KP three o'clock in the morning, working with kitchen stuff, big pots, with an apron on turning eggs. Someone came to me and told me that they wanted me to report back to my base. I knew right away that it was time to go home and so I threw the hat, threw the apron, threw the spatula and ran back to my base.

The rest of my army career was here in Alaska. I was not really in active duty; it was just every two weeks a year that we would go training. I trained and was pretty good at it but I had never been in a foxhole. During one of our annual trainings they showed me where the target range was. I went into the foxhole and set up real good, shot real good and made sharpshooter. My MOS was radio and telephone. I could speak my native tongue. When people came up to train with us who didn't understand Eskimo, they couldn't understand what I was saying. So I got away with a lot.

Anyhow, I got out of the Army right after those whales were rescued over near Barrow. When we heard about it, me and my husband volunteered because they were looking for people to help. I knew the military was going to get involved because the whole world got involved. I volunteered and worked in the hangar and could translate English and Eskimo because that was what I trained for.

After the whales were saved, I even got a letter from Reagan and his wife. I also got interviewed by an Alaskan magazine asking about what I thought about it. I told them that we aren't as inhumane as what people think we are. We don't kill all the whales. But people always want to stereotype and that's not good.

I got a whole bunch of letters from sixth graders from down South asking if I liked Garfield the cartoon and thanks for saving the whales. I answered every single one of them and it was really exciting.

In 1988 Robert and I moved from Barrow to Nuiqsut. That was before the Alpine oil field was established. I liked it better than Barrow right away and my dad-in-law accepted me right away. He kissed me on my cheek and hugged me and we got along real good. As you can tell, my husband is half white and half Eskimo, but he was raised up by real Eskimos and that's all he knows. That's what attracted me, because I am really Native and he is raised up really Native. I knew he would be a good provider, and he is.

Here in Nuiqsut, I really love the hunting. If I were really rich and had that unlimited plastic card that could just get the money to pay for the gas, oil, and groceries, I would be out in the bush hunting, and just stay out there.

I grew up hunting before with a .22 for ptarmigans, muskrats, rabbits, and ducks. That experience with a gun is the main reason I could shoot so good in the Army.

I learned how to hunt from watching my brothers and dad and my friends and relatives. I am the one that always saw the game. They would always ask me where. Even my husband likes to take me; he bought me a really good pair of binoculars because we go hunting every summer for moose, and I show him where it is and he gets the honor of shooting it. But I get to see it first.

I also like to hunt caribou. We just came back last night around nine o'clock and got a caribou. We don't try to overstuff ourselves with lots, just one or two to last us for a couple of weeks. About an hour from now, I am going to go cut up the one we caught last night.

But you know, I've never shot a caribou. I could if I had to, but if it were only me I would have to. I prefer having caribou to a prime steak. Last night I made late supper so I could sleep, I had fried caribou and rice and that was so good.

When I was in Georgia, I really missed caribou meat. I found that I ate that Georgia food, and it didn't take long for me to get hungry again. It's all that store-bought food. It would dissolve already in my stomach because I worked hard. But here, at least I will be full for a while with all the Native food I grew up on.

You know, I think a lot about my kids' future. I want them to have the same life that I had, but I want them to get more education if the schools can make it more interesting. I want them to be more knowledgeable with the high tech stuff nowadays. My youngest son is into mechanics and my middle son is into girls right now, and I don't know what his interests are because he hasn't decided what he wants; my oldest was chosen by this woman. She was interested in him and that's how I have two grandkids.

If my middle child wants to say go to the University of Alaska that would be fine, because I want them to make decisions. I had a mean dad that told me that I wouldn't pass my physical, I wouldn't pass my basic training, I wouldn't pass my AIT. He was dead set on me going to college, but I knew in my heart and mind that I wasn't smart enough and how rigid and strict they can be, and I wasn't about to sit in class another how many years.

I went through 13 years of school already and didn't find it interesting at all. My dad didn't know, but I got sworn in, now look where I am at. I would have been stuck in Noorvik still if I didn't join the military. I know there are options besides school; you just have to look and set your mind to it. I was never a real outspoken person when I was growing up; I was really shy and even cried when I was supposed to talk in front of people, but not now.

I don't know exactly what made the difference. I just finally grew up and became more of a self-sufficient person. I am the oldest out of 10 kids, and I had to take care of them and help my mom because my dad drank and was a mean man. I never forgave him for years but I finally got out of it and forgave him before he died.

You know, if I could talk directly to the people in the Lower 48, I would tell them just to leave us alone, quit pestering us, quit giving us high prices, attitude problems. Let us make our own decisions. Help us when we ask. We are simple people and that's how we are, we aren't naïve. They have this attitude like we still live in igloos. If they would just listen to us, and be patient with us.

Sometimes when I get calls from states down South, and they say Alaska is not the continental USA; therefore, they have to pay more for freight. They say that we Inupiats aren't USA people. The most important thing they can learn from us is this: we may not be continental USA, but we are people.

The Youngest Whaling Captain

Thomas Napageak, 26-year-old man who lives in the village of Nuiqsut, Alaska, on the Coleville River and just a few miles from the Beaufort Sea of the Arctic Ocean. Everybody calls him by his Eskimo name, Kupa, which was his mom's best friend's name. Even at his tender age, he is a whaling captain, an honor he accepted at age 21 from his late father, Thomas Napageak, Sr. http://www.maplandia.com/united-states/alaska/north-slope-borough/nuiqsut/

When I was just a baby, I was adopted by my grandparents from one of their daughters. I call them my mom and dad, because I was raised by them and lived with them ever since. Other than Nuiqsut, I don't remember much.

My father's name was Thomas Napageak, Sr. I first started going out with him whaling when I was 14. It's pretty interesting. It takes a lot of courage and confidence and strength, and you have to know what you are doing.

My becoming a whaling captain at the age of 21 was hard, to start off. But my father had been a great teacher as he was a great whaling captain. Ever since I was a little boy, I'd always had two or three younger boys with me at all times. My dad would always have us get together and do a lot of work. We would always be on the run. We would always check the nets together; we built a few fishing camps together.

Whaling is fun, it's something that I love to do. I do it to feed the people. It is what my dad loved to do also. I have it very strong in my heart to not let it go. You know, I still have a lot to learn because I am only 24, but I do have the strength and family to help me improve my mistakes. I know how to cut up a whole whale, I know how to make the bombs, and I know how to prepare myself to be out there for a good month and a half. We stay at Cross Island, which is two miles long, maybe a quarter-mile wide. It's 14 miles north of Deadhorse, so we have to travel 94 miles to our camp.

I got my first whale out of Nuiqsut when I was first a whaling captain of 21. It was a 49-foot nine- inch bowhead, and that year, we were the only ones that got a whale in the village.

I distinctly remember the circumstances. There was this one Canadian barge that was passing through. There was five whaling boats 20 miles east of me, and I was about seven miles north of Cross Island. The whaling boat crews could see this white spot, which was that Canadian barge. It sounded like a helicopter when you were three to four miles away with your motor off.

The other whaling crews had lost the whale due to the sight of that barge. The whale just disappeared as that barge passed by. My crew had harpooned the whale when I was a ways away, so I had to catch up with them. I was having problems with my boat, but I was making my way there no matter what. By the time I got there, I had to turn off my motor to change some spark plugs. At first I thought I saw an iceberg. But all I heard were these noises that sounded like a helicopter.

I remember I started seeing this whole school of whales, the first time I had ever seen a whole school at one time, and they were on both sides of me. They were blowing and swimming west with the barge that was taking oil to Barrow. After that barge passed by, I didn't see nothing, no more whales.

Now, any kind of activity out there that affects our whale hunt is very disturbing. I have seen quite a bit of oil industry traffic that has disturbed our subsistence activities. In the fog, when we are chasing the whale and a barge comes out from nowhere, we lose the whales.

When I finally caught up with my crew, the whale was already dead, and they were getting it ready to tow back to the island. All five of the boats were there. We towed the whale to Cross Island. Butchering a whale usually takes quite a while, depending on the size. If you have 20-35 footer, it can be done in a day. But if you get a 36-45 footer, it could take up to three days.

When we arrived at the island, my crew told me how they got the whale. I had my three boats: Napageak 1, Napageak 2, and Napageak 3 out there. Number 2 struck the whale. All five boats helped put the whale down. There was a little competition between the boats, but I don't think of it that way. The most important thing is making sure one of our crews successfully gets the whale, and all of our boats make it home safe.

I'll have to tell you, I felt very happy that they had successfully got the whale, but not really till it was landed. When I first went out whaling, my dad had struck a whale right in front of me, and I started getting really happy. He bawled me out right there on the boat.

As soon as I got back to the island, I heard the exact same thing from all the other whalers, because you know the whales will attack you, turn on you because they are trying to give themselves to you but you're overly excited. I have seen a whale turn and try to attack a boat before. Believe me, it's pretty intense to see such a sight. And we don't want this big animal to suffer. But if your tradition is to feed your people and to keep everyone's stomachs full, well, then you have to do it. And you must do it right.

Now a 49-foot whale is a huge animal. We have a winch and a 960 loader; we use both of them to pull up the whale. We also use a 960 loader for many things including to bring all the blubber that is not used to the other side of the island, so it will keep the polar bears away while we cut up the rest of the whale. The bears love the blubber. There is 14 inches of

Homes in Nuiqsut, Alaska

blubber and we only need 4-5 inches of it on the inside of the black skin. Inside that, there's lots of meat.

Before we had the machines, we used a block and tackle. We still have a block and tackle setup in case the winch goes out. We may only be able to pull up half the whale at a time and cut up what we can right there with half of the whale out and half of the whale in. We do this until we can get more situated with a better plan to cut up the rest of the whale.

Nowadays, the barges haul the whale meat from Cross Island to Deadhorse and then we have air cargo fly it here. But back when I was a lot younger, we used to wait until wintertime and go there with our trucks and start loading it up and bringing everything back on the ice road or straight through the river, whichever was easier.

The village is really happy when we return with a whale. The captain sends his crew here with a boatload of meat, and they celebrate that. Everybody is at the river when we come in to celebrate that the whale was successfully caught and we all made it home safely.

About a month from now, I will be out there again. I am definitely looking forward to it. Last year, I missed out and had to go to Fairbanks. I had dreams every night while the whalers were out there and I was in Fairbanks. I had dreams that I went to Cross Island with a barge and I picked up my whaling camp and brought it to my front yard. I also had dreams that I went out and I wanted to go whaling. It felt terrible to miss out on whaling. My other half got mad at me because I wanted to be whaling more than to try to do the right thing and take care of my family. I was really trying to concentrate on one thing at a time.

But really the older guys are okay with a younger guy being captain. They feel that I would be a good captain as long as I want to keep learning and I don't try to give nobody an attitude. I try to treat everyone the same and with respect, and I am always open-minded because I want to learn as much as I can while the opportunity is still here before all our elders are gone. If I were in the position that there was something I didn't know and nobody else knew it, I'd be in trouble. You have to know a lot to be out there. It's not for just anyone to go out and hunt. I try to bring as many people whaling as I can. If it were possible, I would bring out the whole village, but I don't have that many boats.

I often think about how I am going to involve my own kids in whaling. I already have a daughter. I also have one on the way; she will be born in November. My daughter right now has a birthday in the same month as mine. My birthday is July 4th and hers is July 24th. My wife's birthday is in November, and our next baby is going to be born in November.

Umiak awaiting skins

Not many people do this, but I am going to bring my daughters out with me, not anytime soon but maybe when they get 17-18 years old. I would bring them out so they could get a good look at how everything is done in case anything were to ever happen to me. That way, I would have someone there that could take my crew and be successful at whaling.

I'm already training some young guys to whale. I always have a couple of guys out there with me because they are like my little brothers; they used to follow me camping, fishing, and my dad used to put us to work together.

Another thing my dad would do is to take us younger ones out moose hunting. And nowadays I go out caribou hunting every summer. Also we go fishing most every year at our fish camp at Fish Creek, where we put our nets out.

I was maybe 12 years old when I got my first caribou. I used a .22/410 gauge over and under my dad had given me. I remember that so well. The caribou had just made a river crossing when I got him. But by now, I have taken maybe 50 caribou, which is great eating. I am making beef jerky right now with soy sauce. I made some last week and it's all gone.

But hunting and whaling is not the only form of education. I graduated from high school here in Nuiqsut, so I have a pretty good formal education as well. I'm pretty proud of my schooling. Actually, I was able to blend the two, education in school and education in the bush. I always kept a subsistence journal. I had to write one full page in the journal every day, and that's how I got graded.

I graduated four months early and went right out on the ice road and started working. I started work the day after I turned 18. Actually, I went to work part-time before I even got out of high school, and I was making $13.75 doing water and sewer lines. Right after high school, my mom had a stroke, so I moved to Anchorage for two years. But we would still come back for whaling. I have had several jobs including welding, which I am now certified in.

I'm not for sure what I will do long-term. Right now, I want to try to get into politics. I want to help this village keep putting its foot down and maintain the subsistence that we have around here. I want to make a footprint for myself and for others.

But no matter what I do for employment, there's no question that I will continue whaling, hunting and fishing. It is something that I will always do and I love. I can't wait until next month to go whaling. My favorite subsistence is hunting for bowhead whales. I got a brand new outboard on my boat. It's a 225.

Like I said, I have learned from the best; I am not afraid to go hunting for bowheads. I am not afraid to come up to them and take them on. Sometimes whales get a little spooked, and they go really fast or get a little crazy. I know how to keep my distance and I know how to come up to a whale without spooking it.

Speaking of whaling, I am very concerned about the government leasing offshore for oil exploration. I definitely oppose offshore drilling. Cross Island doesn't even have a buffer zone, and that's where our whaling camp is. The drilling activity is planned to be between Kaktovik and Cross Island. For that to happen is just like them pushing out our subsistence

This cabin had to be moved back from the river to avoid toppling in.

right there. In 1974-76, they were drilling right there, and Nuiqsut whalers didn't get any whales. We had sued them and the wells got pulled out of there. Nuiqsut whalers had won that lawsuit against them because they didn't get any whales that year due to the offshore activity.

The loud noises from boats and the well drilling are what spook the whales. But when we go whaling, we keep our engines idle until we spot one. As soon as we do, we speed up right to it and we stay behind it and then it doesn't really spook. But I have seen bigger boats and oil and gas activity spook whales.

I know that this year the whaling captains were negotiating with Shell about offshore exploration. I personally think Shell should find a way to drill onshore instead. I don't like oil wells in the water. It may be good for our country. But is a little pocket of oil as valuable as bowhead whales for our village? I would rather pick bowhead whales for our village than to get a million dollars. A million dollars would make everyone rich but our tradition of bowhead hunting is what's valuable to me. I don't think all that money is worth anything compared to a bowhead whale.

When I go to Anchorage sometime, I see people selling beluga fat or something like that, but you should never give out fat. My dad always had it cut up and brought it to his friends and let everyone eat it all of the time because it's something to give to the people, not something to sell. It is always for the people and that's how I feel. For the oil industries to make an impact like that would kind of ruin it.

I'm not sure all the whaling captains feel exactly like I do. I know a few people that are whaling captains and that are working with Shell to try to get oil activities going. That's something I don't want to see. My point of view is that these people are in it for the money. I might be wrong; that's what it appears to me. If they offered me money instead of going out whaling, I wouldn't take it. Where would our tradition be? Where are we going to be?

You see, when these guys drill, they want to have seven things out there. They want two drilling pads, three ice cappers, and two more boats for daily routes. And they want a helicopter too. All that activity would divert our bowhead whales directly north away from the shore, and I know that for a fact. Take just the noise. Cross Island and the onshore rig at North Star are 12 miles apart, and you can hear the flare at night when we are on the island.

Another effect of oil and gas activity is that many things are changing. I would say that it seems like there is a lot less water nowadays in our little creeks. The rivers are starting to spread here near Nuiqsut. In one place, a 20 by 50-foot piece of Coleville River bank is ready to drop. That's where you can see all the permafrost melting. It was on the news that at Kaktovik or Kotzebue that lakes have drained out, and that looks like part of global warming as well. And with all these oil activities, you see brown smoke pollution. We see that all of the time. I think that helps cause global warming.

If my interview gets in your book, I would want to be sure that your readers understand that my life is very interesting, and I have a lot to live for in this community. This is where and how I want to live. It's pretty hard to live here at the cost of everything. But there is no price tag on my life. I want to live as free as I can subsistence-wise, and I want to keep my people and our tradition going.

Mr. Mayor

Steve Oomituk was born in Point Hope in 1962 in the old town. He lived there most of his life. When the North Slope Borough was formed in 1972, his father took a job as Housing Director and the family moved to Barrow. After graduating from Barrow High School in 1980, he moved back to Point Hope shortly thereafter and started a family in the village. Steve explains the impact of commercial whaling for oil during past centuries and why he opposes modern petroleum exploration today. http://www.maplandia.com/united-states/alaska/noth-slope-borough/point-hope/ http://en.wikipedia.org/wiki/Point_Hope,_Alaska

I learned the ways though I was taken away from my hometown and moved to a bigger community. My childhood memories were always the old village, living with my grandparents. I was the oldest son, so my father had me live with my grandparents to help out with chores. We had to collect water, firewood, and we didn't have power all of the time. We had it 12 hours a day. We didn't have any running water or anything like that. I took care of the dogs, got the wood and water as a young boy for both of my grandparents.

When I was born, my father was working out of town. My mother told him that if I was born a boy, my aunt was going to name me. When I was born, my father was gone. So my aunt named me Alfred Steve Oomituk. As I got older, there were times that I got sick and they always have people name you. My Eskimo name is Arsceralio. When you got sick, they always gave you three names and they would make you stronger. They would name you after strong people and help you survive. We didn't have very many planes coming in and people still lived in sod houses. We probably had a plane come once a month.

That is Rock's whaling boat there [as he points to a wooden frame awaiting its skin shell]. It's an eight-man boat. Point Hope people still hunt their whales in the skin boats. It takes about five to six sealskins, and we sew them in a waterproof stitch. We still paddle and throw a harpoon at the whale. The way we mark the whale has always been the way it has been for the last 2,000 years. We have another site over here called the Peacot, which is between 2,500 and 4,500 years old.

As you can see, our graveyards and our houses were made of whale bone. The whale was always the center of our lives and still is today. The population of Point Hope in the 1860's was about 4,000 people when the commercial whalers started coming around and brought in all these diseases. By the time it was 1905, within 30 to 50 years, the population of Point Hope was 126 people. They died off from starvation, diseases, and people moving. These houses were lived in up until the 60's and 70's. 1975 is the last time one of these houses was lived in, the whale bone sod house.

Steve points out whale-bone feature in Point Hope, Alaska

I was in Barrow when they were moving out of the sod houses. My grandparents lived in them and my parents were born and raised in them. This is a whaling ceremonial site, and they have the whale feast for three days in celebration to the whale. Every two bones that you see is one whale, whether they are upside down or whatever. All these are whale jawbones, just like the houses right here.

You will want to keep an eye out for polar bears! [as we sit on the point feet from the frozen sea in March]. We don't feel like feeding them today! Ice cellars are still being used today; there are ice cellars in these mounds right here where people store their whale, walrus, beluga, seal, and so forth. They don't store caribou or anything like that there.

Commercial whalers have always hunted the grey whale and the sperm whales, but every once in a while they would come across a polar whale which is a bowhead whale, and these bones you see make all these ice cellars and houses.

The head is about a third of the whale. The bigger bones are just bigger whales and smaller, just smaller whales. All the houses were built the same but erosion has caused this. We had nine different clans and now we only have two left. That is why they moved the town in the 70's because of the erosion problem. They were going to build new houses and new structures, but there wasn't enough land because they knew it was eroding away, so they moved it two miles further.

They built a big gravel pad so they could be on a level ground. They would form ridges like this, and the ridges are on the south side. We lose a lot more land on the north side than what we gain on the south side. The point used to be a lot further than it is now. We get that northwest wind that erodes our land away.

We still hunt the whale the same way we have always hunted it. We have a few minor changes, like what they yank the whale with and the black powder bomb. You throw a harpoon, which is like a trigger. It's a model of the 1880's one, and we still use a model harpoon that the commercial whalers were using.

Point Hope is still really traditional how we mark a whale, how we distribute it. We do a lot of hunting out here. This point is very popular for the hunters. In the night, it gets a thin layer of ice, and you can walk on it, salt water ice is flexible. You can see polar bears walking on it. If the wind comes from this way, it will come through and break it up.

You can see seals out there if you look with binoculars. They are out there sunbathing. The polar bears lay flat on the ice and use claws to glide on the ice and go right to the seals. This is where the two seas meet, the Bering and the Chukchi. One hundred and fifty miles that way is the borderline to Russia. Two hundred miles this way is Wrangle Island.

There are three different currents out there. The first current goes up through this way and curves and you can see how it breaks off that way. It heads up north and you will end up in Barrow. There is a second current that goes straight out that way by Wrangle Island. There is another current on the south side of Wrangle Island that brings you back to the point. Point Hope people used to go to Wrangle Island on the Russian border.

This is who we are. We are a very traditional community with our songs, our dances, our drums of skin. We do a lot of our dancing that tells stories of the animals that we hunt. So when I heard of the leases of Chukchi Sea, I opposed it. To me, we don't want to put our way of life in danger. We don't want to put the animal in that type of situation. I want my children and my grandchildren to hunt the same animals I have always hunted in the same manner that I've always. My son has been whaling since he was six years old and he is now 24. He still whales.

My daughter is 25 and she's out there. She doesn't like to miss the whaling season. She moved to Anchorage and went to Palmer, but they always come back to go whaling. We have been a whaling family for generations and generations. My parents were from Point Hope. My grandparents were born and raised in Point Hope, and so were their parents.

I became involved in the community for this reason. I was the Vice-Mayor and Fire Chief as well as other things. I was in the tribal Council for 10 years. I was Vice- President throughout the 90's. Some people asked me to run for City Council. So I ran for City Council and they voted me in. They tried to make me mayor right away and I told them, "no, no, no." I needed to know the structure of the municipal government before I jumped in to become mayor. The mayor resigned, and I stepped in there in December of 2007, and have been in there ever since.

It's been challenging. You have to be a people-person and you have to look at the concerns of all people. You try to do what you can do to help out your community. I've looked for funding and grants to bring it in to preserve our way of life. We try to make the city run with the low budget. We stay busy and we have money coming in.

We are fixing up the youth center and the elder/senior center as well. We got a grant so that we can get these buildings back up and going again. It would be nice to work a program to merge them together and work a program where the elders come to our youth center and talk about the old days or talk about hunting, the currents, wind direction, weather, or how to cut up an animal, or sewing, or what you can eat. The youth can go and help the seniors who want to eat their traditional food.

The younger generation can learn how to prepare the food. The younger generation got away from it because we got into the cash economy and got pulled away from that. The younger generation is into the microwavable stuff and fast food, even though we don't have a restaurant. The younger generation need to be more in touch with who they are, and understand that they have a rich life and culture right here in Point Hope that is still somewhat intact. We can get the best of both worlds. We see some of our traditions slowly dying, but we see some of our children stepping up and wanting to preserve it. We don't want our generation to be the ones to lose what we've done for thousands of years.

Oil impact, however, is the biggest challenge. What is going to happen when they have an oil spill out there or a tanker, an Exxon Valdez? Will the animals move to a different area? Will they stay with the cold currents and move? We are looking at that and are curious. We don't want our waters being invaded by oil companies. We had that done before in the 1800's by commercial whalers where they killed off so much of the whales for the oil.

The commercial whalers hunted the grey whale and the sperm whale for their oil. From the grey whale they got 35 barrels of oil and from the sperm whale they got 50 barrels.

When they caught a polar whale, a bowhead whale, they got 150 barrels of oil. But they never knew where these bowheads lived. They hunted all through the Atlantic and killed off all the whales, so they started in the Pacific. Then up North, Roy Thomas came through the Bering Strait and found the bowhead whales.

This started a rush when he came through uncharted waters of the North. Within two months, he had his ship full of oil. It was unheard of. It took almost a year hunting the sperm and the grey whale to fill a ship. There was 24 hour daylight and whales as far as you could see. In 1849, there were no ships. In 1850, there was 250 ships. They figured the population of the whale back then was about 30,000. We see this happening again, the hunger for oil. First it was the whale oil, and they almost extincted the animal. There was starvation and people dying.

You see, the animals come to us. We always believed that the animals give themselves to us. We have never hunted them. That's why we're here today. They talk about the Inpuiat or Eskimos being nomads who followed the animal. Well, the animals came to the Inupiat people. They fed, clothed and sheltered us. They are our identity. They are who we are and we cannot change that. We don't want to lose that.

We have seen oil moving from the land to offshore. We have seen the oil impacts since the 1970's since the Borough was formed. This is our garden. This is who we are. This is it. If we have a a major oil spill, what is going to happen to the small plankton? The ecosystem, as they say, starts with the smallest animals and the smallest plants.

There are lots of things that we don't know about the Arctic. They want to build oil platforms in the Chukchi Sea, out this way, and it's right in the migration routes of our whales. We don't want to see that.

I would rather see them open ANWR before they even go offshore, as much as I oppose drilling in that area. I would rather it be contained on land than with the currents that go everywhere. We oppose this offshore lease 193. It's a shame to see it progressing offshore and to see the money they paid for it. To us, money isn't the issue even though we live in a time where things are changing. Are we going to be the last ones to be the whale hunters of Tikigaq? As you see, our feast grounds, our cemeteries are lined with them.

The Coal Story

George Paneak is the 59-year-old mayor of Anaktuvuk Pass, Alaska. He is an Inupiat Eskimo living in this village, which has as its main food source the caribou of the Western Arctic Caribou Herd. Two years ago, the federal government proposed that the people of Anaktuvuk Pass give permission to develop the coal and other hard rock minerals west of the village. Below is the story of their response to the feds. http://www.maplandia.com/united-states/alaska/north-slope-borough/anaktuvuk-pass/

In March of 2007, the U.S. Bureau of Land Management in charge of the National Petroleum Reserve Alaska (NPRA) came up here to have a public meeting with the residents of Anaktuvik Pass. They asked us about possibly developing the western part of the NPRA. They wanted to develop that part of the territory because there are a lot of hard rock minerals in there, like coal and possibly zinc and copper.

They gave us a presentation on the area and what they were interested in. They had maps, and the coal area happened to be between the Western Arctic Caribou Herd's calving ground and Anaktuvuk Pass. We knew there was hard rock there from the past meetings we had had, and from the times past when we would bring coal back by dog team to our village to burn.

People at the end of the meeting were against developing that part of the area, because once they get into it heavily, they would develop it. In developing it, they would have to transport the coal, and for sure there would be a road involved.

They would have to build a road. That really concerned the residents. How would it affect the herds? Would they find a different route, or would they not exist anymore in that area? We heavily depend on that herd. That's our meat. We would rather have caribou meat.

We know that they are currently drilling some part of the NPRA, especially sections near the coast. They are even drilling in some areas where it would hurt the habitat, like Teshukpuk Lake. There's a caribou herd there and nesting birds, and the people of our village really watch that. For that reason, we opposed the coal mine.

Our testimony to the BLM was by consensus. Different residents of our village told them we opposed it. And you know, even if it meant jobs, we were really concerned about the road that would transport the hard rock. Around here they would certainly make a road. It might run from the hard rock itself to the pipeline or wherever it would be feasible to transport it. Generally, a road wouldn't be good.

To me, it looks like they won't pursue it for several years. For now, it's not in the picture. But in 10-15 years down the road, you never know. Times change. But they need to know that to my people, the caribou is a lasting thing.

Whaling Canadian Style

Freddy Rogers is an Inuvialuit person in his 40's. He lives in Inuvik, but was born out in the bush on the Peterson River, which is part of the massive Mackenzie River delta. He lived out there until age six when he was taken after his mom died to a residential school, where he stayed until age 20. He is a trapper, a fisherman, a hunter, and a whaler. http://www.maplandia.com/canada/northwest-territories/inuvik-region/inuvik/

When we are going after whales, we go out to the area of Baby Island. First, we will spot a bunch of beluga whales (a small whale, 10-15 feet long). Then the head honcho says it's time to head out. Next we sort of herd them into shallow water about four feet deep to make it easier for us to catch them. They try to evade us but we make them go to the shallow water. Then a whale will come up for air, and if you are a good driver like me, you get to them right away. Some people are good drivers, and some are good with harpoons-- I can do both.

If you have a good driver and a good harpooner, it takes about half an hour. That's a good time. The harpoon goes into the muktuk. The harpoon is attached to the end of a rope, which is tied onto a balloon, which acts as a marker as it bobs up when the whale comes up for air. Once this is in the whale, the harpoon head stays in the muktuk, but the shaft comes off. The balloon can be made of anything that floats, but in the old days was made of a seal poke (a bag).

Now the harpoon is inside the muktuk. Once it is in there, if you can try to pull it out, it won't come. You must use a knife to get it out later. Anyhow, once the harpoon is shot and the whale tires out, we drag it in and work as a team. We beach it and then roll it over.

I learned whaling from my dad and my brother. I was about 20, because I had been in the residential school till then. I remember when I first learned to whale. Once you learn something like that, it is pretty hard to forget.

I was never a shooter, but he wanted me to learn how to harpoon. My dad was a very conscientious person with safety. We couldn't touch guns until we were a certain age. Now, people go out there with their grandparents when they are 14. They learn at a young age.

Canadian Independence Day parade in Inuvik

I remember when I first harpooned a whale. You feel good about it. You do something for your family, but it is also hard work. My dad is a shooter. My brother is a driver. They follow the whale after you harpoon it.

You stay beside the whale. When the whole head comes up, right away you see the neck area. You shoot near the neck bones in order for a good shot. You don't want to make a whale suffer. We use a high-powered rifle like a .30-.30 or a .270.

If you have a good harpooner and shooter, it takes about a half hour to one hour to tire the whale out so that you can beach it. After that, we process it, hang it out, cure it, and then it gets ready for the boil pot. Some people have a big vat filled with water. They do only half a whale at a time.

The women are the main ones once you get the whale up on the beach. They cure it for a couple of days, and they make jerky. They put it on the racks. If it is a good warm day like this, it takes two and a half days.

About two or three per family feeds you for a year. We are not allowed to get a cow with a young one. Mostly we go after the bulls. It's no problem telling the bulls. They are bigger and they usually go off to the side by themselves.

It seems like kids aren't as interested as they used to be. But they can be a big help. They can drag up the muktuk. Lay it out in the sun. After that, they have free time. The water is cold, but they go swimming. It could be about freezing, but they go in. After that is time for the cooking part. After everything is cured, we call it mipku.

The Activist

Jack Schaffer is from Point Hope, Alaska. Jack was raised by his grandparents Jimmy and Kate, but he spent some of his younger years in Juneau. After his mother died, Jack returned to Point Hope and eventually became involved in local politics as President and Vice President of Native Village as well as a member of ICAS (Inupiat Community of Arctic Slope). Jack became well-connected with the past and present environmental concerns of the region. In the conversation that follows, Jack reflects on the treatment of Native Village by outsiders and responds to the pressure to lease the Chukchi Sea to large oil and gas corporations.

I came up here after my mother passed away, which I still haven't figured out exactly what happened. There were a lot of sensitive things occurring at that time. I mean there was so much atmospheric contamination by nuclear testing that it wiped out caribou in central

Canada in 1957 and in the early 60's. Palmer had the highest contamination in the U.S next to New York in 1963. That was the environmental issue at that time, and it's remerging in the form of mercury and dealing with climate change.

My whaling captain cousin had indicated that there was a need for reviving the Native Village of Point Hope government in 1985. Our uncle was the one that was pushing it without saying anything. We continued to do that with nothing through 1992. As for ICAS (Inupiat Community of the Arctic Slope), I was drafted when there was concern about lead in adults and children in 1989. http://arcticcircle.uconn.edu/SEEJ/RedDog/index.html

Then, we were distracted by an issue that involved research into the history of military activities like Project Chariot: http://en.wikipedia.org/wiki/Operation_Chariot_(1958)
http://arcticcircle.uconn.edu/SEEJ/chariotseej.html.

They only did a cleanup of top wild projects; the other projects that occurred to them are still under consideration. About 131 experiments found unusually high amounts of fluoride in the teeth of people here in 1957. Fluoride is used for the manufacturing of plutonium [and uranium].

In the mid-nineties, I went and met with 19 other tribes at the UN, and they gave me 30 seconds to indicate the concerns to Secretary General Boutros-

Main Street US Arctic, Point Hope, Alaska that is

PROJECT CHARIOT

The 1950s was a time nuclear advocates were looking for projects that could use the atom for peaceful purposes. One of the most ambitious and perhaps outlandish, was Project Chariot, a plan to use nuclear explosives to cut out a deep-water port in northwestern Alaska along the Chukchi Sea near Point Hope.

The plan was the brainchild of the famous nuclear advocate, Edward Teller, who traveled throughout the state of Alaska touting the harbor as an important economic development for the state. Alaskan political leaders, newspaper editors, the state university's president, even church groups all rallied in support of the massive detonation.

Opposition came from Point Hope, a few scientists engaged in environmental studies under AEC contract, and several powerful environmental organizations. The grassroots protest soon was picked up by organizations with national reach, such as the Wilderness Society, the Sierra Club, and Barry Commoner's Committee for Nuclear Information.

In 1962, facing increased public uneasiness over the environmental risk and the potential to disrupt the lives of the Point Hope residents, the AEC announced that Project Chariot would be "held in abeyance." It has never been formally canceled. The history of Project Chariot is recounted in the book, The Firecracker Boys by Dan O'neill, The Firecracker Boys: H-Bombs, Inupiat Eskimos, and the Roots of the Environmental Movement).

Although the detonation never occurred, the site was radioactively contaminated by an on-site experiment. Material from a 1962 nuclear explosion at the Nevada test site was transported to the Chariot site in August 1962, used in several experiments, then buried. Thirty years later, state officials found low levels of radioactivity at a depth of two feet in the burial mound. Outraged residents of Point Hope demanded the removal of the contaminated soil, which the government did at considerable expense.

Ghali in regards to discrimination of Native people by transnational corporations. He was pretty disturbed and filled with fear, and he had an agreement with President Clinton for which Clinton betrayed him. I guess that agreement must have involved him withdrawing as Secretary General of the United Nations and then was replaced by Kofi Annan. They did accept our case, but we were unable to communicate because of the blockages being done by our government.

There was also seismic work that was being done without our knowledge over a 10-year period, and that may have wiped out a lot of the food chain. We had no idea until last year that that took place. Now we are dealing with the oil and gas becoming a real complicating and difficult issue.

As far as I know, there is no real proven technology for oil cleanup in ice conditions. One other recent comment that I made was that there is no proven way to clean up oil in ice conditions, unless you have superman that can watch flow under ice and track it.

There was no information that was provided to us in regards to any type of environmental impacts stated by the Mineral Management Service or the personnel that was with them. They would not go into providing us with information on impacts from seismic works. They wouldn't go into any type of environmental impacts in dealing with oil and gas.

They said, "We come here to listen to your concerns and we will do what we can." It was before we knew anything about public meetings and consultations. Public meetings and hearings are not taken seriously, and consultation is a discretionary thing that can be considered a public meeting so they don't have to follow through. There was a lot of overriding of responsibilities by upper people against those that are responsible for scientific information and input in dealing with impacts.

These federal employees had their integrities at risk. We are somewhat fortunate that they were finally able to stick up for their interests and their rights in dealing with their concerns and protecting their position. The Department of Interior is still semi-hostile in regards to disclosure of that information and have rejected or altered the information to the point where you couldn't make much of it.

We were considered as non-valuable people of information. The only field of people that were qualified were biologists. Traditional knowledge and first-hand knowledge was not something that they desired and they continued to push it aside to allow development to occur and to meet those other interests.

There are other methods that have been utilized to eliminate the federal government's trust and responsibility toward the indigenous people. They have been able to get around that responsibility by establishing non-profit organizations and non-governing organizations to make decisions and go into agreements and ignore those real issues and environmental concerns. Here in Point Hope, the last frontier-- we are the furthest west you go-- there are many desires of exploiting not renewable resources onshore and offshore.

We haven't talked very much about onshore deals, but the reclassification of some properties is being made from subsistence areas to industrial zones. There is an impact in relation to that and we don't have enough representation or support or process to addressing those things that are taking place. It is very interesting how the Department of Interior works in that regard. There was one that took place here that dealt with onshore, where we did request that those lands remain the same as subsistence areas.

Red Dog mine [the world's largest source for zinc and a significant source

Dave, Harvard & student on Crow Mountain

of lead] has been expanded, and they used up the edge of their outcrop. They will be going into other properties because it is the largest mine in the world. It is 29% of the United States reserve, and they plan on dumping all of that [waste] into the ocean. That has been a major concern, as I had indicated earlier that there was evidence of lead in adults and children in Kivalina. That company had wiped out two other communities in Greenland and in Canada, and that gives you an idea of some of the concerns we have.

As for oil and gas, we are still struggling to deal with that issue, and both the onshore and offshore arrangements have not been made in such a way that it is even close to being acceptable with our tribe and our people, both for environmental purposes and for sharing of non-renewable resources. Other responses need to be made on the side of corporate social responsibility and human rights. Employment is only a very small fraction of any type of benefit that we would receive.

Oil has divided the community to a certain point, but the majority of our people are really concerned about the non-renewable resources in dealing with tradition and culture. Those procedures and religious activities are still being practiced now and are held on to for dear life. I don't know how to express that, but we won't let go of our life. The desire to protect it is a matter of pride and identity. It is just like when you get your cross after you are confirmed in the Episcopal Church, you are 12 years old and to get your cross you probably did a lot of studying.

There are a few that do support it and maybe do not have a choice because of job security; however, there has been no real arrangement that has been made to meet our needs if there was development of a non-renewable resource that we will never see again. We have at least $248 billion that is owed to us from Prudhoe Bay, without interest, up to 1989. We do have a rough life, but we have always been here.

There were thousands and thousands of caribou passing through, and it was literally at that moment that I questioned, "I wonder where my son will ever have the opportunity to bring his children and have a similar experience?"
- Dirk Nickish, bush pilot from Coldfoot, Alaska

Chapter Four: Those Who Come for Business and Pleasure

Each year, droves of people come to the Arctic to hunt, fish, raft, and backpack. We have interviewed these visitors, and those who guide and fly them, to get varied perspectives on the tourism industry in the Arctic. Since these people return in most cases to the "Lower 48" and southern Canada, the opinions they take home with them are particularly influential in the political decisions made about this vast land.

**Biologist Geoff Carroll and team
in northwest Alaska**

Southerners Backpack the North Slope

Laura Beebe (far left) was born in Mobile, Alabama. She remembers her youth as growing up in a very liberal family in a really conservative town. We met up with Laura in 2007 by coincidence in Anaktuvuk Pass, Alaska, as she lead a group of mostly Wisconsin high school females on a trip to the Arctic. Laura has a major in Adventure Education with a focus in Women's Studies and another major in Environmental Studies and a minor in Arctic Geography. She discusses her recent life in the Arctic teaching both natives and non-natives in the region.

When I was 15 years old, I did a backpacking trip, and ever since then, I have been working in the outdoor field with teenagers and teaching. My school was a very small liberal arts school, about 350 undergraduates, and you design your own major. No tests, no grades and it's all experiential-based, so the philosophy is you learn by doing. I was there three years and I spent probably two years studying geography, mountaineering, women's studies, leadership skills in the outdoors.

I first came to the Arctic three years ago in the winter to be a research assistant with the climate change. It was about two and a half weeks that I worked with some scientists out of Canada, and basically we went out eight hours a day for snow samples in February. They were looking at pH levels, snow level. It is part of one point on a graph, about a 15-year study. We went to 11 different sites, some in the trees, riverbeds, and so forth.

Currently, I am leading a trip out of the YMCA based out of Wisconsin. It is my sixth summer with them. I have led three-month-long solo courses for them, backpacking and sea kayaking, and then two summers ago I led this trip which is a 48-day Arctic backpacking course. Last time we went

The beauty of the Brooks Range in the Arctic Refuge

through the Refuge.

These are single-gendered trips and small group expeditions where the kids come to our summer camp when they are in seventh grade and work their way up, doing longer and longer trips. This is the final trip they can do, which is six weeks, so they have all come up through the program. Our camp is almost 100 years old.

For this trip, the cost is probably $4,500, but we have a really great scholarship fund, so any child that wants to come can find money for and get on the trip. For me, I like to travel in the Arctic, but it's about teaching people about culture and natural history here.

When I started working for the Park Service, I got into teaching environmental education in different Arctic villages. I think my travels had set me up really well. I have been working for the Western Arctic National Park Lands. The Department of Interior and the Park Service run it, and I teach in 11 different schools. We teach classes on environmental and natural history, and so forth.

It was definitely a steep learning curve about how to teach in different villages. Some of the social problems and some of the different learning styles of the kids in the villages make it hard. I got to travel to all 11 villages. All the villages are different in their own ways, even though it's the same people.

Well, I am based in Chalkitsik, a bigger village. I go to each village three to four days and teach. It also depends on the village; if it is really small, I might only be there two days. I stay at the schools and bring a sleeping bag and sleep in the gym. Sometimes they will put us up in teaching housing, but most of the time, you sleep in school and they feed you.

Life here is completely different, just a different culture. Even though you are in America, it does not feel like it. The classroom here could have five students, others 17, and their ages could range about five years apart. You could go in an elementary classroom and it could be first to fifth grade, and then you have a handful of children that have fetal alcohol syndrome and so they have special needs. Some can read, and some cannot. Some can do basic math, while others cannot do any math.

We make our curriculum to coincide with the Alaska state standards and what they are working on. So, if they are doing science and looking at microscopes, then we will come in and show how plants reproduce at the microscopic level. If they are learning about the bears or wolves in class, then we will come in with a talk, sing songs, and watch movies to make our classes relevant to what they are learning in school.

Teaching in the classroom in Alaska is also completely different from the summer trips I lead. I think a lot of it is just different because the girls I work with in the Lower 48 have traveled everywhere and are very worldly. You can ask them to name a national park and they can name at least a dozen of them. You come up here and ask them if they have ever heard of the Statue of Liberty and most of them haven't.

I have noticed that the kids are more shy and are less likely to just jump in and try something new. They need an example if you are making a craft project. We make these caribou puppets, and they will not just make one, they have to see your example, and they will make it identical to your example. We encourage them to be creative and think of some new ways of looking at the world.

Sometimes it is hard, because they are so focused on testing, and they have state standards covered every week. It's hard for some principals to let go of that idea. One of the services we provide is just a positive role model. We also talk to them about options after graduation and explain that there are jobs out there for them.

They have a lot of money and they definitely pay for the facilities, pay their teachers, but there is just a lot of pressure from the state for their testing to be higher. I think a lot of the people in the village want their children to be educated in the traditional ways, so it is a big toss-up about what you are going to teach.

And, lots of challenges face the village. I think the rate of alcoholism, drug abuse, a lot of abuse towards women, and child neglect are the big ones. I see a lot of the teachers taking in children that are not fed, and they take them on as their own kids. The village will take care of everyone to an extent, but there are quite a few that fall through the cracks. I think they are also looking at what to do with their teenagers when they are done with school and what their options are. Should they stay at home living sustainably or go work? The more TV they get, the more worldly they become. They want more things and more money a lot of times.

As a teacher, I think working for the Park Service has its challenges, because we come in, almost as a police force. Although they have their hunting separate from the camp, they are hunting off the land, so those two worlds are together. We really work with the people so they can continue their lifestyle. But a lot of times when I come into villages, people ask me if I am a police officer. I wear my traditional park uniform. I think the hardest thing for me is coming in and teaching for a few days and getting attached to the children and then just picking up and leaving. So I worked at the boys' and girls' club, so the children could have some consistency, because people move up here and then leave.

The Dog Musher

David van den Berg is a 41-year-old resident of Fairbanks, Alaska. He has spent almost 20 years of his life with dog teams, driving them through some of the least-populated parts of Arctic Alaska. Over these years, he has led many wilderness trips as a back-country guide. He has also been the Executive Direc-

Dave gives the dogs a free pass

tor of the Northern Alaska Environmental Center headquartered in Fairbanks. He is currently the Executive Director of the Downtown Association of Fairbanks.

The first time I ever mushed was with my friend Sue Steinacher's dog team. She and her team had been in a plane crash after a Russian mushing event, and ended up back in Fairbanks with some dogs who, along with her, survived the crash. Injured, she had no way to look after the dogs. That was my first winter up here, and I was the perfect guy to dog-sit her team.

The next year, she offered me her older, veteran dogs for free: "Such a deal I have for you!" So I started off with some good dogs with good habits. You learn over the years that dogs teach dogs better than people can. That's what I have learned, but I've taught my best dogs everything that I can. I got a lot of that technique from reading a book by Mel Fishback about training lead dogs. It was like a pamphlet, and I was just going through it and finding out what works for me.

There are certain types of dogs that I can't work with very well as a leader, and some that I can. It's a whole bunch of trial and error, but I've been doing it for 17 years, and I have a lot of likes and dislikes and opinions about what makes a good dog. First thing a working dog needs is the will to work. You can cultivate a whole team with leader qualities -- malleable yet independent, smart but not too smart, and a certain zest. But you'll wind up with your top string and put the others where they can still contribute.

Getting into dogs for me wasn't a conscious decision. It was more like a bright-eyed kid arrives in Fairbanks, and here is an opportunity to do something that he has never done before. And soon, I've got a small team of experienced dogs. I had lots of pets growing up, working animals included. Working that first winter in Sue's kennel, I loved everything about it, even the feeding and scooping poop was great.

A dog team is pure energy. As individuals spin on their chains, it's noisy chaos. But harnessed, there's directed power and it's an adventure every single time you leave the dog yard. Then what makes it stick is that I love being with animals.

Now, I'm what is called a "recreational dog musher" who has had as many as 14 dogs, but I usually only have eight. I never raced. But I'd still put one or two thousand miles a year on my team, depending on what I had going. A dog team is a great way to travel if you're fit and patient. I hunt with dogs. We pack with dogs. As a commercial venture, if we have a long trip or marginal people or both, I'll take up to two dogs as pack animals.

You train dogs, and you put on miles and teach them good behavior. Around Fairbanks you run on trails. In Fairbanks, you don't get a lot of wind but rather a lot of snow just falls and stays, so you are always running trails. The dogs kind of know where to go, plus they know all the commands, along with other things.

Preparing for my first trip across Alaska's North Slope, it occurred to me that we don't get to run in the windy, featureless terrain we'd be heading into. So how can I train my dogs for this? How can I replicate this? So I went to the Fred Meyer superstore parking lot for a series of nights after the store closed. It was maybe a four acre parking lot, so it was big enough that I toggled them to myself, and we went jogging back and forth across the lot. I taught them to run more or less straight at my command across a flat, featureless plain. Dogs hook left and right, and they will take you in a circle unless you train them to do the right thing.

Dave's dog team on the North Slope

Nuiqsut is on the Coleville River, the biggest river on the North Slope. Mushing up here, having dogs, used to be an economic proposition, and I'm not talking about dog racing. You just always had a couple of dogs. They were your beasts of burden, and they did everything but give you milk.

After a twenty-some day traverse across the North Slope, we were nearing Nuiqsut, and we ran into some hunters two or three days out. They asked us what we were doing out here. We told them we were running across the slope to Nuiqsut and they thought that was great. A couple days later we are pulling into the village, and people said, "Hey! You're the dog mushers! Oh here you are. We were a little worried about you." The first people had told them that we were out there, and it got around the village.

In town, there are more and more people coming out to greet us. We are almost getting buzzed, there are so many of them. I'll never forget running down the middle of town. It was really fun. We stayed there for four or five days. There was a whaling captain there named Thomas Napageak, who has since passed. He was inviting us to come by and visit him at home. We did, and he was old and had smoked a lot of cigarettes, and he was in failing health.

Interestingly, when you drive a dog team into a Native village, there is an instant recognition of something different than if we came any other way. For years, I don't think Thomas ever knew my name. He just called me the dog musher. When I visited over the years, or called on the phone, I'd ask if Thomas was there, and his daughters would tell their dad it was the dog musher. That was what was so neat. He was truly passionate about dogs – he'd hunted polar bear with them back in the day. As an old man in failing health, what he was trying to do for his grandson was cultivate an interest in dogs. And for as long as I knew Thomas, dogs were our bond – dogs and the great wild country that dogs opened up for us.

On that first visit to Nuiqsut, Thomas pressed me hard to sell him a dog, and I wouldn't do it. He wanted a dog that was my main leader. At that time, Lumpy wasn't quite three years old, and he had just led my team across hundreds of miles of featureless terrain, through ground blizzards and all that. He was a phenomenal dog and would, through the rest of his life, continue to inspire me with his work ethic and verve.

Anyway, Thomas wanted to trade a brand new four-wheeler for the dog. Rather than say flatly and impolitely "no", I said, "Thomas, that machine's not even in Deadhorse. How am I gonna get it there over all this snow?" He said that he would get it there, but I wouldn't give him Lumpy. But I gave him one of the other ones – a dog of my choosing – like Sue did to me years before. It was a good, tough dog from Fort Yukon. I left Nuiqsut with seven dogs.

No-Trace Camping and Bear Tales

No-trace camping came out of the National Outdoor Leadership School. They were the ones who coined the phrase and developed the techniques, as far as I know. It's born of the recognition that there are more people than there are wild acres, even in Alaska. You use to be able to cut all the green limbs you wanted and sleep on a bed of boughs. You could make a great big fire and dig a trench around your tent.

But now people realize that there is a diminishing resource here. For me, it makes a lot of sense. Who really wants to go through a pristine landscape and leave a heavy imprint? A guerilla fighter would say that you sleep by day, and you move by night, and you do all things that keep you from leaving a heavy imprint. You want to be imperceptible on the land, so that nobody can tell that you were there. To be in the guiding business, likewise, you have got to do that. People would be wide-eyed if you do stuff like dig trenches or allow people to poop 10 feet from the river. You can't diminish it each time you go through. You have to do your very best to keep it the way you found it.

As a practical matter, you try to use gravel airstrips to get into a place or land on lakes. But if it is a tundra strip or a vegetated or sensitive Arctic tundra, it's basically a no go, even if you find a 1,000 foot strip on some tundra bench. If there is a textbook on leave-no-trace, I think you would find some of these things. I'm not saying that we're perfect or that these techniques are widely recognized, because there are pilots and guide outfitters who don't see it that way. But for our company, we don't pioneer strips that aren't on durable surfaces. The point of entry needs to be something that doesn't scar the land.

Dave the birdwatcher

We also try to camp on durable surfaces-- that's gravel bars. If you are going to camp on tundra, you try to camp on the eroding river bank and put the cooking area, the area with the highest amount of foot traffic, on a gravel area. If there are rocks in the tundra when you are pitching your tent, don't just grab some big cobble that has grown in and around with lichen; don't leave a cavity in the tundra. And if you brought a rock from the river to drive tent stakes, don't just leave it lay – chuck it back where you got it.

For going to the bathroom, what we have taken to doing, because we had to police individuals' behavior and we saw some stuff that you didn't want to reprimand a grown person for, we went to group latrines. When we get out there and make camp, the guides go out with a trenching tool and make a group latrine. From our experience, we can say that hydrologically, this is going to be a good place. We can bury it deep enough and it's not going to drain into the water table in any period of time.

Before the days of the latrine, we would have the same tool, and we would give extensive talks about how to do dig a hole and where to dig it. We still give the same talk and we still have the tools for people if there is a line for the group latrine. We try to empower people with the information and show them the basis of our decision making. When they go to dig their own cat hole, they will do the right thing.

Fires are something in the Arctic that we discourage on the North Slope. We try to resist having fires. On personal trips, I have no problems with having small "smudge" fires. But with groups, in areas that don't have anything but willows, you just don't want to be taking all that driftwood.

We'll explain to people that it is light all the time and that they don't need a fire. But if they persist, you tell them that the wood is one of the primary sources of nutrients that is going to be put back into the environment. It's the thing that creates little objects that help collect sand during floods and it helps to re-vegetate. The wood up there is part of a dynamic landscape and ecology, so we don't like to burn it.

If we will have a fire, we will do it right down at the water's edge. You can find me late at night, throwing tiny embers back into the fire to make sure that everything burns. You go and fish through it, and make sure that you aren't leaving anything. You can go to an extreme with fires, and I believe that I and most of our guides do.

Then there is stuff about walking on or off the game trail. Typically, I don't think that matters too much because you have caribou that come through and just hammer an area and just lay down this big trail. Be smart about approaching wildlife, but that isn't something that we have really had to approach anyone about. These aren't the people that get out of their car to feed a bear; these are the people who don't want to see a grizzly bear, to a point. People are anxious about bears, and we don't have to persuade them not to take marshmallows out on the tundra if we have seen a grizzly.

With trash, we used to burn it about halfway through the trip in a big, gross gold-pan. So back in those be-knighted days, we would have a trash fire after the clients went to bed. It was not a pleasure fire. It was stinky, and we worked it to be economical on wood, and we'd poke and prod and blow to make sure everything burned, or at least was captured in a molten blob in the gold-pan. We don't do that anymore. We pack out everything, and we have a system of inserting a compactor bag inside a tear-resistant poly-bag that's capacious enough to handle everything inside.

With brushing your teeth and doing the dishes, it's a little contradictory. When brushing your teeth, we say spit it in the river. When doing your hair, do it about 200 feet from the river. With the suds and the sanitizer, we say put that 200 feet from the river as well. The logic with brushing teeth is that people would spit right outside their tent. We put all the food in the common area along with their tooth brushes and toiletries, so all fragrant items are in the cook area.

Food is tough. Packing all food in bear-resistant containers is really not feasible. Food volume has gotten more and more, from our perspective, when we go in with a party. We eat well, and by that I mean very little dehydrated stuff. If we were to pack all the food in bear-barrels, we would need an additional plane for every trip just to bring these odd size barrels in and out. We figure that with enough safe, steel-barrel storage for at least 65% of our food, we can then use a cooler with fresh stuff and maybe a dry bag of crackers. We'll just be careful as we pack things in the steel barrels as we draw down our inventory. By day three or four, maybe all of our food is at long-last in bear-resistant storage.

About guns- it is really up to the guides. Few of the guides take guns on the backpack trips-- they take bear-spray. The odd thing is that if there is one guide and one client, they are the most vulnerable because it is a small group. But they are carrying the most weight. Some things are irreducible like the satellite phone, the air-ground radio and the medical kit. You can't spread that weight around like in a larger group. I guarantee you that they won't pack a .44. If you have a group of six people, the guide might think that he or she can pack and carry one. On river trips, we take a shot gun because there is no reason not to.

I've only had two bear incidents that have been with clients. Maybe three have been by myself or with a dog. I can only think of one that could have been serious. It was a guy who went out late, late at night to go to the bathroom, and he took a shovel with him. He walked a mile from camp before he dug his hole. As he was squatting, he spotted a bear to his left, across a deep, narrow ravine. The grizz gets his scent and runs down out of sight. The guy thinks he could be in trouble. As he is pulling up his pants, the bear comes at him in a full charge. He sprayed him with the bear spray, and he was hollering. He said that the bear just ran and ran and ran and almost ran toward camp, but when it saw it, it deflected away. He came into camp and woke us all up and told us.

Oh and birders! You have got to watch those guys because they just want to go sneaking around in the woods looking for birds. One morning with a birder, a little and funny guy, he went off and was smoking a cigar at 5 a.m. This guy is walking along looking for the bird with a big stogie in his mouth and he was being quiet and stealthy. But he turns around, and there is a bear sneaking up on him!

Anyhow the bear charged him, and he stood his ground, waved his arms, hollered and shrieked, which worked. He's still with us today.

My Love Affair with the Arctic

Geoff Carroll is a 58-year-old wildlife biologist who has taken the lead in many aspects of Arctic Alaska wildlife studies, especially with whales. This Wyoming born and raised cowboy was bitten by the Arctic Alaska bug in his teenage years and has never looked back. His scientific team, funded substantially by the Inupiat-run North Slope Borough, developed new and accurate techniques of bowhead census-taking that allowed Inupiat whalers to have larger annual quotas for their most important subsistence species. Carroll has devoted his last 20 years to managing land mammals over the western two-thirds of the North Slope from the Coleville River west. http://www.maplandia.com/united-states/alaska/north-slope-borough/barrow/

I guess I've always had a fascination with the Arctic. I always read books about the Arctic. I always kind of preferred winter activities like skiing, winter camping, and that sort of thing. I drove up to Alaska in the mid-seventies just to spend the summer, and it became obvious that that's the place I ought to be, so I began to stay up here.

Geoff and his dog team on sea-ice near Barrow, Alaska

At some point, I came to the realization that a person could spend the rest of their life getting paid to study wildlife. This big light bulb went off over my head, and that got me back into school. I went to the University of Alaska in Fairbanks and I got a wildlife degree. In the midst of that, I got an opportunity to work with bowhead whales along the Arctic coast.

So I went up and started working with National Marine Fisheries and started a bowhead whale census. We would basically camp on the ice, start in mid-April, stay out there the next two months, and count all the whales that went by, both the bowhead whales and the beluga whales. I found that to be one of the most wonderful places in the world. It was just an incredible experience every year.

You would go out on the sea ice, which at that time is completely silent. There are no animals in sight, nothing much going on. Within a couple weeks, leads of open water would appear in the ice, and there would be this explosion of life. You would see literally millions of eider ducks fly by, the bowhead whales would come by the thousands, the beluga whales by the tens of thousands.

Of course when the leads open and seals start popping up, then the polar bears get real interested and will be alongside the leads. You always had polar bears to deal with, and it was just one of the best jobs in the world getting to be out there and run these census camps.

So anyway, that's what got me hooked on the Arctic. Eventually my specialty in life was working and living on the sea ice. I ended up going with a group of people, and we did a dog sled expedition to the North Pole in 1986.

Anyway, that's what got me fascinated with the Arctic, and it took me a long way. It felt like going to the North Pole was my graduate school and my ice education. It was a real feat for me, but there's nothing really better than being on the shore-fast ice and watching all the wildlife go by. The ice dynamics are just about as interesting as the wildlife. You would be in a situation where you're camping out on the land-fast ice and out in front of you, you have the pack ice. You know the ice extends for hundreds of miles across the ocean and moves back and forth with the currents and the wind. Sometimes it would just come and smash up against the land-fast ice and make things real exciting. We then would have to make all these decisions on whether it's safe to be out there, or not.

But I'm getting ahead of myself. Going to school at the University of Alaska was kind of a mixture of studying hard and doing a lot of cross-country skiing, doing some mountain climbing and trying to get through everything academically. Then every spring, I would leave school a month early and go up and count whales, so it was always quite a challenge getting through all that stuff. I usually had to come back mid-summer after the whale count, scramble and make up some stuff. But anyway I got through with decent grades and got my degree.

When I was at the University of Alaska, I had some great professors. It's a smaller school and probably not as well-financed as lots of bigger schools around the country. But because it is in Alaska, and those of us that really like wildlife are attracted to it, they have some really top-notch teachers. Some of the really good teachers I had included Bob Elsner. Then there was a guy named John Burns who worked for Fish and Game that came up and lectured every once in a while. He was a great marine mammal biologist as well. That got me going towards marine mammals in general and whales in particular.

It was one of those things. I should have gone ahead and gotten a graduate degree, but I got busy working up north. You know, I don't have any regrets; work was always very interesting to me, so I continued with that. Well I guess I did a variety of things, actually, for a while; I was building log houses during the part of the year I wasn't out doing whale research or related.

But eventually, like I said before, I wound up going on this expedition to the North Pole and found myself three days after we got done with the North Pole trip right back up on the whale census and counting those whales.

Then the next fall, I was contacted by some people that wanted to attach radio transmitters to bowhead whales and they wanted someone who was familiar with those whales. So I went up and worked with them on that project, which was actually in the Canadian Arctic. I ended up back in Barrow working with some of the people from the North Slope Borough Department of Wildlife Management.

Initially, the whale census work had been through the federal National Marine Fisheries, but then the North Slope Borough took it over and so I switched over. I had worked with them on the whale census, and we had lots of material to write up from our whale work. I decided to stick around another month or two, and that evolved into a full-time job with the North Slope Borough Department of Wildlife Management.

That was 1986 and we'd been doing the bowhead whale census since 1976. The reason we started the census was that initially when I was hired to go up there, it was to collect samples and take measurements from bowhead whales that were harvested.

But it was obvious that there was a great need for an accurate population estimate. Those were very controversial times with bowhead whales, because nobody really knew the answer to the question. For some reason, the scientific community felt that the bowhead whales probably numbered in the low thousands or even less than a thousand. There was a pretty high harvest rate, and the International Whaling Commission basically proposed a moratorium on hunting bowhead whales, and somewhat later, a very, very low quota.

Geoff and dogs at sunrise

I felt from being out on the ice and from everything that the whalers said that there were many more whales than what the scientific world thought at that time. So basically we started from scratch. How do you count a population of whales? That's always difficult. But with bowheads, you have the advantage that most of them migrate past certain points about the same time every year. But there are tremendous difficulties as well, because you're dealing with an ice covered environment. And, of course, it's a pretty difficult weather situation.

So anyway, this gradually evolving project was fascinating to be part of because we made a lot of advancements. For one thing, we would use auto-lights to survey the instruments to track the whales. You would see a whale surface six or eight times, go through a blow series a mile to the south of you down the lead, then a while later see another whale surface off to the right somewhere. And you wonder, is that the same whale? So we used these surveying instruments to determine what speed that animal would have had to travel to get from one place to the other. We knew about the average speed the bowhead whales swam, which is about three knots.

Then we could calculate that that had to be a new whale or not, so it gave us a much more accurate estimate of what was going by. Then the most interesting of it-- you're in a situation where you got a lead that opens and closes depending on the wind direction and the currents. If everything is calm, it can just completely freeze over again. But we didn't really have a good idea as to whether the whales stop moving when the lead closes.

The North Slope Borough was able to contract with an anti-submarine warfare specialist, who developed a system of hydrophones that we could string out. It turned out that fortunately, these bowhead whales vocalize pretty consistently when they are moving along. You could actually hear them going by.

So we had this sophisticated system where there's a string of hydrophones, and the difference in the amount of time that it takes the sound to get from one hydrophone to the other, you could get locations and speeds. So then you have all these tracks of whales going by based on the hydrophones. Then we're able to combine the digital count with the acoustic count; we came up with a really sophisticated system which allowed us to actually count the whales.

We did a fair number of aerial surveys in those days, but mostly we were using that to test our ability to see whales. We knew how many we had counted, and we were always trying to figure out ways to come up with how many we were missing. The acoustics were fantastic for that, because we could hear whales 15 or 20 miles out, while visually we could see maybe only three. We were able to correct our counts for the whales that were going beyond our range of view, and were able to correct it for the whales that were swimming under the ice through the lead when the lead was closed.

Anyway, it gave us lots of different options. Since I've gotten out of the picture in recent years, they have started to send aircraft more and more to photograph bowhead whales, and they found that when they fly right over the whales and take their photographs, they can actually identify individuals by their scar patterns. They all have had a pretty rough life scraping along the ice and getting hit by boats and getting bit by killer whales.

One of our first questions to the acoustics experts was, can we voice-print these whales, and will we know if it's the same one or not? They could never really do that.

Just the fact that we could track them along-- you could see their lines of movement-- you could see which one was the same whale going by. And then we could combine the visual count with the acoustic count. So we went from the estimate of probably fewer than 1,000 whales to showing that there were probably over 10,000 whales now. As a result, the IWC has a very liberal quota now. The Inupiat can take just about as many as they can use.

Eskimo Whalers and Larger Quotas

All of this work put us in the big middle of the controversy about quotas. My first years up here, it was apparent that there were a lot of whales being struck and lost. When it gets hit by a harpoon, the whale swims off and may die or not. And up to maybe a hundred in a year might be lost and die. And there might only be a thousand whales. That was just too many whales being struck and lost.

One of the best things that came out of that whole deal was that when the quotas were re-set, they were set so that you could strike so many whales per year. So a struck and lost whale counted the same as a harvested whale. That was a strong motivation for people to do a better job of killing the whales that before may have been lost.

Thinking back to our success with the count, it made me feel great. That was kind of my life's work at that point, trying to come up with an accurate population estimate.

I also felt that the Native population was being treated unfairly because of the misperception that science was not a part of their concern. One of the amazing things about this group of Eskimo people is they recognize the fact that they can only fight science with science. One of the main things that they have supported is putting up the money and lobbying other people to put up the money to do an accurate count, and then using the factual information to show that you could have a much higher quota than what was originally set.

The North Slope Borough has one of the most amazing wildlife departments in the world. It's probably the only municipality that has a wildlife department at all as far as I know, and it's an amazing combination of really top-notch scientists and subsistence hunters.

Their director is a woman who comes from a longstanding subsistence family. Their deputy director is an excellent whaler, and he's the head of the Alaska Eskimo Whaling Commission. He goes to meetings all around the world with this information, plus he's a good caribou hunter to boot.

Offshore Drilling and Whales

One thing we haven't talked about is offshore drilling and its effect on whaling. There is plenty of scientific literature that proves that noise and disturbance could effect the movements of bowhead whales. In fact, that's one of the great things the North Slope Borough did early on. The federal Minerals Management Service hired a consulting company to do a study to determine the effects of seismic activity occurring in oil exploration at sea. They came to the conclusion that there was no evidence that this activity was affecting the movement of whales.

Every whale hunter could tell you that the year that there was a lot of seismic work done, the whales were way farther offshore. They would have to make dangerous trips a lot farther offshore to get whales.

The scientists with the North Slope Borough looked at the methods and the results of the study that had been done, and they said it was a poor test. The methods of testing were so poor that you couldn't possibly conclude that the noises incident to oil and gas exploration didn't affect the whales. It was a completely inconclusive study, and they made them do a much better job the second time around. It's clear from other studies that the bowheads were obviously avoiding the sonic area around those ships. That's what makes a bowhead whale a bowhead whale. Hearing is their main sensory defense.

Every whaler knows that, and the key to successful bowhead whaling is to be absolutely silent. They use skin boats or wood framed boats covered with skins, because they are silent in the water, not because they are trying to be cool or traditional. They use homemade wooden paddles with little sharp tips so that there's less noise pushing your paddle in the water and pulling it out.

One last interesting fact about bowhead whales: over the years, there have been several tips found in bowhead whales like old stone harpoons and jade spear points, things that haven't been used for a hundred years. This started giving people the idea that these are some really old whales. They have a technique of using the lens of the eye to age bowhead whales and they are finding that some of these whales are 160, 180. I think the oldest one was 212 years old, so they're really one of the longest-lived mammals in the world.

A CEO Goes North

Dave Harman is a 60-year-old businessman from Boone, North Carolina, who visited the Arctic of Canada and Alaska in 2004 with the Appalachian State University field trip. He is an outdoorsman who loves to travel and is interested in environmental protection. He is a co-author of Arctic Gardens who is responsible for Chapter Five, but he was not on the book team at the time of this interview.

I decided to go to the Arctic with an ASU professor, Harvard Ayers, whom I had known for about 25 years. I had done the business route and he had done the academic route and we used to see each other in Sierra Club years ago. I ran into him at a bank lobby and he told me about these trips he was doing to the Arctic in the summertime, and asked if I would have any interest in going. I immediately said, "Yes, I will." As it turned out, the very trip he had in mind, I could not manage to get it to work out to go, but I told him to put me on the waiting list for the next trip.

Dave in camp

The reason why I went primarily was because I saw it as an opportunity for adventure travel. Probably secondarily in the back of my mind, I decided that it was time to learn about some of the issues of that region. I always sort of thought I knew something about the issues in the Arctic. I was to learn later that I knew nothing really, so it was his invitation that made me realize it was time to go.

On our trip there were seven students and four older people and business-types plus the professor. The professor was the leader of the group and there was John Cooper who is the owner of the Mast Store, Hanes Boren who is the owner of Footsloggers and me. We were all fairly close in age and career path. The only difference is that the professor has been an academic all his life, but the three of us business-types wanted to go because we were all sort of environmentally predisposed. We all like camping and hiking, and it seemed like a perfect group. The students were a mixture of males and females, and different courses of study.

We went in August, and it was ostensibly part of an anthropology class. We attended classes for two or three different episodes to learn a little bit about the Native people, and to learn a little bit about the history of the area from an anthropological point of view. The rest of the trip involved travel from Raleigh to Toronto to Vancouver to Whitehorse to Old Crow, the last two being in the Yukon Territory. Then we actually spent 12 nights on the ground in tents in various places. We went to three or four of the small villages, plus we were in a place called Sunset Pass up in the Refuge, actually near the Arctic Ocean. We got to see the ocean and the pack ice right off the coast.

We were prepared for cool weather, but incredibly, we had mostly 70's during the day, mostly 50's at night. Once we got up there, we spent the first night at Whitehorse, got our bearings and ditched a few of our things that we decided we didn't need, which we stored at a hotel there. Then we flew Air North, a regional carrier that is 49 percent owned by the Gwich'in Indians. We stopped in Dawson City, and then we flew on up to Old Crow.

Old Crow has a wonderful landing strip. It was gravel, a long sweeping valley near the Porcupine River, and it was in front of a mountain called Crow Mountain. The view from there was incredible; you could see the river snake its way. We stayed in Old Crow at least four days, as I recall.

One day the locals invited us to get on board a boat and go the three or four miles up the river to Tlo Kut, the ancient meeting grounds, where we attended an annual summer meeting called the General Assembly. Those two days we spent the whole day up at their Assembly watching, what is, for most of us, the only pure democracy we will ever see.

You know we have a republic where we elect people to speak for us, but in that case like this Indian band, anyone who belonged to the band and showed up could vote, and each vote counted equally on such thing as whether to buy a float plane or whether to explore the mineral wealth within their territory, or whether to continue the Gwich'in language for the youngsters, and so forth.

To our great delight, we were there during the height of wild blueberry season. I have never eaten so many ripe blueberries; it was just fabulous. We ate blueberries and wild cranberries every day for breakfast. I would have this instant oatmeal and somebody always had some wild blueberries or cranberries for me to put in it.

Also, we got to have a lot of personal time with the people and they were very inviting, open, and welcoming. They shared their food with us and we got to eat lots of caribou in various forms. I got to eat some wild goose, and got to eat moose meat and salmon. We had caribou stew, burgers. We talked a lot about rites of passage of the young people; the boys and the girls talked openly about it and explained the rituals. I considered those two days to be maybe some of the best.

I met Joe Linklater, the Chief of Old Crow. We talked about what it meant to be chief. I met Roger, who was the assistant chief of Old Crow, and we spent about 90 minutes in an interview with Roger. Roger spent a lot of time explaining to us their sincere spiritual connection with the caribou. He told us about the elders and their wisdom and how they tend to know what is happening and why.

Once we left Old Crow, interestingly, the way we got from Old Crow to our next stop was by the river. The professor had worked out the trip with a local Indian guide, a guy named Dennis Frost, and a nephew of his, Steven. We all loaded up their two power boats one morning on the Porcupine River and we ended up going 300 miles.

We spent one night along the river. I could talk for days about that experience; it was fabulous. We went through a place called Yukon Flats. Lenny Kohm called it the most productive wildlife area of North America. Our destination was Fort Yukon, Alsaka, and by then the Porcupine had merged with the Yukon River, and we spent the night there.

The spectrum of experiences with the Native people varied a whole lot, depending on where you were. On the Canadian side in the Yukon, we saw the folks at Old Crow and it was just my impression that they are a very functional group of folks. The people in Arctic Village and Fort Yukon, on the other hand, were American citizens. They benefited less from their land claim. They were part of the welfare system and it was a very different situation. There was high unemployment and a lot of alcoholism.

We flew from there to Arctic Village via Wright Air Service, which is another regional carrier. There, we helped restore an old church and took some supplies over to the school house and ran into the old principal there. We ended up talking to this guy for about half an hour, and he pointed out to us how the schools are supported normally in American states by the local property tax. You can imagine what the property tax was like there. The only money they got, they shared in the oil dividend every year in Alaska, but per person that could be from $400-$1300. It was not as much money as most Americans think and did not make up for the lack of a tax base or support from a central government.

Those people, in my opinion, have a very desperate situation, so I was really concerned to see these people who have lived a subsistence lifestyle. It was not very encouraging. We came away from there with a lot of feeling that we wanted to do something that would help their situation, and we were very conflicted as to what that might be.

We met a young girl named Roberta who was 16 years old and worked for the Tribal Council in the summers. She was going to go to school in Fairbanks and was hoping to become a fashion model, a real pretty girl. I had my picture made with Roberta while I was up there, and pretty much everybody kidded me about her the whole rest of the trip.

We stayed in Arctic village for a few days, and from there we flew with Dirk Nickish in

**Dave's Photo of a miniature forest on the
Arctic Refuge tundra**

his plane, which is a Dehavilland Beaver, an old-timer of an aircraft. It was built in the 50's. A real stout plane. He had to take us in two loads, and as luck would have it, he had gotten behind because forest fires in the area created lots of smoke. He didn't have time to take us all the way into the Refuge that trip, so he touched us down in a little stream valley known as Marsh Fork, a tributary of the Canning River. It couldn't have been more beautiful to sleep for a night. He took the six of us there, and he went back and got the other six.

The next day, he came and shuttled us to a place called Sunset Pass, which is in the Arctic Refuge. And again it was so pristine, so beautiful. Any surface water we could find, we could drink. Being above the Arctic Circle in the summertime, naturally we had a lot of sunlight. In fact, while the sun did go below the horizon, it didn't go much below. So our days started early, but I got pretty good at sleeping in, maybe waking up as late as eight o'clock. One day, we walked up on a mountain and didn't get back till after 10 pm, and it was still plenty bright.

We were in the most beautiful, pristine surroundings you could ever dream of. There was nobody else around; we just had this lovely and unstructured time to take pictures, hike, to write in journals, and to just contemplate what was there.

I was just blown away by it. I remember one day that a group of the students and Chad Kister, who is an author that has done a couple of books on the Arctic, went for a day to another river a few miles away that they hiked to and fished. Harvard, John, Hanes, and I stayed back in camp. We had the day to ourselves.

We decided to split up, so I walked south toward the Brooks Range. You could see Mt. Chamberlin in the distance and it was just gorgeous. I came across a mountain a couple of miles down the way undoubtedly unnamed, just sort of a rocky-sided mountain. I walked half way up, and just sat there looking at the valley below. I saw some caribou and wrote some notes. It was a little windy and I found a small spot on that mountain, a little depression that had rutted out, a little low spot with moss in it. I was sleepy, so I just laid down in that spot and took a nap. I slept for about an hour and a half.

But at that time and place, I had no weapon, no support system, no communication, nobody really knew where I was. I was in bear country and I was asleep, about as vulnerable as I guess I ever have been and ever will be. Call me crazy but I was thrilled at that moment. Almost nowhere else in North America can you go and have that experience.

Dave, John Cooper, Harvard Ayers climb Crow Mountain above Old Crow, Yukon

The opportune word concerning bush pilots and travel in the Arctic is flexibility, as we had been warned by Lenny; you might think you have a schedule, and you might be sort of counting on that schedule, but the truth is, you have to just go with the flow. And the reality of that is that these bush pilots sort of enjoy and command a sort of authority. And by that I mean they know the weather, they know the hazards, and they know the conditions. If they say we're not going, you're not going. If they say it's time to go, it's time to go. We had a lot of confidence in Dirk and he did a good job for us.

Once we left the Refuge and Sunset Pass, Dirk ended up flying us back to Arctic Village. We caught Wright Air again. In this case, we flew to Fairbanks and we stayed there a night. From there we flew to Whitehorse and we had an extra day that the professor had built in because you have to expect delays on possible places you get stuck. We had a free day and we got to do some exploring.

For a guy who grew up in Western society, I have always been in a protected situation and always been in a controlled environment, always had back-up systems for whatever need I might ever have.

The days had great variety. We were on the rivers, we were in the mountains, towns, had some structure but mostly not. It was pretty much up to us to do what we wanted to do with our time. And for anybody that can get there and indulge themselves in that time, you'll come back a changed person. I took a lot of pictures of wildflowers; I wasn't always sure what they were and anybody who thinks that is a barren place is ignorant. I don't mean that in any pejorative sense; they're just ignorant in a clinical sense-- they have no idea what is there. It is not a barren landscape.

On the animal side, we saw eagles, falcons, hawks, ducks, geese, and we saw a lot of other birds that naturally I didn't recognize. We saw a fox while we were walking on the riverbank heading up north toward the Arctic Ocean. It jumped out of its den but the crazy thing wouldn't run. I think it was curious about us as much as we were about it and we were probably no more than a hundred feet away. It would just sit there and watch us and we would get a little bit closer and she would back up but she wouldn't run. We saw ptarmigan. Some of the guys on this trip had some fishing gear and I don't know if they were good fisherman or there was just a lot of fish, but they were catching fish every day. We saw a grizzly bear and lots of caribou.

I read a fair amount of science and current events. And I am pretty up, as I think most citizens ought to be, on current events, politics, and so forth. But I found I was totally ignorant, really, of the issues of that land. I was totally ignorant of the Gwich'in people and the plight that they face.

So there was this epiphany that occurred to me. There is this whole other civilization that has been there. They've been there a lot longer than we have been here. It has been working beautifully. It's self-sufficient. It's independent. It's fabulous. It's my personal opinion that it's the way humans were meant to live. It's not the way we live now.

These folks are still connected to the land. I think we have lost our connection to the land. I felt great envy for the folks in Old Crow. At least the part of it I saw. I think they have the best lifestyle I have ever seen. They don't ask for much. They have what they need. And it's beautiful. They take care of each other, so I was very envious of that.

I also came away finally understanding the importance of the Refuge, and especially the coastal plain, to the ecosystem and to the Gwich'in people, and how interconnected they are. Once I finally realized and understood, something that is probably not obvious at all to most Americans, I realized that it is urgent that we deal with this issue in the right way.

I have a lot of friends that are much like me. They work, they are middle class Americans, they live here, they have always lived here. They mean no harm, but just living the lifestyle we do causes a big footprint on the earth.

The kind of cars we drive, the houses we live in and the kind of choices we make. I would have to say, and again I mean this in a clinical sense, most Americans are just ignorant of the effects we cause and most Americans are totally ignorant of the issues in the Arctic and the differences you can make.

I came away with that epiphany that I finally get it. I think I finally realize and furthermore I felt I came home with a sense of obligation. I need to try to explain to as many good, thinking people and make them aware. Awareness is the beginning of the solution; most Americans are simply not aware even after all that has been written. If you ask your average friend or neighbor to explain the issues in the Arctic, they would not know, they would not understand.

So I think that part of the issue is that we need to continue doing the best we can to educate the public on why developing the Arctic, especially for the rest of the oil, why the cost of doing it is so far beyond the little benefit that might be gotten. I came away with all those feelings: a feeling of urgency, a feeling to spread the word, a feeling of envy of how some of the Native people still live, and a feeling of sadness for how some of the Native people's lives have evolved.

I got to see a new land, I got to see beautiful places, and I got to sort of reconnect with the land. Sleeping on the ground 12 nights, living basically on the ground was fabulous for me. If you think about humans today, we are all part of one species. The truth is genetically we are not much different from our ancestors even 1,000 years ago. We are basically the same. Like the Natives, we always had a connection with the land. We lived off the land. The land is what sustained us. We took care of the land. In the last few generations, I don't know exactly when, I guess since the Industrial Revolution, we have begun losing that connection with the land. I think that it is a loss for all of us. I think we miss it; we don't even know we miss it until we go back to it. I think it is a primal feeling and that sort of got re-awakened in me, and I think that's one of the great highlights of my trip.

I am absolutely certain that as this human population continues to grow, that the need for wild places will become greater and greater. This sort of human nature that we have, is to move into areas and change the areas to suit human needs, and we basically begin poisoning wherever we go with our by-products. There have to be places that we just don't do that. The great part of Alaska and the Yukon up in the Arctic is still basically unspoiled, and we need to leave it that way.

From the Outside In

Itai Kah was born and raised in Israel, then immigrated to the United States. When visiting his brother who lived in Tsiigehtchic, Northwest Territories, he made friends with Alestine Andre, a Gwich'in resident of the small town. They had a very good long-distance friendship for a few years, and he eventually moved up to the north. Shortly after, they were married and have been together since 2001. Itai is a painter/artist and house-husband. http://www.maplandia.com/canada/northwest-territories/inuvik-region/tsiigehtchic/

When I lived in the States, I lived in the San Francisco area, and I also spent time in other places. I think there were things in the big places that I didn't appreciate much, but where it really struck me was when I spent two months in the Silicon Valley in California. When I would be walking there, I could sense that 20-30 years ago, the place was mostly orchard and it was just the most beautiful place. In my mind, I could see those orchards and those small communities spread around, and in reality, I would be surrounded completely by concrete and big corporation buildings. It kind of made me sick from something that was very natural and organic into something that was completely industrial, and it struck me that was the way it was done.

The place felt very cold to me and very artificial, so that kind of summed up my time in California. It was very crowded and the lifestyle of people did not make very much sense to me. When I came here [Tsiigehtchic], the contrast was huge. I could just see the land in prime condition, and that is what really attracted me, and it felt like it brought my humanity back up to the surface. I could still experience myself as a human being. For me, that was the major difference.

In California, we had very hot summers, probably in the 90's and 100's where I used to live. The winter wasn't very cold. It was maybe down to 40 degrees, quite a bit of rain sometimes. In the Arctic, the winters are probably 40 below and dark and in the summers, it can get up to 90 sometimes.

When people live in the big cities, I find many times that instead of adapting themselves to nature, they adapt nature to themselves. In this process to me, something is lost. When the weather is more extreme here than California, it's just part of the environment. I really enjoy winter. To look at everything white and frozen; it's just most beautiful. I feel much more alive being up in a place like this than being in a place that was modified to accommodate a certain style of life.

When I first came to Tsiigehtchic, people were pretty suspicious about outsiders. It is hard for them to sometimes feel comfortable enough to communicate, but when you spend time with them and they come to know you, things work better. I am a quiet guy who doesn't speak much, and I think that fits with the culture pretty well. People up here would speak much less than people down South. When people from down South come and they speak a lot in relation to here, it gets too much noise for people. The main thing that I found out with people in town, if you can make them laugh, they would accept you faster.

I'll give you an example. We knew a woman from Fort McPherson who had two little parrots, and they are really noisy. I go in there and tell her that her parrots are making more noise than the white man.

My diet changed, too. It's mainly meat now. I'd say that 70 percent of my diet is meat. Fish would account for 10-20 percent, and the rest is mostly rice, potatoes, and some veggies. In the past, my diet was mostly fruits and veggies and much less meat. Most of our food comes from the land. I guess 70 percent would be caribou. Other meat that we would eat sometimes would include beaver and moose. Caribou would be, by far, the main meat. Every now and then, we eat some muskrat, but we don't eat it very often.

My father-in-law passed away last year, and I learned so much from him. He passed on to me to not worry about the things that are out of your control. I think when I lived down South, it was a much more worrying way of life for me, and a lot of the stuff that I worried about was beyond my control. There are probably other things that I have learned by observation. I have learned how to set a net for fish, and I am practicing my fish cutting.

You learn to respect the environment, and that came out of his stories. When he would go hunt for caribou, it was very important to let the smaller ones go, instead of just shooting. He was always upset when young people would go from town and just shoot, and he was always concerned about the litter. For him, when he would go out, the land provided. But he always made sure that he would do his part so the next time he went, there would still be caribou or fish. There was always this foresight and for me, it was something very good to hear and to see.

Unfortunately today, when people go hunting, they don't have this knowledge anymore, and they do lots of stuff that my father-in-law would never dare do. When he would go hunt, he would actually track the animal down, so there was lots of skill and knowledge in tracking the animal and how to approach the animal. I don't know how many people still do it, but some [youth] would drive down along the highway, and if they see the caribou, then they would hunt.

For me, if I were a hunter, I know that I would want to do it in the way my father-in-law would do it, because it gives the animal much more respect. In order to do it, I must have some real knowledge that I definitely don't have when I am driving my truck and shooting from the highway. Just from the stories, so much knowledge I have gained from him. I think it was also very important for him that I would go hunt. It was very hard to explain to him sometimes, and he was hard of hearing too, that I was not a Gwich'in beneficiary, so I cannot just go and hunt.

To him, hearing that someone couldn't just go hunt was totally foreign. As a human being, in my mind, he was so complete between his mental, spiritual and his body that it was just always a pleasure to be with him.

He never worried about anything, and when he noticed me worrying about something, like maybe a windy day and we wanted to go out boating, he would ask me what I was going to do about it. When it comes to learning, I also think about the context of the culture and the way that they learned compared to the learning done in a Western society where you go to the university to study and you spend many years in your field. The traditional knowledge is based on common sense; you observe and then you figure things out. There is nothing that is that complex about it, and in a sense, that is what makes it beautiful.

It just takes good observation to realize what the most energy-efficient way to do things is, and that is how things are done. I think that is the way that learning and comprehending knowledge is very different than in Western societies. I think that it is a very healthy process, not to say that the westernized way is wrong. But when I look at the observation skills of people up here in the community, I would say that their observation ability is so much stronger. My father-in-law was almost blind and sometimes, he would see things out on the river that would be hard for me to see. It is almost like a spiritual aspect for his observing power, and I don't have any other way of looking at it because his eyesight was so weak.

For now, I can't say that I would stay here for the rest of my life, but for the near future, this is my home. I am the outsider most of the time, and in a sense, I have no voice because I cannot go to the Gwich'in Tribal Council. I do not have the right because I am not one of their people. I try to do what I think I can do. The most important thing for me, if the pipeline project worked, is to know that I voiced my opposition.

I feel like if I voice my opposition, at least I stood up and am known for not approving the project. I had to operate in a totally different way than if I was a beneficiary. I cannot tell the Tribal Council, but I can voice my concern to the National Energy Board. I can write articles for the paper in very simple language and try to help the local people question things that they have been told. I can in a sense, try to explain things for people in simple language, since quite a few people don't have the education to fully understand the concept that is coming from down South.

I explain to some that they are not an owner of the pipeline like they have been told. What has been proposed is to basically run the pipeline from Inuvik down to Norman Wells and then down to Alberta. And I believe it's about 1,300 kilometers. The maximum

Tsiigehtchic, Northwest Territories, on the Mackenzie River

planned capacity for the pipeline is about 1.9 billion cubic feet a day of gas. With the [current] way that they are building, the processing capacity would be only one billion cubic feet a day of gas. In order to get it moving fast, they figured that they wanted to have the aboriginal people on their side.

In my mind, the way they did it was a partnership with the aboriginal groups in the region. Potentially, they can become one-third owner of the pipeline. In order to do that, they [Gwich'in and Inuvialuit] have to bring gas to the pipeline. So they would have to go to an explorer and ask them to ship it. The estimated cost of the pipeline was about four billion dollars and now it is up to 16 billion. But the amount of gas that they would put in the pipeline stayed the same.

In my view, this project is not economically feasible, and the toll is going to be so high to pay for this pipeline, because there is not enough gas to bring the cost down. For any gas explorer, it would be too costly to ship gas down South when the prices of the gas are set on the international market. The farther the gas has to go from the Arctic, the more expensive it will be to buy, so there is a problem there. I think the pipeline is moving slowly because of economic concerns.

The key players from the region are the Inuvialuit and the Gwich'in. The Gwich'in Tribal Council is a big pusher of this project, but they never consulted their people properly in my opinion. From what I see, they just think that it is a great opportunity for us and believe that all of our problems will disappear suddenly. They just decided that they wanted to go with it. For me, there is something very wrong there because the Gwich'in Tribal Council's purpose is to look after their people and not a corporation who has a goal of making money for their shareholders.

Their goal is really to make sure that their people have a good future, and unfortunately, their vision of a good future is the pipeline. The Gwich'in Tribal Council Director is also the chair of the Aborigines' Pipeline Group and part of the oil company that wants to put in the pipeline. Something was very flawed in the whole process.

Development has brought lots of drinking. I have heard about back in the boom years in the 70's that people would go out and come back with lots of money, and then they would basically drink. I have heard of people starting to drink when they go to work for those oil companies. I think that part of it was the amount of money in the short amount of time earned by people that didn't have the skills to manage it properly.

For this community, I think the pipeline would create more damage. The construction time they are talking about is three years, but they will let people from the community be working. They would be removed from their community for a week or two at a time and then come back. You actually take your male population out for a long time, and then after this period of time is over, all of a sudden those men are coming back with lots of money. I just have a feeling that the capacity to manage things like that is not here.

Also, I do not think that they have any value for land [as land]. I think when the oil companies come up to a place like this, they don't interact with the land and it doesn't impact their being; they don't let it influence them. For them, sitting outside listening to the migrating birds has no value. The only value to them is extracting and making money to put in their pocket. It is just a totally different belief system. For me, the value is in the life on the land, and not what is below it.

I don't see myself as an environmentalist, but I think I see myself as just having common sense. I just don't want to destroy a place in order to get something that is going to last 20 years and doesn't build any future. We must have development, but we must develop with common sense to do all we can to protect places. The pipeline is not wise. It is just the short-term big bucks.

Not building a pipeline would offer them a chance to really consider what kind of future they want for themselves, and a chance to prepare for a better future. It would give them a chance to become their own master, instead of carrying someone else for 20-30 years. It would give them a chance to really create a stronger and healthier community by developing small and economical enterprises in the communities.

None of that is going to happen until a big chunk of the population goes and gets educated, in my opinion. I am talking about PhD's, engineering, nurses, doctors, lawyers, and mechanical people, but it will take some of the really highly-educated in the society to have a vision that they can build toward. I hope that would give them the opportunity for people to sit down and think about what they want for their future.

The 40,000 people that live here in this region get one billion dollars from the government. I don't know anywhere else on earth that people get that kind of money. Yet without education, nothing is going to be changing in the North, and it will remain the same 20 or 40 years from now.

One thing that I am noticing that is missing from the community is leadership about where they want to be in 50 years, and then figuring out how to get there. In my mind, there is no reason why a community like Tsiigehtchic couldn't have three doctors and one lawyer, etc. Until they understand the importance of their people being educated, they will never be independent. It will just always be the same story. The good jobs will be given to people from down South brought up here. The only way they can really protect their beliefs and values is education.

In terms of drilling of the U.S. side, I am very annoyed, because it is pure double face when I hear that the Gwich'in leadership here in the Delta tell the Americans they cannot drill there. They are very supportive of a project like the one here. They don't have any credibility to tell the American not to do it when they support development just as big, and the impact on the land is just as severe.

The proper way for the group to deal with it is uniting. It is almost impossible for them to do because there always seems to be lots of fighting among the group. They must unite as one voice and say, "This caribou is important to us, and all of their ground must be protected." And then we have the same leadership talking about doing something for global warming, but it starts at home. It has to start with you, and you can't support a pipeline like this if you want to do something about global warming.

In Israel, the first one going to war was the officer, not the soldiers. It was always the officer that led the way and those people had the rights to tell people what to do because they put their life on the line the same way. I don't have much respect when they say you can do it here but not there because it is the same thing. There are other ways of building the economy. There are smart ways to do things, and then there are stupid ways of doing things.

I am not saying don't drill for oil. It's the way it's done, where it is going to go, and is there no other alternative. When I look at the gas here, there are so many other alternatives and possibilities. If it was really just the last place, and beyond any doubt we needed it for our survival, then I would say go and do it. It's not the last place, and it's not that we are desperate for it, because just by a little conserving we can probably produce much more than what they ever will see from here.

My house is about 1200 square feet. It's built for a northern climate so it's heavily insulated. We try not to waste, and we do not have TV, so it's cut our power consumption down. I change all the light bulbs to the efficient compact fluorescent bulbs, and when I am not in the room, I cut off the lights. If I read, I try to read by the light. I try to just have the area where we are lit up.

I changed my washing machine to energy efficient, and that has cut lots of power. My fridge will be replaced in a few years. We bring our usage down to 300 kilowatts of power a month, and it was not hard to do. At one dollar a kilowatt, it's really a big savings. I think that there is more to be done. I think it would make sense for the government to provide high efficiency appliances to the communities, and those things would pay back in two years, and then they would be cutting their subsidies. I don't think they would do it, though.

One Man, Two Loves, Three Lives

Lenny Kohm is a 69-year-old environmentalist from Todd, North Carolina, a small village in the Appalachian Mountains. Lenny began his working life playing in bands as a percussionist, morphed into a photographer, and 20 years ago found his stride as an environmentalist traveling the country to protect the Arctic National Wildlife Refuge coastal plain from petroleum exploitation. He now works as Campaign Director for Appalachian Voices, an environmental group headquartered in Boone, North Carolina.

My First Love

I'll start the story with my life's first love, music. I started playing when I was 14 and as a 14-year-old kid, rock and roll music never really interested me. I enjoyed some of it, but when I first really began to listen to music and think about it was when I started paying attention to what is referred to as jazz.

When I was 16, my family moved from Seattle to Japan. Fortunately, I got to spend some time with some of the better known Japanese jazz musician groups and got a chance to hear people play who were really top drawer. I mean they were really good! These Japanese musicians were my first exposure to that level of professionalism and it seemed to me like an impossible dream. I thought I was slated to be an accountant, or a doctor, or some other professional. It just wasn't part of how I was raised to be an artist or a musician.

The first two years of my university experience was at the University of Washington in Seattle where I majored in Jewish Engineering, otherwise known as Business Administration. Then I transferred to Berkeley College of music in Boston for my two upper division years. I finished there in 1962 with a Bachelor in Fine Arts. My major was in percussion, and I played the drums for my entire professional musical career. Over those 15 years, I played with Barney Kessel, who was one of the premier jazz guitar players in the 50's, 60's, 70's, and 80's. I played with Gabor Zabo, another jazz guitar player. I played with Jim Hall for a while, who is the father of modern jazz guitar.

It was near the end of the 15 years that I came to realize that although I was good, I was probably the 238th best drummer in the world, but I wasn't a phenom. So I began to think about what my life would be like when I was the age that I am now, 67. Can you still see yourself pulling the drums up the stairs?

My Days as a Photographer

So, I decided that I had an opportunity to sort of relax and take a look around and decide which direction I wanted to go, which I did. Then my marriage ended, and I moved to Sonoma, California, because of my interest in photography that I had had for a long time.

After a short time, I conned my way into a job running the photo department at this drug store and actually learned on the job. When I went in there, I was a con-man, and when I came out six years later, I was a photographer.

Over those six years, I was learning photography sort of by osmosis just in dealing with people and their snapshots and became really interested in it. I started getting some freelance photo assignments and was doing okay. I had worked with this writer on one of the projects that I did, Mark Twain's centennial celebration. We were given the assignment to photograph the whole Mississippi River.

The following summer, I got a call from that same writer asking me if I would be interested in going up to the Arctic to photograph Discovery Days in Dawson, Yukon. I had never been to the Arctic and I was curious. I called Audubon, and they said they were going to do a whole issue on the Arctic Refuge, which I had never heard of.

The Love of My Life

Now strange things happen in strange places. As we were doing laundry in Dawson City, there were Native people doing laundry. It turned out to be people from Old Crow, the most northern community in the Yukon.

They gave me this fact sheet on the Arctic Refuge that represented the environmentalist perspective. It was a much different approach than I was familiar with, and they told me how they felt about it. I thought it was interesting, that sort of human approach to it. I decided at that point by hook or by crook that I was going to go to the Refuge. There was just something about the whole combination of the ecological values that I kept hearing about so prominently, plus the human angle. I couldn't ignore it.

So, I got hold of a couple pilots, and they hooked me up with other people within the environmental community who were going up there. We were able to secure a charter, and it became less expensive. We stopped at Prudhoe Bay, Alaska, and we got a chance to see what that was all about. I do remember spending a few days in that area and it was really shocking.

The limited research on the oil companies I had done before I left stated what a terrific job they were doing, being good stewards of the land. But this place was a waste dump. I just thought, that's par for the course.

We flew over to the coastal plain of the Arctic Refuge, and the pilot dropped us off. I had had a perception, because it was the Arctic, it had to be all ice. I actually had visions of photographing these weird ice formations. But it was August, and there wasn't any ice.

The first thing that struck me really was that it was the wildest place that I had ever experienced. We all have heard that the world ecosystem was sort of something separate from us. What I realized on that initial trip there was that I wasn't separate from the ecosystem, I was part of it. Certainly Mr. Bear had a hand in that. The first time I saw a bear, it was just myself and this grizzly bear standing maybe a couple hundred feet from each other. Right then and there, I had the realization that I may not be at the top of the food chain.

That moment was frightening but at the same time, I was awestruck with just how it felt. I was seeing the caribou interact with the bear and the mosquitoes, and the ducks, and the wolverines, and all the other critters that live up there, and realizing that they all depend on each other to survive. That is what sort of led me to believe that it was all interdependent, and I was not separate from it.

When we left the Refuge, the bush pilot stopped in a Native community called Arctic Village, Alaska, to refuel; how many times have I told this story? Something happened that day that has in many ways directed the rest of my life. There was to be a congressional field hearing because there was a proposal to open up the coastal plain, the place that I had just been, for oil and gas development, which in my view, could turn it into what I saw at Prudhoe Bay. I thought that it was unfortunate that that was even being considered.

The Gwich'in Indians live in 15 villages in Alaska and Canada, and they sent representatives from all the villages to state their concern. The big moment came as the congressmen arrived. The first person to testify was an elder from the village of the Old Crow, Yukon, a man named Alfred Charley. Alfred gave a 12-minute speech in his own language.

The next person to testify was a younger leader whose name was Stanley Njutley, also from Old Crow. He got six minutes into the translation of Alfred Charlie's speech, and the chair person of the delegation stood up and said, "We got to be back in Fairbanks in an hour and a half, thank you all for coming and have a nice day," and that was it. A 30,000-year-old culture had 18 minutes to defend itself!

That moment for me was an incredible epiphany. I can distinctly remember sitting there thinking that 500 years ago, Cortes and Pizzaro swept across Central and South America and wiped out the Aztec and the Inca, and it was because they wanted the gold. Then 150 years ago, we swept across the Great Plains and slaughtered the buffalo because we needed the land. And now, in 1987, we are getting ready to do it again because we need the oil.

Lenny and protégé Darius Elias

I always had an interest in Native people and found that being Jewish and coming from a sort of a tribal culture myself, I had an understanding of how that works, and it was interesting to me. After that epiphany hit me, I walked up to another leader from Old Crow, and asked her if I could take her picture. She said, "Yeah, you can, but what difference does it make? You will just go home and forget about it like everyone else. If you really cared about this, you would come to my village in Old Crow, and you could see why this issue is so important."

So, I went to Old Crow myself and spent 10 days there which were phenomenal days. Nobody knew who I was, just this funny-looking guy who had three cameras hanging off his neck. They looked at me just like I was anybody else who came to study or look at them.

I can remember driving home to the Lower 48 after that experience. I had parked my car on the Dempster Highway maybe 30 miles above Eagle Plains where the plane had picked me up to take me into Old Crow. I retraced my route down the Dempster to Dawson, then to Whitehorse, then British Columbia, and all the way home to California. I don't think that I spoke to one person on that trip. Mostly I camped out and thought. I was so moved by that experience of being in Old Crow that I had to digest it all, because something was changing for me.

At first, I thought, "Here we go again? Let's see, I have been a musician, a photographer, and now, oh my God, this is happening again." But no, it was very different, because when I was a musician, I had a plan.

I was going to do this and I was going to become educated in the craft itself of playing. Even with photography, there was a clearer plan than with this. I had no idea how this worked. I made the decision on my way down to California that I was going to try and do something to help stop it, but had no idea what that would be.

In a way, I was pretty intimidated, because I didn't know where to begin. I didn't know even the steps that I would take to protect it. What was wilderness? Wilderness was the woods as far as I knew, and how did Congress work? This was in 1987 and I think the last time that I had voted before that was for Hubert Humphrey in 1968.

I was living in Sonoma, California, which is 40 miles from San Francisco. I knew the Sierra Club office was there. I ended up sitting in Bruce Hamilton's office at the Club still

Lenny relaxes in Fort Yukon, Alaska

thinking that he worked for the magazine and after about 20 minutes of me ranting and raving, he said, "We would be interested in you going to D.C. and testifying in front of the U. S. Senate." I thought, "I'm not sure if that's appropriate. What if they asked me how long I have been working on this? What am I going to say, a month?" He said, "No, we want you to go, because you have been there, and you are obviously quite passionate about it." I decided to go.

I prepared my testimony and was really anxious about it. The testimony was however long it was, and you were to prepare an oral summary and submit your testimony. Then you would have three minutes to do the oral summary. The Energy and Natural Resources Committee was less than dazzled with my presentation.

But I do remember clearly sitting there and saying to myself, "Wow, here I am in Washington, D.C., talking to the U.S. Senate, and I really haven't lifted a finger. I thought, what would happen if I really applied myself?"

Again, I didn't know what to do, so I went to somebody who has been a part of my life ever since then, Sierra Club staff person Mike Matz. I said to him, "I want to do something with this issue, but I really don't know what," and he said, "Where do you live?" I told him and he said, "Well, Congressman Boscoe from there is very important. He is one of our top targets, so maybe you could help influence him."

I went back home and called together a group of my friends who started making slide and video presentations in our friends' living rooms, and shortly, people were starting to call us to make presentations. The venues started getting bigger, and soon we were talking to the Santa Rosa Sierra Club, and then Audubon, and then the San Francisco Garden Society. We were getting a lot of letters written to Mr. Boscoe.

After a short time, some reporter at the Santa Rosa Press Democrat found out about us and wanted to interview me. I had never done a newspaper interview before. He asked me a number of good questions, and I thought I came up with the right answers. We talked for a long time and then at one point he said, "Well, let's go have some lunch," and I thought that meant that the interview was over. At some point after lunch he said, "Well Lenny, you haven't told me what's in it for you. What are you trying to accomplish?" And I said, "Well, I want to deliver Congressman Boscoe."

The next day, it must have been about noon, and the phone rang. I picked it up, and the voice at the other end said, "This is Congressman Boscoe's office, and we would like to know what you mean by 'deliver Congressman Boscoe'?" I was terrified. I had visions of concentration camps and then I hung up the phone, and it didn't stop ringing through the rest of the day. People wanted to help me "deliver Congressman Boscoe."

The first summer that I was in Old Crow, I had spent 10 days there. I met Stanley Njutley, whom I had seen at the Arctic Village hearings. He was one of the leaders for Old Crow who was negotiating their land claim with the Canadian government.

I was really curious to interview him. I was after him that whole time trying to interview him, and he was always putting me off. So finally one day he said, "Well okay." So, I went in his house and he sat down in a recliner chair. I was sitting there and had a little tape recorder and was asking him questions. After about 20 minutes, I looked up from my note taking, and he was asleep. He was ignoring me.

Then the next year is when I decided to do a slide show and went back up to Old Crow and spent four months. When I got to the community, the first day I was walking down the road, I heard a door open, and it was Stanley running after me saying, "Hey, hey!" He ran up to me, gave me a big hug, and I thought, "Hmm, this is different."

On the last day that I was there, I was walking down the road to the airport. Stanley came up to me again and said, "You're leaving. Well, thanks for coming and I hope to see you soon; let's stay in touch." So I said, "Stanly, I got to ask you, last year when I was here you wouldn't even give me the time of day, and now this year we have become really good friends. Why?" He said, "You came back!"

Well, switching gears to discuss my slide show. It's titled, "The Last Great Wilderness." Basically I feel that with a presentation like this, first, you need to establish a sense of place, then demonstrate the threat and who is threatened, and then what the solution is. The slide show didn't necessarily cover the solution, because that's something personal that you have to make an "ask" by looking into someone's eyes and saying, "Please write a letter or make a phone call." I found you can't just leave it to some written notice that somebody can throw away. You can actually look them in the eye and intimidate them into writing a letter.

I was on the road for a dozen or so years pretty constantly, and it was towards maybe the last half of it, I got smart enough to take off half of November through beginning of January, and pretty much from the middle of June until the beginning of September. The rest of the time, I was either on the road or recovering from being on the road. It's really hard physically.

After 10 days, the Gwich'in people with me on the road would hit the wall and start to become disoriented. That would happen to me after about three weeks, but I found out that if I stayed out no more than two weeks, I was much more efficient and much more effective as far as being sharp and on my game. I found that after that point, exhaustion really sets in. I remember giving my talk and then finding myself at the end of it not really remembering getting there.

Concerning having a Native person with me or not, I think it was night and day. One thing that was really important was just having a Native person there. It really didn't matter what they said. There were some people who were with me that just froze up, start to say something, and then look at me and freeze. So I would pick up and say some stupid thing to shift the attention of the audience. But just the fact that they were there, I think, had a tremendous impact on the audience.

It has an incredible impact both in just talking to people and getting press. You know, here is this guy from North Carolina who is here in Detroit. What does anything that he is talking about have anything to do with us? Why should we interview him? But for some reason, when you have a Native person, suddenly it's different.

It's the same thing visiting a congressperson. It helps them put it all in a different light. They weren't just talking to some old lobbyist hack that they see around all the time. They saw it from a person who was in a sense really desperate and really passionate about what they are trying to accomplish, and I think that really made a difference.

For instance, in 1991, I asked the people of Old Crow to send a young woman named Glenna Frost down to travel on the road with me all summer. She is an incredibly stunning and beautiful woman. When she would get up to talk, she was usually crying within a minute or so, and everybody would start to cry too. There was not a dry eye in the house wherever we were, and at the end of that, both of us were exhausted.

Just before an important vote came up on the Arctic, there was a newly elected Republican from Maryland, Congressman Gillcrest, who held an influential committee seat. Everybody felt that we had a really good chance to get his support. We got an appointment with Congressman Gillcrest, and I went with Glenna and three environmental leaders.

The Sierra Club leader started off the presentation to the congressman and went through what an environmentalist is concerned with: wilderness and wildlife values. A lobbyist gave his spiel countering oil industry claims about how much money would be generated for the federal treasury.

My job was to get Glenna there on time. All of us were there to hear what Glenna had to say. Near the end of our appointment, the Congressman said, "Well, you're definitely passionate, and it's definitely a very compelling argument, but just last week there were two Inupiat women here who also gave very compelling and passionate pleas FOR drilling. So I am curious if those women were sitting here right now, what would you ask them?" I realized at that moment that our whole effort depended on Glenna's answer. She stopped for a minute, thought about it, and said, "I would ask them when your children come to you, and ask you who they are and where they came from, what are you going to tell them?"

Time froze, everything stopped! It was almost like if you had been pouring a glass of water, you would see the water in mid-air. I looked over at the activist leader, and there were tears running down his cheeks. I looked at the Washington lobbyist and tears were running down his face. Glenna was sobbing uncontrollably by this time. I looked at Congressman Gillcrest and there were tears running down both cheeks. The first thing he did was to run in his private bathroom and grab a towel for Glenna to dry her eyes. He came back out, she calmed down, and he put his arm around her. "As long as I am in this Congress, I won't let anything happen to where you live or the people you love."

There was a documentary made several years later, and they went to Congressman Gillcrest and asked him about that and he said, "It's something I will never forget, and it was the most refreshing moment of my congressional career." Almost always, there is this parade of slick pasty lobbyists who have slick presentations and slick brochures. But there is very seldom that somebody, who is just coming in with their heart on their sleeves saying, "This is why I am here."

You know, I have learned a lot about the Arctic, its natural resources and especially its people. But I've also learned a lot about me. I now realize that the only limitation that I have ever had was the realization that I am not perfect, and I am probably less perfect than most.

I have learned that I don't consider myself to be overly bright or certainly not intellectual. I am not a policy person. I don't like going to meetings. But, you know, you may win or lose battles, but the war is never lost until you quit. My interest right now is somehow imparting that sort of confidence in other people.

Just like when I go up to D.C. to speak at Wilderness Week, I start off now by saying, "Look, I made a decision 20 years ago that if the oil industry is going to get into the Arctic Refuge, they have to go through me." But, the success that I have had is being a good deliverer and messenger. Nothing that I talk about is original; it has come from somewhere. I was accused by a Sierra Club member a few years ago of writing a book about how to do grassroots, and my response to that was, "No I didn't write it, but I did read it."

This Economist Flies a Bush Plane

Dirk Nickish is an accomplished bush pilot in Arctic Alaska who lives in Coldfoot in the summer and Fairbanks in the winter with his wife Danielle and two children. He has a degree in economics. They live off the grid and have their Coldfoot cabin within a few feet of the runway. http://www.maplandia.com/united-states/alaska/yukon-koyukuk-census-area/coldfoot/

My wife and I run a small air taxi business, and we predominantly fly into the Brooks Range and north coast regions of Alaska. We live in Coldfoot where there is the trooper and his family, the truck stop across the road and that pretty much sums it up. I have two kids, ages 10 and eight. We predominately live in the bush, but we have a cabin outside of Fairbanks. We live a kind of seasonal lifestyle. During the winter, things slow down, so we go there and travel quite extensively to developing nations as vacation.

We home-school our children because the nearest school in Fairbanks is five hours away. Rather than Danielle and the kids leaving to go to school, we decided to home-school. It works better with our lifestyle. Both Danielle and I are third-generation pilots. Both Danielle's grandfather and father were Northwest Airlines captains. I am also a third-generation pilot. My grandfather used to deliver mail in North Dakota from the airplane back in the 40's where they used to just fly over the farm and drop out the mail sack. My dad commercially flew for us for a couple of years but now flies for himself.

I moved to Alaska in '94 from North Dakota, and my wife is from Washington. We actually moved there the same month but didn't know each other until a year later. Before moving to Alaska, I was a crop duster, and I had several friends who hounded me incessantly to move to Alaska, and they said that I would like it and fit in just fine there. They were right. When the company that I was flying for sold out, I started thinking of running my own operation, and I decided to go up and check out Alaska. I went up for the summer and never did leave. It's now home since that's where we live, and that's where my kids were born. Every time I come back down to the Lower 48, I am very anxious to get back home.

Only recently we became a seasonal business. We used to fly year-round, but there are

**Dirk lands the Beaver at Marsh Fork,
Upper Canning River, Alaska**

not a lot of bush people left anymore to provide winter service. We operate two Beavers and we operate them on tundra tires. We haul backpackers, rafters, hikers, and hunters. But, we do some work with the National Park Service, the U.S. Fish and Wildlife Service, and the National Science Foundation.

Ecotourism is predominantly what our industry is, however. In season we start about six in the morning and we get going with the air-planes. A lot of times the planes shut down around midnight again. My wife works on the airplanes a lot during the day, and we rotate on maintenance of the planes. Between flights I help her look at things and tell her which way to go from there. The kids basically run the office and their lemonade stand, which is really quite possibly more profitable then the air taxi business.

We sleep about 50 feet behind from where the airplanes are parked at night, and when the airplanes start in the morning, everyone wakes up whether they are ready to or not. It really is a family business, a lot like being on the farm where you have to make hay when the sun shines.

During the summer is when we work. We conduct our business a lot over the internet now, which is a wonderful tool because you can log on almost anywhere and answer emails. Our winter work consists in complying with regulations by 19 government agencies now, all of which have some new reports or new edition to comply with. So we spend more time with regulations than we do flying.

We have a small dog team, and we run dogs almost on a daily basis. We eat predominately caribou, and we hunt caribou in the spring. We do it as a family activity. We all go out, and we hike through the woods until we find caribou. We all work on cutting them up, and bringing them home.

There are about 47 commercially permitted operators in the Arctic Refuge, so there are 47 small businesses directly tied into the Arctic Refuge. Often, I look at the fight for the Arctic Refuge as a small business versus big business. In the Arctic Refuge, we always consider it a really unique place because all the air taxis are very small. There's Shannon Air which is Tom out of Kaktovik. Kirk Sweetzer with Yukon Air is also a single-pilot-operator. The largest one is Wright Air Service who has several airplanes. They are kind of small in the bush operations, and we have a great relationship with them.

As a matter of fact, we talk to each other on the radio all of the time, and we're constantly working with each other to get people moved when one person gets jammed up or has a problem. You just think nothing of calling the other guys and going, "Hey, can anybody do this?" On a daily basis in mid-June or mid-August when things are really busy around seven or eight in the morning, we'll talk about who's got people where and if you

The trusty Beaver at home in Coldfoot, Alaska

can grab these people for me, I can pick up yours out there. We all kind of work together, and that's very unique.

I loved Ted Stevens' classification of us as green extremists because like I said, I'm from rural North Dakota. We didn't eat any oatmeal or hug any trees while growing up. I started out my flying career as a crop duster and came to Alaska with no preconceived ideas that anything had to be saved. I actually flew for a geophysical firm out of Houston in South America for two winters back in the mid-90s. It wasn't until my son was about three months old that we flew in the Arctic Refuge. One morning, I had an empty leg going out, so I took my wife and son out and dropped them off with camping gear with the idea that I'd do my flying and come in that evening to spend the night with them and start off the next day from there. So I dropped them off; it happened to be on the Aichilik River in mid to late-June.

By the time I returned, there were so many caribou out there that I couldn't land. I had to just fly around for awhile and wait. There were just thousands and thousands of caribou passing through, and it was literally at that moment that I questioned, "I wonder where my son will ever have the opportunity to bring his children and have them have a similar experience?" From that moment on, my perspectives on a lot of these things started to change. This is not about me. This is about my kids and their kids, and the real question of how much is enough.

Tom Brokaw wrote a book called "The Greatest Generation." I read that book and it was very interesting to see the challenges that those people surmounted and the sacrifices they made. Then I think about my generation, and I think someone is going to write a book titled something more to the effect of, "The Generation that Rested on Past Generations' Successes to Make the Future Generations Pay the Price." It frightens me, and I feel truly guilty about it. I don't care if gas hits $4.00 a gallon because then more people would quit just driving everywhere, and they would actually get out and walk, and we would have to quit spending so much on research for heart attacks.

More than that, we have the opportunities and certainly our forefathers have proven that we can come up with answers. I find it a little disheartening that I fly airplanes manufactured in 1952 and if you equate out the pounds carried by the speed per gallon burned, it's more efficient than most of the planes that have been built in the last five years. I still don't really consider myself an environmentalist, but my wife likes to think of herself as a humanitarian. I don't think we are going to destroy the earth, we are just going to ruin it for us to live in. Something will still be surviving here; maybe it's the cockroaches. We should be looking at it as a humanitarian effort as much as an environmental, because it's our own necks we're hanging and certainly the necks of our children.

Much oil development on the North Slope is occurring today where you have basically three directly-linked user groups: the air taxis, the commercial recreational guides, and the commercial hunting guides. Outside of that, you have the commuter airlines, the shuttle services that drive people up and down the Dalton Highway, as well as Alaska Airlines and the hotels in Fairbanks. Several thousand people a year come through to see these areas who all spend a fair amount of money on their way.

A lot of people promote drilling in the Arctic Refuge as being good for the economy, and I don't actually see it that way. It would certainly be good for investment companies or overseas companies, but as far as small companies go, there are very few benefits.

Almost all oil service companies are out-of-state based companies. If you look how often a dollar turns around in the economy, we see small business' dollars tend to re-circulate 17 times in the local economy. If you compare that to a dollar spent at Wal-Mart, it equates to about 60 cents on the dollar. So it's quite dramatic, and applies also to these big companies that are in the mineral extraction industry.

By and large, the employed work force there is all out-of-state. I think the impacts on small businesses that are operating there are absolutely huge. I heard that $600 million is what they figure the business contributions are of the Arctic Refuge to small businesses. Certainly we can't compare to big industry dollars, but I believe we are businesses that are being operated and earned on a sustainable basis.

We hear that we need to develop these resources for jobs for our children. Maybe that's true for the children that are ready to hit the work force right now, but what about their children? I mean the mineral exploration industry does not provide long-term benefits. All you have to do is go check on the coal industry in Kentucky or in bigger contrast, go to places like Chile where there was the huge phosphate industry, and now there's just thousands of miles of toxic waste sites.

Furthermore, if you look at the way leases are written, it's private property once it's done. You cannot actually drive the Dalton Highway all the way north and then step your foot into the ocean because the leased lots start at Deadhorse. You have to take an oil company tour. You cannot privately go through any oil-leased area. Essentially by opening up the 1002 area, you have the potential for absolutely cutting off all recreation from the foothills.

I can speak for both Kirk Sweetzer and I, when we have days off in the summer, we typically find ourselves somewhere in the Refuge with our family, hanging out, playing on the beach, or if we have extra time, we go camping. Most other bush pilots share similar sentiments. There isn't a single one of our air taxis that couldn't sell out or go fly for someone else and make a quick buck if they drilled in the Refuge, but none of us are there for the quick buck.

I certainly do not push being a pilot on any of my kids, but certainly if one of my kids wanted the business, I hope the opportunity for them exists. The family farm was everything growing up, and that way of life is gone to a large extent. It still exists in Alaska, but it's slipping away fast to the almighty dollar. It's really quite sad because we run a family-operated business.

Although we all burn a lot of gas, I wish that we would be devoting more of this energy to come up with better technology. I'd be the first person to sign up for it. We're off-grid in Coldfoot. We generate our own power; we got rid of our old generator and got a new generator that burns essentially less fuel, but we hardly run it because we run on solar all summer long. We start our generator whenever we have to run heavy shop equipment.

We do not have a large system, but if we can run our business that way, then certainly there are other answers besides drilling. I don't think anybody here is prepared to start living out in

Dirk does his job

the cold again, but we have to find what is truly responsible mineral extraction. Can you imagine the jobs in the industry involved in alternative energy? We are a tech country so we should be teaching and leading others.

As far as the positive effects of drilling, I don't see any at the current level. One of the arguments that I hear for drilling is that the oil companies are responsible because it's in their best interest to do a good job. I have found that to be completely false, helped mostly by great advertising campaigns by the oil industry. Both Exxon and BP have proven time and time and time again that they would rather pay fines than comply with regulations.

A few years ago it came out and it was hushed up incredibly quick that less than half of the check valves on the pipeline are working at any given time. I know that people are quick to point out that there have been thousands of spills in the Deadhorse /Prudhoe Bay area, but the oil companies respond, "Well you know we have to report a quart of gas spilled or a quart of anything, and let's face it, who here hasn't spilled a quart of gas while filling their car, dropped the can while doing their lawn mower?" But in the last three years there have been three spills in excess of 15,000 gallons, so that's kind of a little bit unacceptable. If I spilled 15,000 gallons, you can dang well be sure I'd be out of business. I'd be gone. I'd be wiped off the map tomorrow.

For them, it's just a little PR blip that gets covered up and then they get to negotiate their fine. The Exxon Valdese spilled twenty-some years ago and they're still fighting the law- suits that they lost 20 years ago on it. We don't hold them responsible, and certainly government has no real interest in holding them responsible. If you could prove to me that all of this could be done in a way that there would not be spills, in a way that they would not be producing waste, you could start considering the pros and cons of economic development. We always hear about all this great technology, but why isn't it in place? And if it is

**Dirk and the Beaver on a sandbar along the Canning River
across from the Arctic Refuge with fall colors on the tundra**

in place, then it's failing.

Ted Stevens once asked me about receiving the permanent fund. I said, "Yep, we sure do." We put ours in our kids' college fund, and I mean I didn't move to Alaska for the permanent fund and when the permanent fund goes away, I will still live in Alaska.

I look at the permanent fund as blood money; it's bribe money. A lot of people use it for fun money, but I look at it as the money to pay back our kids for what we are taking away from them, and it's not much of a payoff. I truly wish it would just go away, so that argument would also go away.

Oil company promises are what kind of brought me to D.C. for the first time. Several years ago was when Arco and BP started this huge media campaign in Alaska. They had all these songs about how everything's great and we're doing so well, full page ads in the paper, big bucks. You know, BP doesn't have a gas station in Alaska. Immediately you start going, "Okay, so what do they really want?" Well, they are literally trying to buy something from us, and the oil companies only buy when it's a good deal, which means it's a bad deal for you. So anytime I see a huge media blitz, I immediately think that it's far cheaper for them to spend all that money on a media blitz than it is to either take the current terms of the lease or deal with the consequences. I think certainly the promises they make are to labor, and I hate to say that they tend to court the less-educated with all sorts of promises.

The fact is, on the North Slope, they only hire as many Natives as they need to fill the quotas, and they give them the worst jobs where they very seldom will get promoted. They're the guys that will get to grease the Caterpillars. If you shut down the oil patch today, I venture to say that half of the Wasilla-Anchorage area would just move out. They do add jobs to the economy, but the largest percentage is imported.

Concerning Natives, there's nothing better you can make as a statement as to wave the discrimination flag and say we're going to provide jobs for Natives in these villages that have no money. They hire a few to fill quotas and more of the Native culture becomes lost. I mean we convinced them to move into these towns with oil money. Houses are built that all have oil heat in them, and now you talk about taking away the ability to heat their house. They're in a lose-lose situation, and I find it really sad that they are used in this way.

Frank Murkowski, when he got elected, talked about the next global oil boom and how great the oil boom was going to be. I think it'll boom, but isn't that where inflation rocks a place? All sorts of labor come in, the locals can't even hardly afford to live there anymore, and they have to leave. Then, the boom leaves, the riffraff that came in and spent their money stay, and the economy craters. I mean, you don't have to read a lot about history to realize that that's what a boom is. There are a few people that come in and make just a ton of money and leave.

I don't really know what to make of the future. Every year we have more bureaucrats that make being small businesses harder. Every year big business gets bigger, and in just the last couple of years in Fairbanks we went from having no box stores to almost no small businesses. Everything's a box store. You know we have Home Depot, Lowe's, a big Wal-Mart, a Sam's Club. All the local grocery stores are closed now, but we have Fred Myers and Safeway.

In the big picture, we have seen a great change in the environment. The tree line is steadily moving north. We're constantly in a bit of an argument with the Fish & Wildlife Service about allowing us to brush out air strips and they say, "Well you can't brush out any air strips because it has to be left in its original state." We go "Well that's cool except there was never any brush on these gravel bars until five years ago." In the last five years, it has been an issue because the alders have grown from foot-high plants to where they are now knocking off the lights at the wing tips of the Beaver, which is eight and one-half feet in the air.

A few years ago, we had three to four inches of snoe in Coldfoot on the second or third of June. It was the first time in June that I had gone out there that it was completely blanketed white. We got within 10 miles of the coast and there was no snow and all the lakes were open. I ended up landing them on this lake which is what we have always landed on. We taxied over to the far side and I said to my passengers, "You guys can carry the stuff from here. You got sleds to drag it on over."

Interestingly enough, a couple of days later another plane went in there to haul in the rest their gear. He taxied in over and fell through the ice. That lake is normally hard frozen and sure ice through the first week of June. As a matter of fact, I've landed as late as the 16th of June, so whether that was a freaky year or not I don't know, but normally you fly across the coastal plain that time of year, and the snow is all gone until you get within 10 miles of the coast, which is still winter for another two weeks.

Gikhyi Susan

Susan Oliver is a 34-year-old Anglican priest originally from Toronto, Ontario, who had the St. Matthews Anglican church in Fort McPherson, Northwest Territories. She is seen here in Fort McPherson with two children from the community. She departed her labor of love in Fort McPherson in fall of 2008, after three years as the village Gikhyi (priest), and now lives in Edmonton, Alberta. http://www.maplandia.com/canada/northwest-territories/inuvik-region/fort-mcpherson/

My First Two Years in the Arctic

Many people ask how I ended up in Fort McPherson from Toronto, and it's a valid question. I often begin by telling them that I was in my third year of my seminary degree at Wycliff College in Toronto, and each student between their second and third year has to do a three-month internship in a parish.

I had never been to the North, and I thought that for a summer adventure it would be nice to go to a northern parish to do my internship, as opposed to Toronto. So our college got in contact with one of the bishops in the Arctic, and we set up that I would come to Fort McPherson.

I arrived in May for a summer internship, and soon after I arrived, I had an overwhelming sense of having arrived home. It's hard to put into words. It was a real strong sense and calling, a homecoming that was like nothing I had experienced before.

All summer I struggled with what this sense of home meant. This place was very far from home and my family. And then there were the discomforts of living in an area that is so remote. As I lived in this place and continued to feel the call, I wrestled to discover what this would mean. Eventually, I was talking to my mom and she said, "Sue, there is something you aren't telling me." Moms always know. I had to tell her that I had to come back here and that God was calling me to be here.

No one expected this to happen. I asked the bishop what it would mean for me to apply to be a priest here. When he picked up his jaw off the floor, he said they could make it happen, and we began to talk. At the end of the summer, I returned to Toronto for my final year of school, and I had to go back to the bishop in Toronto and undo the process that had been started there. Over that year, I made the final decision to come here. I applied and was accepted to the diocese of the Arctic, and I said I would go anywhere, but I would really like to be in Fort McPherson.

There hadn't been a rector here for five years. There certainly was a need in the community, and it was a good fit that summer. People enjoyed my time here, and I enjoy the people here, and I knew they would appreciate having a full-time minister. They have two full-time deacons, Anna and Mary, who are Gwich'in ladies who have served for over 20 years. They were ready for some energy and some youthfulness in leading the church.

So that is how it came to pass. The following summer, I drove from Calgary to Fort McPherson. The journey took about seven to eight days to get here. Canada is a very large country. It was 3,500 kilometers.

I arrived here two years ago and settled in. The first year was incredibly difficult. It was very hard, much harder than I thought it would be. I had recently been ordained a deacon. You are ordained twice in an Anglican Church: first as a deacon; and then a year later, you are priested. So I was ordained a deacon in Toronto before I came but was very new to ministry. Not having a curacy, which is like an internship when you are finally ordained, was very difficult. You usually work with an ordained priest; not having that and being on my own was difficult. I was unsure of what being a priest meant, let alone in a remote northern community where none of the trappings were the same, and I wasn't trying to run five programs a week or have services all the time; anything that you would think of for what it meant to be a parish minister was not the case.

I struggled with incompetence. The first year I thought I was a terrible priest. It felt like I wasn't doing any of the things that needed to be done. I lived in a house that had quite an old furnace that was constantly breaking, so I was worried about pipes freezing when it was -40, getting the wood chopped for the wood stove in the middle of the night, and getting the water tank fixed so that I could have water. It was just a house that was very large for one person to be in.

That was part of the first year. It was also a culture shock, being in a completely new culture and not being prepared for the fact that I was living among a people who were completely different than I was and who had lived a different life. It took a while for doors to open, doors of my heart and doors of their hearts for us to really understand one another, but now we have come a long way together.

I think one of the ways that I was able to connect with the people here was through doing funerals, as odd as that seems. There were 12 people, an unusually high number, who died in the first year that I lived here, and many of those deaths were tragic. There were suicides and many teenagers who died. We got to know each other by burying members of our community who shouldn't have died. Within that, there were moments of connection with all members of the community as I served them.

Interestingly, there were no weddings. I have yet to do a wedding in Fort McPherson. I have done a few baptisms, but mostly funerals. That was just a difficult cycle that our community went through a year ago.

There was a point last summer when I opened the doors, literally, to the kids of the community and had them in for tea and cookies and baking and hot chocolate and bananas, which are a very popular item in this community. As I allowed the kids in the door, there seemed to be an open door to the adults as well. My heart certainly softened to not be as afraid of letting people into my life.

There was just a remarkable change that took place as I allowed that to happen. Becom-

ing a foster parent last year was also a big part of that; again, literally having kids coming with their Northern Store bag of stuff, all their worldly possessions, arriving at the doorstep needing a safe place for a week or two, or a month, or several. That too has opened the door to different relationships with adults as they see me with their own kids. That has been quite something.

I was able to establish a couple of support avenues, but I had to be creative. I had a spiritual director/counselor person who I had known in Toronto, and I had already established a relationship with this person, as he was someone that I talked to on a regular basis during seminary. As I was leaving Toronto, I sort of figured that relationship was coming to a natural end. He suggested that we could try it by phone, and I decided to give it a chance, despite thinking it odd.

I don't actually know how my time would have gone had I not talked to him every two weeks. There was an hour every two weeks when I could share the hurt, the joys, the awkwardness, all of that with this person who took a genuine interest in learning about this place that I lived, so he could better hear what it was that I was saying. That counseling was incredibly supportive, and it still exists as I continue on here. That was a main support and a very important one.

Then there was a group of teachers who were roughly my age who were from the South, Prince Edward Island, B.C., and Saskatchewan. I formed a group of friends who I would get together with on Friday nights when we would play board games. When you live in Fort McPherson, that is what you do on a Friday night. We would get together and play games and have a meal.

None of them went to church, which was actually very helpful. It was an avenue where I could let my hair down and just be Sue in a different way than being the gikhyi (pronounced geehee), which is the Gwich'in word for minister.

When you live in the small town, you are always on; you are always the minister in everything that you do. With this group of friends, there was an opportunity to just be Sue. They were just good friends I could talk to openly. Those were the two supports for me during that first year.

While I didn't think of it as a support, I have written a series of 10 letters home since I arrived. At first, I would send them home every month or two to a list of friends and supporters to let them know what was going on here. As the time got longer, the gaps were greater. Every three or four months I would write down the stories of funerals, of moose hunting, and of children. It has been a very good way for me to synthesize what my time here has been like and to give people a sense of what living in the North is like.

Sue's church in Fort McPherson

Also I could explain who these other people are who are still Canadians, but who live such a different life than what we would understand. People at home are incredibly receptive to hearing the stories. It's part of Canada but a part that we don't understand very well at all. Everyone understands on their own level. Some people want to just engage at the "oh what a good person you are" level, very surface. But very few will want to engage the harder questions around some of the social problems, what it means to live in isolation, and my struggles. Everyone is different in how they choose to relate to the stories. But, yes, the stories are documented.

It was a good effort in terms of writing the stories, but I think writing the stories was more helpful than getting the feedback, in that I was getting it off my chest. It's lonely here, so there is a natural thing that you are receiving emails back from people who want to connect with you in some way. It was helpful and nice, because it is easy to be forgotten or to forget others and not stay in close contact. It's definitely nice to have mail in my inbox, for sure.

[Postscript of July, 2009] I left my priest position in October of last year (2008) after three-plus, intense years. My time in Fort McPherson was definitely a hard time in many ways. I still have flashbacks to that challenging time and have regrets that I couldn't do more than I did to change some of the negatives of life there.

But on the other side of the ledger, I do feel the children who were in my care learned a lot about life, as did I. I finally decided to head back south when the oldest one of my foster kids, age 16, returned to her parents after one and a half years with me. I feel I did make a positive contribution to those kids and to the village as priest. The time also gave me a great life experience that has no doubt made me a stronger person across the board. I feel I have learned greater compassion and will continue to place those three years in the context of my life as I go on to perhaps marry and have a family of my own.

What Would You Tell Them? [This section is Sue's response to the interviewer's asking what she would tell people in the South about her years in Fort McPherson.]

At first, I would describe the beauty, that it is a beautiful place. I have a wonderful view of mountains, trees, a river, and a willow out my window. There is a quiet and peacefulness that someone from Toronto would know nothing about. It is an untouched land. When I go hiking, I know I'm not going to see another soul for my entire time out. The vastness of the land, how uninhibited it is, and how beautiful it is-- that's what I would want people to know.

What I find most fascinating is that when I complain to my church elder Elizabeth about having four foster kids, she says well, I raised nine children in the bush and we didn't have running water.

But she is also sympathetic. On one hand she is compassionate, and on the other, she puts it in perspective. We have people who are living history of a time when they were in the bush, traveled by dog sled, and followed the caribou herds so that they would have food to eat.

There are people still today who have led such a different life. Many who lived here 50 years ago are in fact still living in the bush. For me, I just love hearing those stories. I love living amongst people, who in their lifetime, tell me what it was like to travel by dog team. The people who tell those stories are just beautiful, and I appreciate living in a place where I can be a part of that, or at least have access to the stories and the handiwork that still goes with it, be it the caribou that are still hunted, or the slippers that are beaded, or the martins who are still skinned and sold.

I love it when someone asks me to go look up a baptismal record because they need a new one. Those records are still at the church, and I look back in the history of the beginning of the 1900's where I read about people like Lucy Rat and Sarah Drymeat , who they were, the children that they had, and stories of Hudson Bay Sundays at church where people would bring their (musk)rats in, and in that year they collected 100 rats for the church. They would then sell them as a way of donating money to the church through their trapping.

I would want people in the Lower 48 to know about those stories and about the wonderful richness in the history and in the town. People ask the obvious questions about the North based around alcohol and social problems. I think that would need to be addressed in a way that doesn't dismiss a whole group of people as a bunch of alcoholics or whatever derogatory way that you would like to describe that. I would want people to know that it is not simply a matter of choosing not to drink or that they can just get it together and make better choices. There is a cycle and a history that is embedded in this place that is not as easy to fix as some might assume. The Dempster Highway has brought in much more than "progress."

Why We "Go North" to Alaska and Canada

Shirl Thomas is a 75-year-old retired educator who lives with her husband Bill Thomas in Cedar Mountain, North Carolina. She and Bill have traveled to the Arctic of Alaska on several occasions, having made the Arctic an important part of their lives. Their first trip, in 1990, was a 10-week drive up the Alcan highway in their trademark VW camper. Bill is an 81-year-old retired engineer. Both Bill and Shirl have been very active with the Sierra Club for many years.

Shirl: The trips Bill and I have made to northern Alaska and Canada have had a profound effect on our lives. I feel privileged to have been there. Thinking about it almost makes me weep, because it is so wonderful. I wish everybody could do it. I not only feel privileged, but I think it gives a deeper meaning to your life when you have exposures to places that most of our population just has a very vague idea about.

I remember one time when I was on the Tatshenshini. I was sitting in the raft and I just turned around, looked and counted all the glaciers that I could see coming toward me. Thirteen glaciers, I mean that's an awesome experience, and I guess it just taught me that there are some places that need respect and care, and you got to leave them alone. We have to limit ourselves and say no to some things.

You understand the significance of places like this and how important it must be to the Native people who live there, to the animals, because it's a whole ecosystem that lives there, and it needs respect. It is very fragile, and it bothers me that we would let it all go so we can drive around in our cars. Of course, it all so much depends on the political climate and our need for oil and how we are unwilling to change. To see it destroyed would be like saying goodbye to everything. It is very sad to think of it because I love that part of the world.

It really bothers me when I see Hummers flying down the road. I just want to give them the bird but don't dare, because the kind of people that drive Hummers would know how to retaliate. Showing the world that engine power is more important than a fragile ecosystem which would suffer with oil extraction seems like upside-down values.

To me, it's a direct insult and a way of saying that they have no respect. They haven't seen that area, and I feel sorry for them, but I am angry at the same time for their disregard for what has the right to exist. They don't seem to get the connection.

Bill: Shirl, I'd like to add something about a very pleasant experience I might use to explain why the area

Shirl and canoe

Bill at rest

is so important to me. It was the end of a long day and we had a lot of spitting rain and wind in our faces and it was kind of chilly. We finally found a sand bar that was going to make a nice campsite. We got all our things out of the raft and took it to our campsites. Down to the south on the horizon, we could see this humongous black cloud coming in, and so we really scurried to get our tents set up and everything thrown into them. As soon as we climbed into that tent, it rained, it snowed, and it blew and stormed for a while.

Shirl and I had a bottle of whiskey and we were sitting in our chairs in the tent, the storm is outside and it's pleasant inside. We are having little sips of whiskey and I'm thinking, "Now this is living, now this is really living." After the storm blew through, there was this light dusting of snow on the hill and the trees, and it was just gorgeous.

The sun was just setting. It could set for hours and hours because that is what it does in August. It sits there for a long time. There we were, and one of our friends climbs out of his tent and looks around and says, "I can't stand it, stop it God, it's too beautiful," and a bald eagle flew up the river.

That was a high point for us, really exciting. Of course that is the way it is on trips in the wilderness. You go through some really uncomfortable times and then you have these peak times where you have suffered to get there. Maybe suffering to get there is part of the whole thing, because you will appreciate it and then you are treated to this incredible display of beauty. You are in this place that not too many people have been or have been privileged to see. To me, that's a really moving experience, and it's really what I am looking for on these wilderness trips.

You know, in a sense, it's sort of serendipity. Put yourself into places where it can happen, I guess, and then if the weather and the light are right, there you go. Yeah, it certainly is some kind of accident, but of course it never would happen if you didn't decide to go to those places.

Chapter Five
The Warming of Arctic North America

No geophysical phenomenon has emerged in recorded history with the potential to change life on planet Earth like global climate change. Now accepted to be caused substantially by human activity—principally the burning of fossil fuels to generate energy, and the deforestation of enormous areas of the planet to develop agriculture—global climate change is already creating economic, political, health, and social disruption, and will dramatically affect the web of life that supports humans and every other living organism on the planet.

While society is still debating the specifics, it seems that the human inhabitants of the planet are slowly and reluctantly beginning to comprehend the reality that the Earth is warming, which leads broadly to climate change, with its potential adverse effects on life on the planet. According to the IPCC Fourth Synthesis Report (more later), while the vast preponderance of evidence (Bernstein et al., 2007, p. 30) states unequivocally that the planet is warming and that the warming is changing the Earth's climate by changing the temperature, rainfall, wind circulation patterns, ice cover, sea levels, fire frequency, and ocean circulation—many do not understand and are still reluctant to accept the threat that climate change presents, with the inevitable changes to society required to mitigate and adjust to its effects.

The concept of climate change is proving to be a tough sell for the average American. Scientists now have accurate measurements of temperature trends and levels of gases in the atmosphere and how those gases affect temperature. We now know what is happening, and why it is happening. The scientific method is the process that, over time, arrives at truths in our physical world. But the American population is anxious about losing jobs, and industry is adept at portraying measures to mitigate climate change as threats to one's job. If you will read the following pages, you can arm yourself with the facts so that this society can arrive at the right answers before we cross thresholds from which we cannot return.

Background and Discussion of Climate Change: Geologic time is measured in thousands, millions and billions of years. The Earth has gone through countless geologic eras where the climate warmed and cooled over periods of thousands or tens of thousands of years. But the increase in global temperatures in the last 150 years has no analog in the geologic record (Maislin, 2009, pp. 6-8). In that blink of the geological eye, the 12 warmest years on record have occurred in the last 13 years. As reported by the Intergovernmental Panel on Climate Change (IPCC) Summary for Policymakers, "Average Northern Hemisphere temperatures during the second half of the 20th century were very likely higher than during any other 50-year period in the last 500 years and likely the highest in at least the past 1300 years." (Bernstein et al., 2007, p.2) (More about the IPCC later in this chapter.)

The smoking gun in this scary tale is the dramatic increase in carbon dioxide (CO_2) in the atmosphere over the past 200 years, coinciding with the start of the Industrial Revolution, the era where we humans learned that we could invent power machines to do work for us. Machines do the work, but require energy to do so. That source of energy has been plentiful fossil fuels, like coal and oil. Burning of fossil fuels has released enormous amounts of carbon dioxide and other complex molecules into the atmosphere where they trap heat from the sun, and prevent its radiation back into space.

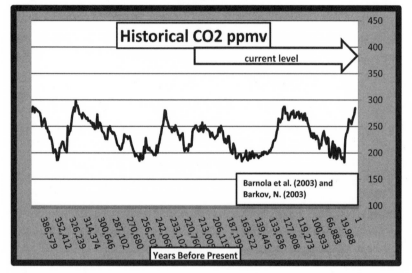

Decades ago, scientists learned that the Earth maintains a historical record of the atmospheric content of gases like carbon dioxide and methane. That record exists in the form of tiny pockets of trapped air that result when snow falls in areas of Greenland and in Antarctica, when the snow is packed down to form ice that has been preserved for thousands or hundreds of thousands of years. Since the 1950's, scientists have been drilling down into the ancient ice deposits, even to depths of over two miles, to retrieve samples of the ice and, using sophisticated instruments, to discern which gases were present and in what concentrations in those past years. According to Maislin, the evidence based on ice cores shows that atmospheric concentrations of carbon dioxide are higher today than at any time in the past 650,000 years. Scientists have compared the levels of carbon dioxide and other gases with Earth's temperature for the same periods to find that temperature changes are very closely related to changes in those gases. (Maislin, 2009, p. 6)

There has been much debate over whether the current climate change trends could be related to natural phenomena such as solar cycles, rather than the measured increases in carbon dioxide and methane. Scientists now know that without the increase in greenhouse gases in the atmosphere, the climate today would likely be cooling, not warming. Scientists call the source of an effect on climate a forcing, and a *forcing* caused by human activities is called *anthropogenic*. In its Summary for Policymakers, the IPCC stated this conclusion regarding greenhouse gases: "During the past 50 years, the sum of solar and volcanic forcings would *likely* have produced cooling. Observed patterns of warming and their changes are simulated only by models that include anthropogenic forcings." (Bernstein et al., 2007, p. 5) In other words, human activities are overpowering the natural cycles and events and causing temperatures to warm, not cool.

While human societies have been burning fossil fuels for energy, human societies have also engaged in rapid deforestation of tropical forests for agricultural uses such as cattle grazing and growing crops like soy. That decline in forest cover, along with the stress to boreal (northern) forests caused by warming, are reducing the carbon dioxide being soaked up by growing trees which use carbon dioxide as a source of carbon for their wood structure. Instead of being carbon absorbers, the boreal forests promise to become carbon emitters.

Now being recognized as another primary cause of warming, especially in the Arctic regions, is the accumulation of soot, or tiny particles of black carbon created when power plants burn coal, when diesel engines burn diesel fuel, when natural or planned forest fires occur, and when people in Africa and Asia burn wood and animal dung for fuel. Soot blackens surfaces on which it settles, and that causes the absorption of more solar energy, and more heating.

Together, these major factors, which are ongoing, portend badly for the near and the long-term future for climate change.

Climate change is the effect and global warming is the cause.

We now know that the primary cause of the cause is carbon dioxide. But carbon dioxide is just the first of a one-two punch from greenhouse gases. While carbon dioxide alone is more than capable of taking the planet to temperatures that will change the environment faster than humans and all other organisms can effectively adapt to it, scientists are beginning to sound the alarm that the Earth is bracing for a more potent second punch—methane. ... *methane may prove to be the greater menace*

Frozen and locked away out of the atmosphere, methane may prove to be the greater menace. It is up to 25 times more potent than carbon dioxide molecule-per-molecule in trapping the heat of the planet. Its increase opens the door to effects that could be much worse and happen much faster than those of carbon dioxide. The IPCC's *2007 Synthesis Report* states that because of human activities, "the global atmospheric concentration of methane has increased from a pre-industrial value of about 715 parts per billion (ppb) to 1732 ppb in the early 1990's, and was 1774 ppb in 2005." (Bernstein et al., 2007, p. 37) In its Summary for Policymakers, the IPCC goes on to say that the atmospheric concentration of methane in 2005 exceeds by far the natural range of the last 650,000 years (320 to 790 ppb) as determined from ice cores. (Bernstein et al., 2007, p. 5)

Incredibly, scientists are concluding that another major source of atmospheric methane is the leaked gases from natural gas wells, including storage facilities. As reported by Andrew Revkin and Clifford Krauss in the New York Times (2009), the EPA estimates the amount lost to be as high as three trillion cubic feet annually, making this source of greenhouse gases as much as one-third of the total of all sources. This source of methane could be eliminated by retrofitting gas wells and storage facilities, but companies will not undertake such retrofitting until the benefit in their estimation from doing so outweighs the costs.

Methane is also being released now by agricultural practices such as raising livestock and rice farming, and from burning fossil fuels, but it may also be increasing by several mechanisms brought about as a feedback of warming. A *feedback* is a process that is itself changed by the response it produces. That is, it is a process that builds on itself. The most obvious of these mechanisms adding to the threat of increased atmospheric methane is the thawing of the permafrost in Arctic regions.

By definition, permafrost is that soil which remains frozen through at least two annual seasonal cycles of the planet, and lies below the surface material, called the active layer, that thaws annually to various depths. According to the IPCC *Fourth Assessment Report*, warmer temperatures are extending the active layer deeper and deeper into the permafrost each year, leading to the decomposition of billions of tons of organic matter. "Temperatures at the top of the permafrost layer have generally increased since the 1980's in the Arctic by up to 3°C." (Bernstein et al., 2007, p.30) When that decomposition happens in an oxygen rich environment, carbon dioxide is released into the atmosphere, which is bad enough. When that decomposition occurs in an oxygen depleted environment, such as the bottom of Arctic lake beds, methane is released into the atmosphere.

The reason scientists prefer the term *climate change* over *global warming* is that climate change encompasses such effects as prolonged drought, plus regional climates may change in ways other than steadfast warming. An example of this is global warming's potential to change ocean circulation patterns, and the effect it may have on regional climates. *The Global Ocean Conveyor* is a term describing the continuous currents of ocean water around the planet driven by colder, denser, saltier water that tends to sink, and warmer, less dense water that tends to rise. They use the term *thermohaline* to describe those currents affected by temperature differences and salt concentration differences. Historically, one part of the conveyor belt has circulated warm surface water from the equatorial regions northward in the Atlantic Ocean, causing northern Europe and northeastern North America to be warmer than they would otherwise be, given their latitudes. As that surface water gives up its heat, it tends to sink and is returned in deep currents to the south where it is again warmed, and so on. But, melting of ice packs on land (such as the Greenland ice sheet), and increased rainfall and river flows both release fresh water into the oceans. The influx of fresh water will make the ocean water with which it mixes become less dense, keeping it from sinking and causing the currents to slow and eventually to stop. Without the warm water from the south, northern Europe and northeastern North America would cool considerably as the remainder of the planet continues its relentless warming.

Other serious impacts of predicted climate change include mass extinctions of animal and plant species, more frequent and severe heat waves, more drought and disruption of the hydrological cycles, increased tropical cyclone frequency and severity, increased ocean acidification, migration of tropical disease vectors, and the potential for irreversible negative changes to the planet's climates and ecosystems.

While all parts of the globe are already experiencing the effects of climate change, the Arctic regions, for reasons explained below, are recording the greatest changes. Climate change is already affecting the lifestyles of the human populations there, and threatens the long-term viability of the Arctic ecosystems. Scientists are documenting the changes in technical fashion, but indigenous peoples are documenting the changes in how they live and cope with lifelong patterns that are changing right before their eyes. They see it in changing river freezing and thawing patterns, reduced ice cover, melting permafrost, changes in animal migrations, and in vegetation species migrating into previously inhospitable areas. As numerous indigenous people in the Arctic report in their interviews below in this chapter and in other chapters, they are living with the immediate effects of a changing climate.

People still living off the land are being impacted now, and as Steve Oomituk said in

Chapter 3, "This is our garden," because the Arctic is just that. All other humans are just a step from feeling the same effects because the planet as a whole is literally humanity's garden.

In the Intergovernmental Panel on Climate Change 2007 Fourth Assessment there is *very high confidence*, (which is a probability of 90%) "based on more evidence from a wider range of species, that recent warming is strongly affecting terrestrial biological systems, including such changes as earlier timing of spring events, such as leaf-unfolding, bird migration and egg-laying; and poleward and upward shifts in ranges in plant and animal species." (Bernstein et al., 2007, p.33)

No one can predict every consequence of this run-up in carbon dioxide and methane and other complex molecules, but we already know that it has the potential to create some very undesirable results, and in fact is doing so now. This emerging crisis portends winners and losers in terms of economics, quality of life, and sustainability of life itself, and thus has been politicized, leading to doubts and delays.

What to do about global climate change, or whether to do anything at all, is now being debated in America in our living rooms, up and down our main streets, and in the halls of Congress. Governments of other countries are considering whether or how to take action, although the only major country not to ratify the Kyoto Protocols yet is the United States. The Kyoto Protocols: http://unfccc.int/resource/docs/convkp/kpeng.html are an international treaty passed in 1997 which went in force in 2005 devoted specifically to limiting the human caused effects to climate, primarily by the reduction and control of greenhouse gas emissions. Until December 2009, the Kyoto Protocols represented civilization's only formal recognition of the need to act together to reduce or limit the effects of climate change. The Kyoto Protocols will expire in 2012, to be replaced with a new framework. It was anticipated that the new framework would be adopted at the United Nations Climate Change Conference, in Copenhagen, Denmark, in December 2009. What emerged from Copenhagen was a weak, non-binding accord that does not require any country to reduce emissions. There is no requirement to turn the accord into a treaty. At the last minute, a few countries agreed to try to limit cumulative temperature increase to 2° centigrade. Copenhagen demonstrates the overwhelming challenges involved in effecting meaningful change now, which carry perceived costs now, but will benefit some difficult-to-define future.

Like any bargained-for result, policies for change will not come easily or quickly unless or until governments decide that mandating painful policies of change will return at least as much in benefits as those changes cost. Governments of countries which are just now arriving at robust economic growth and burgeoning middle classes feel that they should have the right to burn fossil fuels just like the already-developed nations have done for two centuries. That argument would be logical if it were not for the fact that these emerging societies have the most to lose with climate change. Examples of this outcome are the rapidly-shrinking glaciers of the Himalayas, the primary source of drinking water for hundreds of millions of people in Asia, and the Andes, the primary source of drinking water for millions of people in South America.

Governments can estimate the costs of making changes, but have difficulty estimating the costs of inaction. The problem is compounded by the human propensity to delay changes in the present to prevent possible calamity in the future. And yet while governments posture, study, and delay, each year the levels of carbon dioxide and methane continue to increase.

The developing countries have billions of hungry mouths to feed, and doing so will require the expenditure of enormous amounts of energy. The cheapest energy route is to burn still abundant fossil fuels such as coal, oil and gas. But such actions exacerbate the warming problems. Maislin believes that "... to deal with global warming, we must deal with developing countries, and thus we must for the first time in humanity's history tackle the unequal distribution of global wealth. Hence global warming is making us face the forgotten billions of people on the planet, and we must make the world a fairer place. In the 21st century we must deal with both global poverty and global warming." (Maislin, 2009, Preface)

Informed people of goodwill differ over how severe the effects of climate change will be and how soon they will appear. And there are less well-intentioned people who are spreading doubt and obfuscating the facts in order to slow the process to mitigate the crisis. Eventually, human societies around the globe will agree that climate change is a common threat that no one is immune to. The evidence shows that time is of the essence—action is urgently needed. Each year without change is a lost opportunity. While human society has not yet reached consensus, ***this global challenge must be the one common threat that ultimately requires all humans to bond together to find a solution.***

The potential of global warming caused by the greenhouse effect has been documented for over a century. The record shows that many people saw this possible outcome many years ago, but lack of instruments and data, reports of confounding observations, and belief that mitigating factors would always re-balance the equations for any perceived minor imbalances caused by humans, kept the issue from gaining traction until very recently.

Swedish scientist Svante Arrhenius is credited as the first to publish in the scientific literature a paper stating that burning fossil fuels to generate energy will tend to cause the climate to warm. He and a colleague, Thomas Chamberlain, made this prediction *in 1896* when they published "On the influence of carbonic acid in the air upon the temperature of the ground." The research allowed Arrhenius to discern the effects on absorption of long wavelength radiation, which we are more familiar with as heat, caused by carbon dioxide and water vapor. He deduced that carbon dioxide and water vapor act as a natural greenhouse by keeping some of the warmth of the Earth from radiating back into space. Without such greenhouse effect, he calculated that the Earth would be about 59° F cooler on average than it is, and life as we know it would not exist.

It took until the 1940's and 50's, with development of better instruments, for the exact relationship of carbon dioxide to be calculated and to conclude that water vapor acts in a different way than carbon dioxide in trapping heat.

Other observations and research up to the 1970's began to show that average global temperatures seemed to be cooling from the 1940's through the 1970's (see chart below), and popular opinion embraced a belief that the Earth could be heading for another ice age. The famous *Newsweek* article from April 28, 1975, stated in part:

The central fact is that after three quarters of a century of extraordinarily mild conditions, the Earth's climate seems to be cooling down. Meteorologists disagree about the cause and extent of the cooling trend, as well as over its specific impact on local weather conditions ... They concede that some of the more spectacular solutions proposed, such as melting the Arctic ice cap by covering it with black soot or diverting Arctic rivers, might create problems far greater than those they solve. ...

Importantly, only four years after that article (1979) the temperature trend resumed its rise that continues today. This chart (Source: NOAA): http://www.esrl.noaa.gov/psd/data/ gridded/data.noaa.oisst.v2.html shows the annual average global temperature by year compared to the average for the period 1901-2000.

Scientists now have a perspective on the noted warming of the last 120 years. As James Hansen (more later) and others reported in the *Proceedings of National Academy of Sciences*, http://www.pnas.org/c tent/103/39/14288.full, "Global warming is now 0.6°C in the past three decades and 0.8°C in the past century. It is no longer correct to say 'most global warming occurred before 1940.' A better summary is: slow global warming, with large fluctuations, over the century up to 1975, followed by rapid warming at a rate of 0.2°C per decade (since then). Global warming was 0.7°C between the late 19th century (the earliest time at which global mean temperature can be accurately defined) and 2000, and continued warming in the first half decade of the 21st century is consistent with the recent rate of +0.2°C per decade." (Hansen, et al., 2006, p. 2)

The reason scientists are so confident of the trend line now is the correlation of global temperature changes with the recorded changes in levels of carbon dioxide in the atmosphere. Of course, *correlation* does not necessarily mean *causation*. However, when the underlying causation

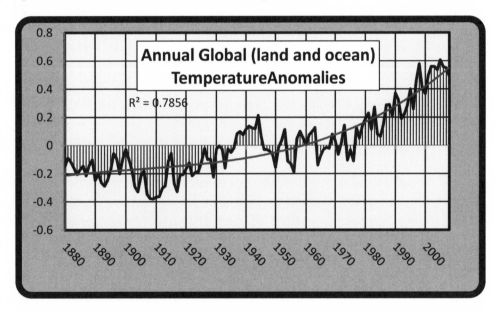

is discerned—that is, when one event can be shown to cause the other event in theory, then the correlation becomes a valid observation of related phenomena. Now that scientists know how carbon dioxide and other complex molecules block infrared radiation, keeping it from escaping into space, the correlation in the rise of global temperatures with the rise in carbon dioxide in the atmosphere describes a compelling relationship.

Scientists now note that in the 1970's, the science of climate change was new and most scientists overestimated the effect of aerosols in cooling the atmosphere and underestimated the effect of the buildup of greenhouse gases in warming the atmosphere. This episode points out that the pursuit of truth by using the scientific method does not follow a linear path, but rather a jagged, self-correcting path that is always under scrutiny and always subject to better measurements, better technology and changing circumstances.

The greenhouse effect was considered decades ago by American astronomer, author and lecturer Carl Sagan, whose first major research effort following his formal education, was an investigation of the surface and atmosphere of Venus. In the late 1950's, the general scientific view was that the surface of Venus was relatively cool and that life of some sort might exist on the planet. Radio emissions had been observed and it was thought that they came from the activity of charged particles located in an atmospheric layer. Sagan overturned these ideas in 1961 by showing that the emissions could be caused by a very hot surface temperature, over 300° C (572° F), in which life could not exist. He said the high temperatures were caused by a "greenhouse effect," in which the sun's heat was trapped between the planet's surface and its carbon dioxide cloud cover. These ideas were confirmed by an exploratory space vehicle sent to Venus by the Soviet Union in 1967. Scientists now know that Venus' surface temperature is approximately 900° F, much hotter than that of Mercury, the planet closest to the Sun, because of Venus' greenhouse effect.

Sagan wrote a blockbuster description of the universe *in 1980*, in terms we could all understand, called *Cosmos*, from which the following prescient excerpt was taken:

> *Like Venus, the Earth also has a greenhouse effect due to its carbon dioxide and water vapor. The global temperature of the Earth would be below the freezing point of water if not for the greenhouse effect. It keeps the oceans liquid and life possible. A little greenhouse is a good thing. ... The principal energy sources of our present industrial civilization are the so-called fossil fuels. We burn wood and oil, coal and natural gas, and, in the process, release waste gases, principally CO2, into the air. Consequently, the carbon dioxide content of the Earth's atmosphere is increasing dramatically. The possibility of a runaway greenhouse effect suggests that we have to be careful: Even a one- or two-degree rise in the global temperature can have catastrophic consequences. [Emphasis added] ... Our lovely blue planet, the Earth, is the only one we know. Venus is too hot. Mars is too cold. But the Earth is just right, a heaven for humans. After all, we evolved here. But our congenial climate may be unstable. We are perturbing our poor planet in serious and contradictory ways. Is there any danger of driving the environment of the Earth toward the planetary Hell of Venus or the global ice age of Mars? The simple answer is that nobody knows. The study of the global climate, the comparison of the Earth with other worlds, are subjects in their earliest stages of development. They are fields that are poorly and grudgingly funded. In our ignorance, we continue to push and pull, to pollute the atmosphere and to brighten the land, oblivious of the fact that the long-term consequences are largely unknown. (Sagan, 1980, pp. 102-103)*

In consuming our fossil fuels at a prodigious rate, our civilization is conducting a grandiose scientific experiment.

Even before Carl Sagan had finished his doctorate, as reported by Spencer Weart (2007), the National Academy of Sciences in 1957 published its first general report on climatology in which it noted a report by Roger Revelle: http://www.aip.org/history/climate/Revelle.htm an oceanographer and geochemist who said in part: "Human beings are now carrying out a large scale geophysical experiment of a kind that could not have happened in the past nor be reproduced in the future." When he wrote those words, Revelle apparently had no idea how prescient his remarks were, but "His 1957 paper with Hans Suess is now widely regarded as the opening shot in the global warming debates."

As early as 1970, the United States began observing Earth Day each April 22, to focus on the planet and what humans are doing to it. While this mass movement was focusing attention on all things environmental – progress on the political front dragged. Congress did not hold its first hearings exclusively devoted to climate change until 1976. That same year, a Harvard postdoctoral researcher asked Jim Hansen, now with the Goddard Institute for Space Studies, to help in calculating the greenhouse effect of human made gases in the Earth's atmosphere. Jim Hansen would go on to become an outspoken figure in the effort to mobilize efforts to mitigate the climate change of which he had no doubt.

A Daily KOS article by Meteor Blades (2008) reported, "In 1977, the National Academy of Sciences published and widely publicized the work of a panel of experts, 'Energy and Climate.' Chaired by Revelle, the panel said there was a possibility that average temperatures might climb a dangerous 6° Celsius by 2050. They urged more spending on research. On the heels of that report, Congress passed the National Climate Act in late 1978 to set up the National Climate Program Office as part of NOAA. A meager budget, a weak mandate and a kind of we-did-our-part attitude from Congress hampered the office from the beginning." (p. 2)

By mid-1988 James Hansen testified before the Senate Committee on Energy and Natural Resources. He testified again 20 years later, in 2008, and made the following observations, as reported by the *Huffington Post* (November 24, 2008, p. 1):

> *On June 23, 1988 I testified to a hearing, organized by Senator Tim Wirth of Colorado, that the Earth had entered a long-term warming trend and that human-made greenhouse gases almost surely were responsible. I noted that global warming enhanced both extremes of the water cycle, meaning stronger droughts and forest fires, on the one hand, but also heavier rains and floods.*
>
> *My testimony two decades ago was greeted with skepticism. But while skepticism is the lifeblood of science, it can confuse the public. As scientists examine a topic from all perspectives, it may appear that nothing is known with confidence. But from such broad open-minded study of all data, valid conclusions can be drawn.*
>
> *My conclusions in 1988 were built on a wide range of inputs from basic physics, planetary studies, observations of on-going changes, and climate models. The evidence was strong enough that I could say it was time to "stop waffling." I was sure that time would bring the scientific community to a similar consensus, as it has.*

Because of the increased alarm and growing awareness of global warming, a new organization, the **Intergovernmental Panel on Climate Change**, was created in 1988. This one organization is now the recognized worldwide source for information regarding climate change. From its website, the IPCC is a scientific intergovernmental body set up by the World Meteorological Organization (WMO) and by the United Nations Environment Programme (UNEP). Its constituency is made of:

This intergovernmental body satisfies the need for an unbiased, science-based panel to examine and report on all the research being done regarding the subject of climate change. While the IPCC does not actually carry out research, its panel of distinguished scientists, sociologists and economists digests and summarizes the findings of all aspects of climate change. Members look at observations of climate change, the causes, and the likely effects.

- The governments: the IPCC is open to all member countries of WMO and UNEP. Governments participate in plenary sessions of the IPCC where main decisions about the IPCC work program are taken and reports are accepted, adopted and approved. They also participate in the review of IPCC reports.

- The scientists: hundreds of scientists all over the world contribute to the work of the IPCC as authors, contributors and reviewers.
- The people: as a United Nations body, the IPCC work aims at the promotion of the United Nations' human development goals.

They are the epitome of expert witnesses whose intent is to help policymakers arrive at appropriate decisions.

The IPCC produces its assessment reports approximately every five years, with its most recent report, the Fourth Assessment Report: http://www.ipcc.ch/ called *Climate Change 2007*.

- Climate Change 2007: *The AR4 Synthesis Report*
- Climate Change 2007: *The Physical Science Basis (Working Group I report)*.
- Climate Change 2007: *Impacts, Adaptation and Vulnerability* (Working Group II report).
- Climate Change 2007: *Mitigation of Climate Change* (Working Group III report).

These documents are lengthy discussions of the various topics, and provide the enormous background to each conclusion and its probability of occurring. To introduce you to the IPCC reports, however, a good place to start is with the *Summary for Policymakers: http://www.ipcc.ch/pdf/assessment-report/ar4/syr/ar4_syr_spm.pdf* which is a document under The AR4 Synthesis Report.

The Fourth Assessment Report takes most uncertainty off the table about the observed phenomenon of global warming and its cause. From the *Summary for Policymakers*, the following conclusions are evident:

- All evidence makes the compelling case that "warming of the climate system is unequivocal."
- Natural systems of the planet are being affected by climate change.
- The primary cause of climate change is the accumulation of greenhouse gases in the atmosphere, and most of the increase in greenhouse gas concentrations is due to human activities.
- Greenhouse gas concentrations will continue to increase with human activities and policies presently in place.
- Climate change effects will continue to increase with present human activities and policies.

Former United States Vice President Al Gore produced a documentary film in 2006 called *An Inconvenient Truth*, in which he presented in visual and dramatic fashion what he saw as the effects of global climate change. The film was viewed by millions, and has been cited as one of the prime efforts to educate the public to the ravages of global warming and climate change. Gore has been active in efforts to fight global warming and climate change since the 1980's.

For his efforts to alert the public to climate change generally, Al Gore shared the 2007 Nobel Peace Prize with the Intergovernmental Panel on Climate Change.

The **American Geophysical Union** is an association with a membership of 50,000 researchers, teachers, and students in 137 countries. This esteemed organization has left no doubt regarding its position on the reality of climate change in its revised statement of *Human Impacts On Climate*: http://www.agu.org/outreach/science_policy/positions/climate_change2008.shtml published in 2008, which states:

The Earth's climate is now clearly out of balance and is warming. Many components of the climate system—including the temperatures of the atmosphere, land and ocean, the extent of sea ice and mountain glaciers, the sea level, the distribution of precipitation, and the length of seasons—are now changing at rates and in patterns that are not natural and are best explained by the increased atmospheric abundances of greenhouse gases and aerosols generated by human activity during the 20th century. Global average surface temperatures increased on average by about 0.6°C over the period 1956–2006. As of 2006, eleven of the previous twelve years were warmer than any others since 1850. The observed rapid retreat of Arctic sea ice is expected to continue and lead to the disappearance of summertime ice within this century. Evidence from most oceans and all continents except Antarctica shows warming attributable to human activities. Recent changes in many physical and biological systems are linked with this regional climate change. A sustained research effort, involving many AGU members and summarized in the 2007 assessments of the Intergovernmental Panel on Climate Change, continues to improve our scientific understanding of the climate.

During recent millennia of relatively stable climate, civilization became established and populations have grown rapidly. In the next 50 years, even the lower limit of impending climate change—an additional global mean warming of 1°C above the last decade—is far beyond the range of climate variability experienced during the past thousand years and poses global problems in planning for and adapting to it. Warming greater than 2°C above 19th century levels is projected to be disruptive, reducing global agricultural productivity, causing widespread loss of biodiversity, and—if sustained over centuries—melting much of the Greenland ice sheet with ensuing rise in sea level of several meters. If this 2°C warming is to be avoided, then our net annual emissions of CO_2 must be reduced by more than 50 percent within this century. With such projections, there are many sources of scientific uncertainty, but none are known that could make the impact of climate change inconsequential. Given the uncertainty in climate projections,there can be surprises that may cause more dramatic disruptions than anticipated from the most probable model projections.

With climate change, as with ozone depletion, the human footprint on Earth is apparent. The cause of disruptive climate change, unlike ozone depletion, is tied to energy use and runs through modern society. Solutions will necessarily involve all aspects of society. Mitigation strategies and adaptation responses will call for collaborations across science, technology, industry, and government. Members of the AGU, as part of the scientific community, collectively have special responsibilities: to pursue research needed to understand it; to educate the public on the causes, risks, and hazards; and to communicate clearly and objectively with those who can implement policies to shape future climates.

The Science of Climate Change: Everyone knows that solar radiation reaches our planet and warms it—the more solar radiation, the more warming, and the less solar radiation, the less warming. We now know that a certain amount of the warming that occurs is trapped near the planet by greenhouse gases.

But what are the greenhouse gases and why do they cause a warmer planet? The most significant greenhouse gases known are carbon dioxide, methane, nitrous oxide, chloro-fluorocarbons and ozone that is in the troposphere (ozone that is in the stratosphere is not a greenhouse gas and in fact protects the Earth from harmful ultraviolet rays). The troposphere is the layer of the atmosphere nearest the Earth, up to about 10 or 11 miles, and the stratosphere is the layer above that, up to about 30 miles.

Light coming from the Sun is composed of many different wavelengths, some of which are visible to humans and some of which are not. The acronym we learned in grade school, *ROY G BIV*, helps us remember how visible light breaks down into its component parts: red, orange, yellow, green, blue, indigo and violet. Light on the red end of the spectrum consists of longer wavelengths at lower frequencies and that on the violet end of the spectrum consists of shorter wavelengths at higher frequencies.

To the left of the red end of visible light is infrared radiation with even longer wavelengths, and to the right end of the spectrum, beyond violet, is ultraviolet. Infrared light is not visible to humans, but it is apparent when you encounter it because you feel it as heat, such as the sensation of holding your hand near the cooking element on the stove after you have just warmed soup.

It is this infrared light that matters most. As explained by a University Corporation for Atmospheric Research (UCAR) document (n.d.): http://www.ucar.edu/learn/1_3_1.htm when the sun's rays strike the atmosphere surrounding the Earth, about 26% of that light is reflected back into space by clouds and particles. About 19% of that light is *absorbed* by clouds, particles and certain gases like ozone. The remainder gets through the atmosphere to strike the Earth, and of that amount, 4% is reflected back into space by surface features. So the remainder, about 51%, of sunlight is absorbed by the Earth and warms it, melts snow and ice, promotes photosynthesis in plants, and evaporates water into water vapor, among other things.

Here's where it gets interesting.

As the Earth warms, it becomes a radiator of infrared light, or heat, back away from the planet. Scientists agree that at present about 90% of that radiated heat, or long wavelength radiation, is blocked by the greenhouse gases in the troposphere.

We remember from high school science that our atmosphere is made up mostly of nitrogen (about 78%) and oxygen (about 21%), with all the other gases, including greenhouse gases, making up the final 1%. The elements nitrogen and oxygen allow visible light to pass through, but the greenhouse gases in the final 1% of the atmosphere are made of complex molecules that powerfully block the heat, or infrared radiation, on its return trip from the Earth's surface back into space. According to the UCAR document, " The ability of certain trace gases to be relatively transparent to incoming visible light from the sun, yet opaque to the energy radiated from the earth, is one of the best understood processes in the atmospheric sciences."

The heat that is trapped and sent back to the planet, is again absorbed and radiated, again blocked, and so on, until no more long wavelength light remains either unabsorbed or radiated back into space. This process is continuous, and one can see that the greater the concentration of these greenhouse gases, the more efficient is the eventual heating of the Earth's surface.

As already pointed out, the single largest identified human caused factor is the emission of the greenhouse gas, *carbon dioxide*, which accounts for about 55% of the change in the intensity of the Earth's greenhouse effect even though it makes up only about 387 parts per million (ppm) (.0387%) of the atmosphere.

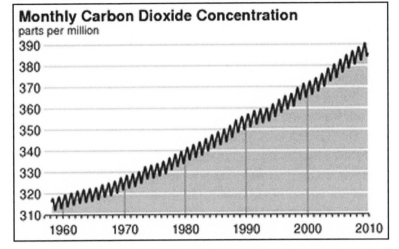

Primarily because of the work of Charles David Keeling in the 1950's, scientists have the means to accurately measure CO_2 in the modern era. Keeling's Curve is a chart: http://scrippsco2.ucsd.edu/ that shows the relentless increase in CO_2 since 1958 (Keeling, 2008). Studies of ice cores taken from both the Arctic and the Antarctic regions indicate a pre-industrial level of CO_2 at about 280 ppm.

Scientists like Vincent Gray (1999) also point out the incredibly complex factors that influence how much free CO_2 remains in the atmosphere. For some periods of high output of CO_2 by an industrialized society, the levels in the atmosphere rose in a linear fashion rather than a much-faster geometric fashion, and possible explanations for this apparent anomaly include faster absorption of the excess CO_2 by the oceans or other carbon sinks (physical elements that absorb carbon dioxide, such as trees). Scientists have even noted the complexity of measuring CO_2 on a monthly basis, as they see a decrease in CO_2 when deciduous trees produce leaves in the spring and an increase when the same trees shed their leaves and go dormant in the fall, as shown in the chart above.

Source
NOAA

Since 1958, the average annual rate of increase in CO_2 in the atmosphere seems to fall in the range of 1.4 ppm per year. The last 10 years, however, have

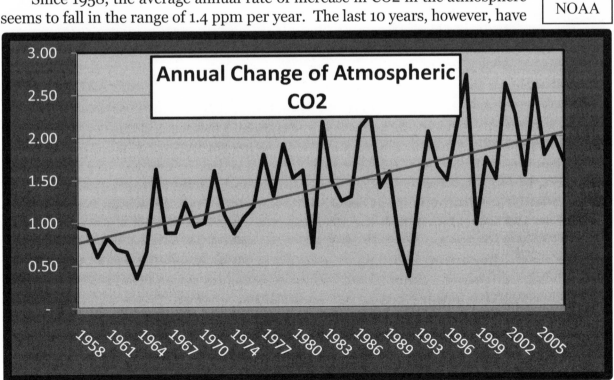

averaged 2.02 additional ppm per year; the 10 years before that averaged 1.45; the 10 years before that 1.52; and the 10 years before that 1.16 ppm. According to the CO2now.org home page (November 2, 2009), at least since the 1958 start of atmospheric CO2 measurements with high-precision instruments, the rate of increase in atmospheric carbon dioxide concentration has accelerated from decade to decade: http://co2now.org/index.php?option=com_content&task=view&id=36&Itemid=1 This chart shows the data from the National Oceanic and Atmospheric Association (NOAA) since 1960 on atmospheric change in CO2 parts per million each year. Note that no year had a negative change—some simply had a smaller positive change. The trendline which shows annual changes is rising.

Scientific research involves painstaking design and execution of studies or experiments to discern what is causing some effect that has been observed. Principles of the scientific method require objectivity and often tedious documentation of the study and its results. Many such projects can take years in the field and in the laboratory in order to arrive at a supportable conclusion. Our interviews with Dr. Baker Perry and Dr. Mike Mayfield of Appalachian State University, in Boone, North Carolina, provide insight into the process by scientists who work in the field. They also illustrate how scientists carefully withhold judgment until they are satisfied with the preponderance of evidence.

Dr. Baker Perry is an assistant professor in the Department of Geography and Planning at Appalachian State University. He teaches a variety of introductory and upper level courses in geography there, including Introduction to Physical Geography, Weather and Climate and Environmental Remote Sensing. He also teaches courses on climate and tropical glaciers in the Andes, global climate change, Mountain Weather and Climate, and

Mountain Geography. Most of his research has been in the area of climate, particularly synoptic climatology and snowfall. Along with four other faculty members at ASU, he is a founding member of the Appalachian Atmospheric Interdisciplinary Research (AppalAIR) Program, a group trying to better understand atmospheric processes and patterns in the Southern Appalachians, particularly related to weather, climate variability, climate change and air quality issues. He spent approximately three years of his childhood in Bolivia at 13,000 feet, which piqued his curiosity about the study of snow and ice and about glaciers he could see every day.

Dr. Perry spoke to Arctic Gardens in April 2009:

As a synoptic climatologist, I'm interested in those aspects of atmospheric circulation that influence high impact weather events, primarily dealing with synoptic scale, or sub-continental scales, like the circulation over Eastern North America and the Southeastern United States. Most of my work has focused on the type of synoptic patterns that influence snowfall events, and in the differences in synoptic scale circulation between heavy events or light events. In the sense of synoptic climatology, I look at longer periods. So in developing a synoptic climatology, sometimes in my data sets I have as many as 500 snow events. And I find commonalities in that sample set, to improve scientific understanding and ultimately provide clues to allow meteorologists and climatologists to improve forecasts.

We work within the scientific method, where we develop hypotheses and try to go about testing them. It's somewhat more difficult in Earth and atmospheric sciences because we don't have a controlled laboratory within which to work. Ideally we would have a spare Earth in which to conduct climate experiments, but we don't. So as a climatologist, I try to develop hypotheses and then develop studies to test them that use historical data to try to understand which factors were most important in the development of heavy snow events in the past, for example, and then use that knowledge to help improve forecasts of future snow events.

In order to test a hypothesis, it's critical to have quality data. That's a big challenge. And any sort of climate-related work requires observations that are spatially representative of a given area, and that are themselves accurate and unbiased. They can then be compared to other observations. There's been so much effort and attention focused on numerical modeling, but if you don't have good observations with which to validate your modeling, then it's a real struggle to say anything about model accuracy. That's a missing ingredient in a lot of atmospheric research. Oftentimes what suffices for observations are model analyses. They take a few observations and just let the model say what it thinks about a given location, and they extrapolate from that. I do focus a lot of my work on gathering quality observations and quality data so we can test hypotheses and make informed analyses from which to draw conclusions.

When discussing this field, I tend to prefer the term Global Climate Change, because we're dealing with more than just temperature. There are changes in precipitation, changes in cloud cover, and changes in other factors, so climate change is a broader term to encompass what is actually happening.

There's no question that the climate has warmed, that surface temperature observations show that warming is occurring. And I think that human activity is playing an important role in the documented warming, but there are likely some natural components at work, too. And the fundamental question here is how large a role each is playing.

Determining the relative contribution from human activities is an evolving process. I have significant questions about how much natural variability may be at work, becase when you go back and look at the northern hemisphere temperature records, in particular, there was a break point that occurred in the late 70's. This coincided with a phase change in the Pacific Decadal Oscillation (PDO) and the North Atlantic Oscillation, (NAO). So there are lots of things that happened in the late 70's with the ocean and the atmosphere. It just so happens that the positive phase of the NAO has dominated in the last several decades. And prior to that period, the 60's and 70's—which were much cooler and snowier here (in Boone)—coincided with the negative phase (cold phase) of the NAO.

There are some other examples from the tropical Andes and Kilimanjaro indicating how atmospheric circulation is driving a lot of the observed changes there. So, I guess the fundamental question in my mind is how are anthropogenic activities influencing atmospheric circulation? The question is how to separate the perturbed state of the atmosphere in its natural variability and its linkages with the ocean from what anthropogenic greenhouse gases and aerosols may be doing to change that atmospheric circulation. It's a question of whether the changes in circulation patterns are a cause or an effect of the climate change we see.

A concern that has been discussed for the last 10 to 15 years is the potential impacts in the thermohaline circulation in the North Atlantic, and the effects that could have on Eastern North America and Western Europe. With the increased meltwater, the freshening of the North Atlantic could disrupt the Great Oceanic Conveyor Belt and lead to cooling in Eastern North America and Western Europe. The North Atlantic drift of warm water could be blocked. There is strong evidence from ice cores in Greenland showing where this has happened in the recent past. There was a big event 8,200 years ago that was believed to be caused by rapid intrusion of fresh water into the North Atlantic, and that brought dramatic cooling across eastern North America and Western Europe.

Another concern is the likely decreases in melt water from glaciers and the effect that will have on large human populations. The primary factor driving glacier retreat in the Andes from Ecuador to Bolivia appears to be El Niño Southern Oscillation—the warm phase of El Niño, called ENSO. So the fundamental question is: how are greenhouse gases and anthropogenic activities going to impact ENSO? That's where it gets a little more complicated and uncertain.

*The melt water from the glaciers is absolutely critical for many of these populations in large cities and semi-arid regions that have a pronounced dry season. **The ironic side to this is that because melting has increased over the last few decades, there has been increased runoff—so people have adapted to the increased water levels.** Well, pretty soon, if current rates continue—if we continue to have diminished precipitation, decreased cloud cover, increased sunshine in these areas—this is mainly in association with the warm phase of ENSO—then a lot of these glaciers are going to disappear.*

I mentioned Mt. Kilimanjaro earlier. We see it as a poster child for the global climate change debate, where it is commonly suggested that the retreat in the glaciers on Mt. Kilimanjaro is being driven by warmer air and just higher temperatures seen in the last 50 to 100 years. But there are some pretty well-respected, very prominent glaciologists and climatologists that have taken a different view and have shown through regional analysis of precipitation and temperature records that it's the decreasing precipitation of the last 100 years or so that is driving the de-glaciations on Kilimanjaro. So that just again points to the fact that what seems so simple—a glacier retreating—must surely be evidence of global warming or climate change. When you get down to it, it is a bit more complicated, more ambiguous. Yes, human activities may be playing a role, but it is perhaps through a more complicated process.

*The Intergovernmental Panel on Climate Change (IPCC) has reviewed the current state of knowledge related to climate change and made specific policy recommendations. But, I think there are plenty of other reasons in addition to what the IPCC has done that are as important, or perhaps more important, for why we need to reduce our dependence on fossil fuels and to reduce our emissions. Those relate to the costs of doing business in the Middle East, foreign policy issues, national security, health, international justice, and environmental pollution of other sorts, and the impacts that these forms of energy have on our communities, on our families, on our lifestyles. We already have over a billion people living in misery and there are a lot of simple things we can do right now to reduce that burden, to respond to child health and help more children survive. And respond directly to basic development needs—these could help people respond and cope with climate extremes, and people have greater control over their own destiny and have increased education, for example, and countless studies have shown these factors to improve their well-being and their ability to cope with different sorts of anthropogenic and natural disasters. And so, **it's important to recognize that there are many forms of injustice out there already, and when we have climate events, they tend to impact those folks disproportionately.** So, in addition to reducing emissions, we need to be doing all we can to respond to basic needs that people have around the world through development focused primarily on health and education.*

Dr. Mike Mayfield also spoke with *Arctic Gardens* in April 2009. He is a professor of geography at Appalachian State University. He is also the faculty coordinator for general education, and for about 10 years worked in global change related research. His interests include hydrology, geomorphology, and especially remote sensing of glaciers. He grew up in Charlotte and spent a lot of time in the Appalachian Mountains, and decided that geography is the focus he wanted to pursue in college. He earned his undergraduate degree at Western Carolina University, and went to the University of Tennessee in Knoxville for his Masters and Doctorate. He worked at Oak Ridge National Lab during that time, where he was able to experience geothermal energy, a form of renewable energy.

I'm in full agreement with the majority opinion of the IPCC, with the Union of Concerned Scientists, with the National Academy of Sciences, with the vast majority of Earth scientists and climate scientists—that there is a well-documented pattern of warming starting in the late 1800's that has accelerated in the 20th and 21st centuries. And I believe human activity is playing a very important role. That is the opinion of all the groups I have just cited. Personally, I don't think there is much doubt about it whatsoever.

I do think we have to be careful suggesting how far it will go, or whether other naturally-occurring cycles could offset part of that. I tend to take a cautious point of view. But I like the position taken in a book written by climate scientist Steven Schneider with the National Center for Atmospheric Research, called The Genesis Strategy, in 1976. That's when people were just becoming aware of the potential for major climate change that could be related to human activity. He made a point using a Biblical analogy. A prophesy was made that there was going to be a decade of drought and famine, and so the response was, "Alright, I'm not sure if I believe this prophecy—you may be a complete kook—but the cautious thing, the appropriate thing to protect my family and the generations after me, is to take the threat seriously."

The theme I'll come back to repeatedly is to respond with great confidence to what the science indicates for us, despite the skeptics, despite the people who have genuine concerns about the role of natural variability, the role of feedback mechanisms, the uncertainty in our climate models, the degree to which short-term changes in heat distribution are confusing the overall picture of climate change tied to human causation.

Sure, all those things are important issues.

But I think there are great benefits to responding as if it were all caused by human activity. Err on the side of caution and invest in technologies that will benefit American society and American industry and the economy of the U.S.

Specifically, benefits are clear: 1) becoming less dependent on unreliable and unfriendly sources of energy; 2) improving air quality; 3) minimizing disruptions that would be tied to rapid warming, if that's what we see.

Another real concern is methane. The reports I've read about methane locked up in frozen tundra and solids called methane hydrates scare the heck out of me. You know, that's one of those feedback loops that would be a non-linear response if we do warm the tundra enough to release those sources of methane, we could pull the trigger on a rate of change that is unprecedented, and the feedbacks on top of that, as I understand the literature, could really be devastating.

The release of methane in particular could make a very unfriendly climate for our agricultural systems that we are currently dependent on. So my question and concern is whether we adapt rapidly enough to a rapidly warming climate so that we don't have massive drought, starvation, all the dislocations tied to that. For large numbers of people, places like Bangladesh, places throughout Asia are really problematic; for largescale migrations, coastal areas throughout Asia, it could really be catastrophic.

Aerosols present a bit of a conundrum. Aerosols tend to block some of the sunlight striking the Earth. But, we're going to remove aerosols like sulfates from the air anyway to improve air quality and to reduce acid rain. So the accidental benefits of having sulfates in the stratosphere that offset some of the radiative forcing of the other greenhouse gases can't argue for adding them back to the atmosphere. It's going to exacerbate the problem, but I don't think anyone in their right mind would argue that we need to burn coal without scrubbers in order to keep injecting sulfates in the atmosphere.

There is no debate that the largest factor in the increase of CO_2 is the widespread adoption of coal as an energy source. In considering limits to use of coal there are equity issues, but I would hope that through technology transfer that we could look at ways of providing energy to those emerging middle classes in South and East Asia. We can't say we've achieved this level of lifestyle and economic development in the U.S., but you *shouldn't do the same because it's going to hurt our air, and because it's going to cause our climate to warm. There have to be more compelling reasons for them to move forward with less impactful sources of energy.*

The whole idea of clean coal is so appealing, but our history so far suggested that there is really no such thing as clean coal, whether it's extracted with mountaintop removal or by deep mining—there are huge consequences to all those things.

We do have to be sympathetic to the poor that are reaching our levels of economic attainment throughout Asia and elsewhere, but we can't just blithely say we will have technological solutions in the near future.

I think another really big worry is the condition of western forests. The situation in the West includes the rapid expansion of the pine beetle outbreaks. There is very clear evidence that those outbreaks are cyclic, that there's about a 500-year cycle in pine beetle outbreaks. A lot of people want to say that's global warming. The immediate cause is these insects that do go through these cycles. But, the proximate cause is apparently the fact that winter temperatures have not been as cold for a decade or more. What I've been told by forest scientists is that they need sustained temperatures of about 20 below zero in order to put a real dent in those populations. But for whatever reasons, when you look back through the long history, these outbreaks have happened from time to time. And when they happen, that pumps a lot of CO_2 into the atmosphere and it resets the forest ecology of those regions. Of course, one could argue that this is another manifestation of global warming, but the degree of warming that is the absence of those long sustained cold spells is more immediately tied to patterns of circulation than it is to the roughly one degree of warming we have experienced.

Conversely, Eastern North American forests have been sucking up carbon at a faster than expected rate, and until these outbreaks of insects have sort of reversed the course in Western forests, scientists had shown in their findings that climate explains part of it, but carbon fertilization is part of the story also. A lot of skeptics like to point out that a carbon-rich world is a greenhouse world, in the sense that plants thrive—but it has its limits. We may be approaching some of those limits.

A natural mitigating factor for CO_2 is something called carbon sequestration in the natural carbon cycle. Atmospheric carbon gets absorbed by natural carbon sinks, like the oceans, the forests, and the soils. But it appears that the biomass/soils sink for carbon could very rapidly be approaching that saturation point. So for all the surplus carbon that we're putting in the atmosphere, about half of it is accumulating in the atmosphere. The rest of it is going into ocean sinks, vegetative sinks, or soils sinks. There is emerging evidence that there is probably no true limit to oceanic sinks, depending on what model of ocean circulation you believe is operative. If you can get a deep circulation, you could put an awful lot of carbon into the ocean. If, however, it's just surface waters, then increasing acidification begins to change the balance of chemistry and we've got some real problems there as well.

Nonetheless, relying on geo-technology, or geo-engineering, for man-made carbon sequestration troubles me. I really think we ought to continue with research, because I think we'd be foolish not to consider ways of capturing carbon dioxide at smokestack level and injecting it into places where it is likely to stay for long periods of time. But the law of unintended consequences says that we shouldn't be naïve about that. The energy cost and the thermodynamic efficiency of extracting CO2 has to be addressed, and there are people hard at work about that.

But my concern about that is, we always seem to want to take the technological solution. If we simply keep on with business as usual, building more and more coal-fired power plants with the unsubstantiated assumption that we can strip it out of the exhaust stream and then put it magically somewhere it will do no harm—we can't just assume all those things.

The present level of CO2 in the atmosphere, about 387 ppm, is a known fact that no physicist would dispute. The fact is that gases in very small concentrations, so-called greenhouse gases, are very effective at increasing the resonance time of solar energy in our atmosphere. In other words, they slow the return of that energy to space. What that does is to drive up the temperature. It's often stated that a better analogy than a greenhouse is a leaky bucket. The analogy there is: you've got a bucket of water and the height of water in the bucket is the global temperature. But, there are holes in the bucket. The gases in the atmosphere tend to plug up those holes, and those gases are being increased by human activity. By partly plugging the holes in the bucket, the level of water in the bucket goes higher, which increases the hydraulic pressure, which means we need to reach a new equilibrium where the pressure exerted by the water at its higher level means that the same amount of water escapes. So, you still have the same solar constant, in essence, but in the short term, because of the greater concentrations of these gases, even at those low levels, the temperature of the earth has to go up to drive the radiated transfer into space. That's undisputed. I don't know of any legitimate scientist who disputes the role of the so-called greenhouse gases.

One thing we do know is that even fairly dramatic reductions in CO2 emission rates will have a very slow impact on CO2 concentrations in the atmosphere. That is one of the most discouraging things about the science of greenhouse gases. For example, one big study that came out in Science some years ago said that if the U.S. adopted the Kyoto Accords of reducing greenhouse gases, that we would reduce the CO2 concentrations by about three ppm, which isn't enough. The radiative forcing of three ppm is insignificant. My personal view is that if we don't start at some point soon, we'll never get where we need to be.

Unfortunately, the evidence is very clear that the biggest losers brought about by climate change are always going to be the people with the least technology and the least in the way of economic resources to respond. For example, disruption of agricultural output for farmers who are prone to adaptation and with financial resources to adapt can be minimized in a really meaningful way. But it would be very different if you were looking at Bangladesh and very different if you are looking at northern India. A factor there is the local groundwater they are using for irrigation, and it is highly likely they will have depleted that source of water in the next couple of decades.

We're also looking at decreased melt water from glaciers. There is a lot of evidence that shows that some of those glaciers have already retreated to the point that even if we had El Nino Southern Oscillation phases that favored their development, they have retreated so far that it would be impossible for them to recover. Bolivia is an example. It would take a huge abrupt change for the glaciers there to remain. Again, it gets complex, but basically it's the change in albedo (the ratio of light that is reflected by a surface compared to the light that is received by a surface), as you melt away more snow and ice and expose more dark rock that absorbs sunlight, it just becomes impossible without major abrupt climate change to bring those glaciers back.

Even the Bush Administration, through the EPA, has said to Congress that the debate has essentially been finished and we are now ready to move on to what policy implications emerge from that. Certainly the new administration takes it very seriously. So I don't think it's at all wrong-minded to look at adaptation at the same time that we are looking at ways of minimizing our emissions. Because for the next 20 years or more, we are basically going to be living with an energy economy that is going to be putting CO2 in the atmosphere along with the other gases that we've been talking about, and I would like to think that for many other reasons, we would be moving away from that.

One possible solution I think is a cap and trade system, which would be better than nothing. But it basically guarantees that we don't move forward rapidly--that's the down side I see of cap and trade. I'd like personally to see stronger measures that have more immediate effects. I think that there are very few scenarios that would allow us to quickly reverse our course in terms of our atmospheric chemistry changes for primary greenhouse gases. I think it makes perfect sense to move as quickly as we can, but in the meantime, what else are we going to do? That includes adaptation, it includes technology transfer, and it includes all the environmental justice issues, which bear directly on that.

I think we should be very careful—we shouldn't be in the business of misleading the public to think that we can make minor adjustments and greatly change the radiative forcing that's been brought about by well over a century.

The science of global climate change is developing rapidly and improving our understanding of the interconnected nature of climate systems. Almost daily, new studies are published which add to the body of knowledge regarding climate change, and they are beginning to clarify the often counterintuitive findings with cause and effect.

An example is a very recent study by the National Environmental Research Council (2009), which reported that cleaner air tends to make sunlight strike the leaves of trees with sharply defined patterns of sunlight and shade. Apparently such an effect results in less photosynthesis than if the light is more diffuse after passing through more polluted air. What does this clarify? Should we want more polluted air so photosenthesis is encouraged?

Another example is a recent University of Miami Rosenstiel School of Marine & Atmospheric Science report (2009) that suggests that warmer temperatures result in fewer clouds over the oceans, resulting in more heating—that is, warmer air creates another positive feedback by causing fewer clouds, which means less blocking of sunlight striking the Earth's surface, which means more heating. We may need some indication of a major change in topics, i.e. methane.

Another critical area with rapid knowledge gains is research into methane emissions that is rapidly raising awareness of the huge potential of warming caused by its release from ancient stores in the Arctic and under seafloors.

Methane (CH_4) is a simple hydrocarbon consisting of carbon and hydrogen atoms, and it is the largest component of natural gas. Methane is produced by decomposition of organic matter without the availability of oxygen. A significant modern source of methane is rice cultivation, where paddy flooding creates anaerobic conditions suitable for methane production. Other sources include digestion of plant matter by livestock and other grazing animals and termites. Scientists believe that termite activity has increased with the increasing deforestation of tropical forests and resulting land use practices. Methane is also produced in landfills by material that decomposes in oxygendepleted environments, and is released as a by-product of gas and oil drilling, and from coal mining.

Methane in the atmosphere is fairly short-lived, with a half-life of seven to ten years. That means that half of the methane will have changed into something else in that time period. That's the good news. The bad news is that when methane breaks down, it picks up oxygen and morphs into CO_2. Even with its short lifespan, its concentrations have increased drastically. The IPCC Fourth Assessment (Bernstein et al., 2007, p. 37) reports that known sources have contributed to the increase of methane in the atmosphere since 1750 by more than 150%. As Dr. David Stang reports (2009), "Atmospheric methane levels of the past 150 years are far higher than those of the previous 420,000 years, and are currently 2.5 times as high as any previous level." Talk about small concentrations having a big effect—at 1774 parts per billion (2005), it is less than .0002% of the atmosphere.

In addition to rice cultivation, digestion of plant matter by livestock and termites, landfills, gas and oil drilling, and coal mining as sources of methane, **scientists now include two significant new sources of methane in their book of worries—thawing permafrost and methane clathrates.**

Both represent positive feedbacks from the warming caused by carbon dioxide.

Because of the potential of methane to greatly accelerate global warming, the public will begin hearing the terms *clathrate, yedoma*, and *thermokarst*. And the public will hear about the work being done by researchers at the University of Alaska at Fairbanks, among others. Our interview with Dr. John Walsh from the University of Alaska is presented later in this chapter. Other researchers at the University include Dr. Vladimir Romanowsky, Natalia Shakhova, and a rising star, Katey Walter Anthony.

Permafrost thawing is now well documented. Dr. Stang goes on to report (Thawing Permafrost in southern Alaska Section, 2009) that in southern Alaska, the permafrost has gone from zero days per year above freezing in 1987 to 139 days above freezing in 1993. More recently, Laura Shin (2009) of SolveClimate.com reports: http://solveclimate.com/blog/20090702/thawing-permafrost-could-emit-massive-amounts-greenhouse-gases "A study ... shows that the amount of carbon locked in the Arctic permafrost is more than double previous estimates. Additionally, other research shows that the permafrost is thawing, meaning this enormous amount of carbon could be released into the atmosphere as the greenhouse gases carbon dioxide and methane. The thawing of the permafrost is especially dangerous because it could cause a domino effect of more warming that, for now, cannot be checked by human engineering or policy."

In Siberia, the permafrost is melting rapidly and scientists are beginning to study and measure the methane production. Frozen, ancient, organic permafrost, called *yedoma*, is melting and decomposing, causing methane seeps. Studies now predict the possible thawing of the top several feet of Arctic permafrost within this century, releasing vast stores of carbon dioxide and methane into the atmosphere. We simply do not yet know how significant the releases may be, but some speak of *irreversible warming*, a terrifying prospect.

Scientists have known for years that methane has been bubbling from Arctic lakes, but the variability of the emissions, in combination with difficulty and costs of accessing the sites on lake surfaces, has led to a lack of empirical information about the emissions. Importantly, this source of methane has not been included in models reported on by the IPCC up to now, making the scenarios described by the IPCC at best, conservative, if the methane threat is as serious as many now believe. Because of the enormous potential impact of methane from permafrost, several groups are working to gather enough information to make this source useable in climate models. From the University of Alaska website: http:// www.alaska.edu/uaf/cem/ine/walter/

Katey Walter Anthony is emerging as a leading researcher who speaks of climate changes based on warming in the Arctic regions. She is an aquatic ecologist and bio-geochemist interested in carbon and nutrient cycling between terrestrial and aquatic systems, the cryosphere and atmosphere. She conducts research on methane and carbon dioxide emissions from Arctic and temperate lakes and wetlands. She is interested in processes that govern greenhouse gas emissions from lakes, including thermokarst (permafrost) thaw, modern plant productivity, geology, and landscape-scale changes in lake area that result in both positive and negative feedbacks to climate change.

Anthony has developed methods to provide basic data regarding methane emissions caused by the thawing of the permafrost and its decomposition in the lake beds, among other places. She has perfected a methane trap, a device to collect methane bubbling up in a lake, so that precise measurements can be made and recorded. In 2006, she and colleagues published an article called "Methane bubbling from Siberian thaw lakes as a positive feedback to climate warming," in which they describe methane ebullition, or bubbling, as the chief source of emissions in Arctic lake environments and in which they have determined that the source of the methane is the decomposition of ancient carbon. The article concluded that North Siberian lakes are a globally significant source of atmospheric CH4 (methane), and that the CH4 is quite old, having been formed during the Pleistocene Age, to which geologists assign dates of about 2.5 million years ago up until about 12,000 years ago. As stated by Walter Anthony and Zimov (2006), "Furthermore, the Pleistocene age (35,260–42,900 years) of methane emitted from hotspots along thawing lake margins indicates that this positive feedback to climate warming has led to the release of old carbon stocks previously stored in permafrost."

What they, and others, including Dr. Vladimir Romanovsky (2009): http://www.uaf. edu/geology/Facultyn/romanovsky.htm have learned is that thawing of the permafrost produces lakes, called thermokarst lakes, because the melt water cannot percolate down through the remaining permafrost below. At the lake edges, material slips to the lake bottom, where it decomposes in an oxygen-free environment, producing methane. They also know that these lakes are increasing in size, resulting in more decomposing organic matter. Once summer melting creates a small layer of water on the ice surface, the water will tend to warm faster than the frozen material in close proximity. As it warms, the melting reaches even greater depths. Over the Arctic winter, pools of water that reach more than two meters in depth tend to remain unfrozen at the bottom, allowing for a continuation of the thawing.

Dr. Romanovsky focuses on measuring temperatures at various depths in the permafrost for the same reasons that Walter is capturing data on methane emissions—to establish databases against which to compare future measurements. His work is increasingly relying on remote sensing.

The topic of methane emissions is critical. If only 1% of permafrost carbon were to be released each year, that could double the globe's current annual carbon emissions, Romanovsky notes in an *LA Times* article: http://www.latimes.com/news/science/environment/la-na-global-warming22-2009feb22,0,646220.story by Margot Roosevelt, "We are at a tipping point for positive feedback," he warns, referring to a process where warming spurs emissions, which in turn generate more heat, in an uncontrollable cycle. (Roosevelt, February 20, 2009).

A 2009 *Science Daily* article from the Global Carbon Project reports on a new study published by Dr. Charles Tarnocai, Agriculture and Agri-Food Canada, Ottawa, and Professor Ted Schuur, University of Florida, about the amount of carbon now estimated to be stored in the Arctic. They are the messengers of this bad news: "We now estimate the deposits contain *over 1.5 trillion* [emphasis added] tons of frozen carbon, about twice as much carbon as contained in the atmosphere". They go on to say "Radioactive carbon dating shows that most of the carbon dioxide currently emitted by thawing soils in Alaska was formed and frozen thousands of years ago. The carbon dating demonstrates how easily carbon decomposes when soils thaw under warmer conditions." This new information can only mean that the feared feedbacks of warming causing melting causing decomposition causing more warming causing more melting and so on is underway and accelerating, and the amount of stored carbon is vastly more than previously estimated.

Methane clathrates are the other methane source now rapidly coming under scrutiny. Because methane clathrates exist in such enormous quantities, and because so little is known about them, they are now the giant wild card in the climate deck. If early indications of methane release from clathrates are even remotely correct, the outlook for climate change is dire.

The chemical term *clathrate* means a molecular structure where molecules of one compound trap molecules of another compound, or trap elements. Where the compound doing the trapping is water, that clathrate is called a *hydrate*. Methane hydrates, therefore, are crystalline structures of water ice that trap molecules of methane. Scientists now have reason to believe that warmer ocean waters are causing ancient methane hydrates to become unstable, releasing the molecules of methane to the seawater. Scientists have located, and are studying, voluminous seeps of methane from shallow sea beds.

In 2008, Volker Mrasek wrote an article titled, "A Storehouse of Greenhouse Gases Is Opening in Siberia," in which he reported: "It's always been a disturbing what-if scenario for climate researchers: Gas hydrates stored in the Arctic ocean floor -- hard clumps of ice and methane, conserved by freezing temperatures and high pressure -- could grow unstable and release massive amounts of methane into the atmosphere. Since methane is a potent greenhouse gas, more worrisome than carbon dioxide, the result would be a drastic acceleration of global warming. Until now this idea was mostly academic; scientists had warned that such a thing *could* happen. Now it seems more likely that it *will*." http://www.spiegel.de/international/world/0,1518,547976,00.html

In the permafrost bottom of the 200-meter-deep sea, enormous stores of gas hydrates lie dormant in mighty frozen layers of sediment. The carbon content of the ice-and-methane mixture here is estimated at 540 billion tons. "This submarine hydrate was considered stable until now," says the Russian bio-geochemist Natalia Shakhova in the same Mrasek article, currently a guest scientist at the University of Alaska in Fairbanks, who is also a member of the Pacific Institute of Geography at the Russian Academy of Sciences in Vladivostok. http://www.spiegel.de/international/world/0,1518,547976,00.html

Now it seems that the methane locked up in clathrates is thawing and seeping into the ocean water. Science editor Steve Connor wrote: "Scientists aboard a research ship that has sailed the entire length of Russia's northern coast have discovered intense concentrations of methane – sometimes at up to 100 times background levels – over several areas covering thousands of square miles of the Siberian continental shelf." (Connor, September 23, 2008)

And Alexis Madrigal published an article in *Wired Science: http://www.wired.com/wiredscience/2008/05/could-methane-t/* with the ominous title "Could Methane Trigger a Climate Doomsday Within a Human Lifespan?" "If global temperatures continue to rise, massive amounts of methane gas could be released from the 10,000 gigaton reserves of frozen methane that are currently locked in the world's deep oceans and permafrost. Passing this climate tipping point would result in global warming that would be far worse and more rapid than scientists' current estimates." (Madrigal, May 28, 2008)

The Arctic: The Arctic region of planet Earth is the area generally north of the Arctic Circle (66° 33'N), where the average temperature for the warmest month (July) is below 50° F, and where winter temperatures often drop to -40° F, but have even been recorded as low as -90° F. While much of the area is snow and ice-covered most of the year, average precipitation is only about 20 inches, although some areas average as little as seven inches. The Arctic encompasses enormous land masses in North America, Asia, and parts of Europe. Nations with Arctic territory include the United States, Canada, Russia, Norway and Denmark (Greenland).

The Arctic has been undergoing climate changes much more rapidly than the remainder of the planet. The independent Pew Research Center reported in 2009: http://www.pewclimate.org/global-warming-basics/faq_s "While the world as a whole warmed about 1°F over the entire 20th century, parts of the Arctic have warmed by 4-5°F just since the 1950's." And the Natural Resources Defense Council added in an article on its website called *Global Warming Puts the Arctic on Thin Ice* (Part 2): "The polar ice cap as a whole is shrinking. Images from NASA satellites show that the area of permanent ice cover is contracting at a rate of nine percent each decade. If this trend continues, summers in the Arctic could become ice-free by the end of the century." (NRDC, 2009)

While the surface area of the Arctic ice cover has been shrinking, data from military submarines, now confirmed by NASA satellite data, indicate that the average thickness of the ice has also decreased over two feet in the four year period from 2004-2008. Scientists now know that the ice that remains over many years (multi-year ice), is shrinking and is being replaced by thinner seasonal ice. NASA recently reported in the *Journal of Geophysical Research-Oceans:http://www.greencarcongress.com/2009/07/nasa-20090708.html* that "During the study period, the relative contributions of the two ice types to the total volume of the Arctic's ice cover were reversed. In 2003, 62% of the Arctic's total ice volume was stored in multi-year ice, with 38% stored in first-year seasonal ice. By 2008, 68% of the total ice volume was first-year ice, with 32% multi-year." (NASA, 2009)

Importantly, temperature bands called *isotherms* are moving northward, especially in the Arctic. As the average temperature increases, the ecosystems are challenged to adapt to the change or perish. As Hansen and others reported in the Proceedings of the National Academy of Sciences, *Criteria for Dangerous Warnings* (2006), "More rapid warming in 1975–2005 yields an average isotherm migration rate of 40 km per decade in the Northern Hemisphere ... exceeding known paleoclimate rates of change."

"While the world as a whole warmed about 1°F over the entire 20th century, parts of the Arctic have warmed by 4-5°F just since the 1950's."

The increasing loss of sea ice negatively affects populations of polar bears and seals who feed at the ice edge. It also affects the Native people who maintain their subsistence lifestyles with reliance on the sea. Increased melting exposes more coastline to storm surges, resulting in significant erosion of land into the sea. In an article by CIEL (n.d.) called "Climate Change and Arctic Impacts:" http://www.ciel.org/Climate/Climate_Arctic.html thawing permafrost in the Arctic has damaged houses, roads, airports and pipelines, and caused landscape erosion, slope instability, and landslides. Local coastal losses to erosion of up to 100 feet per year have been observed in some locations in the Siberian, Alaskan and Canadian Arctic. In Shishmaref, Alaska, a small Inupiat village on the Chukchi Sea, seven houses have had to be relocated, three have fallen into the sea, and engineers predict that the entire village of 600 houses could disappear into the sea within the next few decades. Shishmaref's airport runway has almost been met by rising seawater, and its fuel tank farm, which seven years ago was 300 feet from the edge of a seaside bluff, is now only 35 feet from the bluff. The town dump, which has seawater within eight feet of it, could pollute the nearby marine environment for years if inundated. Advancing seawater has contaminated Shishmaref's drinking water supply.

Darius Elias, a native of Old Crow, Yukon Territory shared his and his family's observations about changes they have seen. Here is part of his interview:

Using a traditional education in a manner that is complementary to western society is especially important today. I find myself addressing global warming and how these changes affect traditional living. I find myself talking about this steadily.

Some elders have told me that mother earth is trying to cleanse herself from the destruction that humans have caused. It is like the immune system has kicked in. I have seen it around here, and it is just as simple as walking on the clear ice. About 12 years ago, I was walking with an elder, Irwin Linklater. He stuck a stick down a muskrat house (a hole in the ice) and pushed it down once, then pushed it down again and said, "Hmm." As he pulled it back up, he said that he had done that since he was a kid and he could maybe push it within 2 inches at the bottom of the lake. Now there was a foot and a half of mud on that pole.

The wood frogs that used to be very plentiful in the lakes behind Old Crow are not so plentiful. The caribou migrations have changed, the caribou patterns have changed, and we are seeing a lot more parasites on the caribou and we are seeing insects we have not seen before. Also, there are pelicans arriving. The vegetation is growing up the side of the mountains. On the coastal plain, the dwarf birches are just invading from the mountains at a very rapid rate which is also alarming.

The weather patterns are especially noticeable. We see summer clouds in December, the fluffy clouds. It rains in December and causes havoc amongst the animal population. The cycles are not as consistent as they used to be. It doesn't get 50-60 below anymore; it's to the point where it is costing people their lives. My grandmother and an elder were walking across a stretch of river that they have walked across the same weekend their entire lives to go fish. She fell through and drowned. We had to find her underneath the ice; luckily we found her. That same stretch of ice for 70 years, they trusted it, and now we can't do that anymore. When we go out in the bush, we don't know if we are going to encounter an overflow or an open lake, so people are hesitant to go out. If so, they have to go with a group of people to make sure they are safe. Things are changing, everything.

I have tried to avoid the topic of permafrost melting because I get emotional. But, I just went up to Crow Flats two weeks ago to a lake at the center of my family's traditional area I spoke of earlier, Zelma Lake. My grandmother protected it like I will never forget. This lake is very central to our family. Recently the permafrost melted on the south end of the lake. It drained catastrophically to the point where it emptied. It's gone. I paddled around that lake with my grandmother in a little canoe many memorable times. She taught me so much on that lake, our whole family from generation to generation lived on that lake. And now it's gone.

Freddie Rogers, Inuvialuit Eskimo of the Northwest Territories, Canada, has seen it.

I have witnessed a whole lot of changes over the years that are due to global warming. Down at Kendall Island, it is getting so warm that it is washing out and eroding. Even before I was born, it used to have its own little bay. But now it's smaller. ... Old Dennis used to live in a cabin, but it washed out. This is happening due to global warming. It is melting the permafrost. The whole island is eroding.

Both these sides of Baby Island are washed out now too. That is where the waves come in. I've noticed that the storms are getting stronger.

We didn't used to have frogs around here. But now we do. I've noticed the last 10 to 15 years that if you go to the pond you hear croaks all the time. They are little things. They migrate from the lake and go to the river. The fish then eat the frogs. It's global warming that's turning this around too.

This cabin had to be moved back from the Coleville to avoid toppling in.

Gwich'in native **Charlie Swaney** of Arctic Village, Alaska, shared his personal experiences that he attributes to the changing climate and "crazy weather" that his villagers talk about: "Another sign of change is that the caribou follow different routes from before. I know part of it has to do with the vegetation that is growing now where their routes used to be. There is so much brush that they can't go through it anymore or don't want to. They don't want to damage the velvet on their horns. Once the velvet on their horns is damaged to any extent, it quits growing and it will stay like that until they shed their horns and start growing new ones. The bulls know that."

These are the words of **Thomas Napageak**, the 26-year-old Inupiat Eskimo whaling captain from Nuiqsut. His name in Eskimo is **Kupa**:

Another effect of oil and gas activity is that many things are changing. I would say that it seems like there is a lot less water nowadays in our little creeks. The rivers are starting to spread here near Nuiqsut. In one place, a 20-foot by 50-foot piece of Coleville River bank is ready to drop. That's where you can see all the permafrost melting. It was on the news that at Kaktovik or Kotzebue that lakes have drained out and that looks like part of global warming as well. And with all these oil activities, you can see brown smoke pollution. We see that all of the time. I think that helps cause global warming.

Here is part of Arctic Gardens' interview with wildlife biologist **Geoff Carroll** of Barrow, where he describes some very interesting and complex relationships. He's lived in Barrow, Alaska for three decades.

AG: So first of all let's talk about global climate change. You're not a Native person, but you have been out here long enough to see some changes and see what's going on. I'm interested in changes you may have seen in sea ice.

Geoff Carroll: Well just from like Barrow perspective you know we are there. It's so obvious that there are major changes going on in the sea ice and you know you've probably seen the information on the Arctic pack ice. Every summer it's farther and farther offshore and we don't see that so much except for longer and longer periods there's not ice around. Ten years ago most of the summer there would be ice within sight and one manifestation of that was when there's so much open water then, when you get an onshore wind, then the waves have so much more fetch, they fill up a lot more fetch and come in and has really increased coastal erosion in a lot of places. So we see that a lot. In addition to that the landfast ice is not nearly as stable as it used to be. Back when I used to work on the whale census you would have these grounded pressure ridges that are formed when the pack ice comes in and smashes against the landfast ice and you know they just anchor that ice and it's there. You know it's there through the spring whereas in recent years we haven't been having those grounded pressure ridges because the ice forms so much later in the fall. I mean actually there have been several events of the ice breaking away and just drifting away with whalers out there and everything else. So it's much less stable and it makes things a lot more difficult for the whalers in the spring and it really has affected their ability to hunt in several of the last five or six years. Now on the other side of that in the fall the ice forms much later than it used to and so that actually has made fall whaling easier and they have been more successful in the fall. Fall whaling they go out with motor boats, kind of larger more powerful boats and basically use heavy equipment to move the whales around once they get them in. So that's kind of it with the ice, as far as land mammals.

AG: Okay, so to the land.

Geoff Carroll: Okay, as far as land mammals, so far with the climate change, you wouldn't really say that it's been particularly detrimental to any of the land mammals. In fact it might have been beneficial. Like I say, the caribou are basically at all time highs right now and most of the herds have gone through a pretty amazing growth spurt.

AG: Except for Porcupine I guess.

Geoff Carroll: Yeah, last 20 years and that could be partially as a result of global warming, but I think that's going to have its limitation because one of the big things with caribou is dealing with insects and being able to get to insect relief areas. For instance, this Teshukpuk caribou herd, they need to be able to get up along the coast on really buggy days and on the other hand they need to be able to move away from the coast easily to feed and when the wind's blowing, then it's less buggy. So they need to be able to move back and forth there, but with these warmer summers it's going to lead probably to more insects and more insect harassment and those caribou, boy, they have a short period of time of the year when they have to put on their fat. You look at their energetics equation and that's only a few months where they're actually on the plus side where they're taking more in then they are using and putting on fat. Most of the year they are just hanging on there, so they need to be able to hit it hard in the summer.

AG: I guess the cows especially need to do that, too.

Geoff Carroll: Oh yeah, you know they're just down to a bag of bones. By the time they got through winter and had a calf, nursed the calf, I mean boy they are just hanging on. They got to get to their food if they are going to make it. So increasingly if it does get warmer and it increases in insect harassment that could eventually be a big factor against them. Other signs of global warming we have seen right here on the Coleville River, are the moose. At the Coleville river the moose are already one of the farthest north moose population in North America and they are kind of right at the edge of habitable range. But that raggedy edge has been moving farther north in the last 10 years and there are more and more moose showing up in my counts than on this downstream part of the Coleville River. Just upstream from Nuiqsut there, even though there's kind of steady hunting pressure there, the number of moose are steadily increasing as the willows are producing more food in this area.

AG: The willows there are increasing?

Geoff Carroll: Yeah, and so it's a pretty good indication, but again it's probably not doing those moose any harm. It is probably providing them some more habitats. Although one thing that happened to the moose population up here in the mid-90's is that they reached pretty high numbers, you know 1600 moose on the Coleville river system in the early-90's. Then they had a series of factors affect them, but one of them was the snowshoe hares moved over the crest of the Brooks Range. They had only been south of the mountains up until that time. Some of them got over the top of the passes and down into the Coleville River system and just erupted. I mean they got into the wide open niche there for them and they expanded through. Just the thing is that they eat the same thing as moose. It's kind of funny to think of hares and moose as competitors but they both are eating the willows. So anyways, this hare eruption came along with some other factors—there were some disease issues and eventually predation issues. But eventually this population had a seventy-five percent decline in the early- to mid-90's. It went from 1600 down to about 400. Since then it has reversed itself again and gradually come back, but part of that was the fact that they were kind of at the edge of the carrying capacity of the range here and then all the sudden this new competitor comes in which was probably the result of warming trends. Anyway, that's part of what pushed them over the edge

AG: Did nature take its course with foxes becoming more abundant and starting to control the hares?

Geoff Carroll: Yeah, yeah, and wolverines as well. I mean we see a lot more wolverines around now. So anyways it seems to be kind of back in balance there and things are never really in balance, they're always in flux. Anyways it's looking more favorable for the moose; their numbers have been increasing together where there is over a thousand moose in the river system. So that's been one thing, another thing we have been seeing just in the last couple of years is we're seeing a lot of red foxes right up to the Arctic coast and for the 20 years before that, I've been observing that basically there was a strip of about 30 to 40 miles along the coast where you would see almost exclusively arctic foxes and then beyond that there were some red foxes. And we have been seeing red foxes right up as far north as Barrow. I mean suddenly they're moving up the coastal regions. So

Fox in the Arctic

that could be partially related.

We have had a lemming high in the past couple of years, lots of lemmings in the tundra. You know they are a small rodent that goes through cycles and when they're high then there are lots of predators around. It's the snowy owls, the yeagers, the ravens. You know everything that eats lemmings. But one of the things that we're sure seeing is that there are a lot more red foxes farther north than they used to be. They really seem to be competitors with the arctic foxes. In fact they eat Arctic foxes. I mean we have seen them take and seen them kill and eat Arctic foxes. Anyways, the dynamics are changing there a little bit. We will see in future years if those red foxes continue to be along the coast or maybe it was more related to those large numbers of lemmings we had there last summer.

As reported by the **Alaska Department of Natural Resources**, warming of boreal forests, including in Alaska, has increased the frequency and severity of forest fires, and fire activity is now regarded as an effect of climate change. In 2004, fire activity in Alaska, with over 600 fires burning over five million acres through August, broke the record set in 1957 (ADNR, 2008). Charlie Swaney experienced it. "Another thing too, is that in the first part of 2000 up until last year, is forest fires. With so much smoke, in 2004 or 2005, you couldn't see some of the mountains during the summer. That's how thick the smoke was here. When caribou get into that kind of stuff, they can't smell, so they don't know what to do. They use their eyes and their noses and their ears to sense danger, but it is mainly their noses. Therefore, they go any direction to get out of the smoke."

Further evidence of dramatic Arctic (and Antarctic) temperature changes is that ice shelves in the Arctic and Antarctic have begun breaking up and disintegrating. The Ward Hunt Ice Shelf, the largest in the Arctic, had been in existence for at least 3000 years, based on carbon dating. It began breaking up in 1992, and today is virtually gone. The smallest Larsen Ice Shelf (A), attached to the Antarctic Peninsula, disintegrated in 1995, and the second largest Larsen Ice Shelf (B), broke up in 2002. A 2008 Antarctic Sun article by Peter Rejcek predicts: "Farther south and larger than the states of New Hampshire and Vermont combined, the Larsen C may disintegrate within the next decade." (Rejcek, October 3, 2008)

When a floating ice shelf breaks up and melts, that melting will not change sea levels because the floating ice displaces the same amount of water it will reintroduce into the oceans as a liquid. However, according to a Queens University study: http://www.science-daily.com/releases/2005/08/050804123855.htm the breakup of Larsen B in Antarctica is affecting land ice that has been held back by the shelf. The result is that once the ice shelf is gone, the glaciers will advance quickly and will move to lower elevations where they will melt more quickly and will calve into the ocean. (Queens University, 2005)

Two enormous masses of land ice that *will* affect sea level are the Antarctic ice sheet and Greenland's ice sheet. The Greenland ice sheet is an unimaginably large body of ice covering about 80% of Greenland, and is two to three km (1.2 to 1.9 *miles*) thick in most places. The Greenland ice sheet's size is second only to the Antarctic ice sheet in mass on the planet. If all the freshwater locked up in the Greenland ice sheet were to melt, scientists estimate that sea level would rise as much as much as seven meters, or about 23 feet.

While most current estimates still calculate that it would take centuries for all this ice to melt, almost all actual research is finding that the results being observed seem to exceed most worst-case scenarios in climate models. As reported by *Science Daily* in the article "An Accurate Picture Of Ice Loss In Greenland," a Delft University of Technology study estimated monthly changes in the mass of Greenland's ice sheet suggest that it is melting at a rate of about 195 cubic kilometres (46.7 cubic miles) per year (Delft University, October 10, 2008). Scientists have also noted rapid movement of parts of the ice sheet leading to significant calving of icebergs into the North Atlantic Ocean.

But *Newsweek*'s science editor, Sharon Begley, reported in 2009: **"Although policy-makers hoped climate models would prove to be alarmist, the opposite is true, particularly in the Arctic."** She went on to state, "More reliable data, however, such as satellite measurements of Greenland's mass, show that it is losing about 52 cubic miles per year and that the melting is accelerating."

There are several reasons that the temperature is rising faster in the Arctic than the remainder of the planet. The factors which tend to increase temperature have a greater effect than those factors that tend to lower temperatures.

According to UNEP, the United Nations Environmental Programme: http://www.unep.org/geo/yearbook/yb2008/ feedbacks that tend to increase temperatures:

- Warming leads to more evaporation and thus more water vapor—a key greenhouse gas—in the atmosphere.
- Warming melts snow and ice, reducing surface reflectivity, thus increasing absorption of solar heat.
- Increased tundra shrubs and soot from increasing wildfires and fossil fuel burning that darken snow and ice also reduce reflectivity.
- Warming leads to thawing permafrost, more rapid decomposition of soil organic matter, more frequent fire and insect disturbances, and increased coastal erosion followed by decomposition of the eroded material. All of these lead to more releases of the greenhouse gases methane (CH_4) and carbon dioxide (CO_2).

Major Arctic feedbacks that reduce warming:

- Tiny particles (aerosols) put into the atmosphere from increasing ?res can reflect solar energy away.
- Warming leads to increased plant growth, which takes up more carbon dioxide. Boreal forest ecosystems that migrate northward sequester even more carbon in vegetation and soils.
- As ice melts and precipitation and runoff increase, there is increased freshwater input to the oceans. This slows the thermohaline circulation and reduces ocean heat transport to the region.

Besides adding water vapor into the atmosphere, evaporation affects temperature in the tropics in a direct way, as explained by Dr. George Woodwell of the Woods Hole Research Center. "There is very little (temperature) change in the tropics, because even though the density of energy received there is very high, it's absorbed by the evaporation of water, and the evaporation of water of course produces water vapor, which carries the energy of evaporation with it. Water vapor enters the circulation patterns of the atmosphere and it's carried in the normal course into the higher latitudes where, as the vapor cools, condensation occurs and the energy is released. So as higher latitudes are warmed differentially, the tropics are not warmed much at all. So if the average temperature change in the Earth is one degree, it's less than that in the tropics and it will be two or three or four times that in the higher latitudes. So in the latitudes that include Alaska, it will be a two or three or four degree change in temperature."

Mentioned above, soot is now believed to be the other major factor regarding the rapid warming of the Arctic compared to the remainder of the planet. Soot is basically pure carbon that is black in color and is produced by combustion of coal and diesel fuel, and by burning wood and animal dung for heating and cooking. As we have discussed, a dark surface absorbs more sunlight and becomes warmer than a lighter color, like snow. So, when the snow cover in Alaska is darkened, even slightly, by soot, it warms more quickly, leading to melting and more warming.

Unlike carbon dioxide, which is a gas that disperses into the atmosphere, seeking equal distribution, soot is a particle of matter that tends to hang in the air and accumulate near its source, only to drift downwind of the source, and then settle onto the ground over time. A *Discover Magazine* article by Peter Fairley (2009) described the climate model results by Drew Shindell, with the NASA Goddard Institute for Space Studies in New York City, which identifies soot that has blown north as the "most likely cause of the Arctic's faster-than-expected warming." Shindell believes that this soot effect is responsible for at least 45% of the 2.7° F warming in the Arctic in the last 40 years. The article went on to say that Shindell's conclusion "dovetails with research by other groups that found soot was as big a contributor as CO2 to shrinking snow cover in the Himalayas."

As the Dr. John Walsh interview below explains, another reason posited for the disproportionate warming of the Arctic is the change in circulation patterns of wind and ocean water.

Rising temperatures are already affecting Alaska, where the spruce bark beetle is breeding faster in the warmer weather. "These pests now sneak in an extra generation each year. From 1993 to 2003, they chewed up 3.4 million acres of Alaskan forest," says the NRDC in their article *Global Warming Puts the Arctic on Thin Ice* (Part 4). The spruce bark beetle has destroyed more than two billion board feet of timber in Alaska in the last 25 years, a process that turns a forest from a carbon sponge into a carbon emitter.

According to the US Fish and Wildlife Service: http://www.fws.gov/Refuges/profiles/index.cfm?id=75635 the third largest conservation area in the National Wildlife Refuge System, the nine million acre Yukon Flats National Wildlife Refuge: http://yukonflats.fws.gov/ is located in eastern interior Alaska. It includes the Yukon Flats, a vast wetland basin bisected by the Yukon River. The basin is underlain by permafrost and includes a complex network of lakes, streams, and rivers. The area is characterized by mixed forests dominated by spruce, birch, and aspen.

The Wilderness Society published a recent study called "Climate Change Implications for Yukon Flats National Wildlife Refuge," by Wendy Loya (2009): http://wilderness.org/files/Yukon%20Flats%20Refuge%20Climate%20Implications.pdf One of the findings is that "... by the end of the [21st] century, the growing season could be one month longer. This would affect wildlife mating cycles, plant growth and flowering, hunting seasons, and water availability in the soil and rivers." (Loya, 2009) Think about the changes to the growing season. Ducks that occupy Yukon Flats for mating and nesting have evolved a pattern where their eggs mature and the hatchlings begin their own search for food usually within a day or two of hatching. Their early diet consists of mosquito larvae, among other things. Availability of adequate food is critical not only to body mass, but also to the regulation of the ducklings' body temperatures. The ducks hatch just as the mosquito larvae are available. It's a beautiful system. What will happen if warmer and drier conditions affect the availability of the mosquito larvae at the time the hatchlings come looking for their first meal? Will the hatching timetable adjust quickly enough to match the mosquito larva availability? It's not difficult to understand that altering this timing over a short period will mean disaster for the ducks.

The Wilderness Society study summary says "The Yukon Flats NWR is likely to become warmer and drier over the next century. Warmer temperatures will cause changes in the condition and health of wildlife habitat. Despite modest increases in precipitation, conditions will become much drier due to warmer temperatures and a longer frost-free season, affecting soil moisture and river levels. Variability in temperatures during spring and fall could also affect the amount of precipitation that falls as snow versus rain."

For insight into research of climate change effects in the Arctic, we present our interview with a prominent researcher of climate change, with a focus on the Arctic.

Dr. John Walsh, the President's Professor of Global Change at the University of Alaska at Fairbanks. He is the chief scientist in the International Arctic Research Center there and is also the Director of the National Oceanic and Atmospheric Center, a cooperative institute that does research for NOAA. The Center is tasked with bridging NOAA research with stakeholder interest, with stakeholders including residents, commercial companies, non-profits and a variety of potential groups.

My research focuses on four major areas, with the first area being ocean and sea ice. In collaboration with Russians, we actually use a Russian ice breaker and each year we have a cruise to the Arctic Ocean and deploy moorings to measure the temperature, salinity and current fields in the Arctic Ocean. We attempt to make sense of the measurements by putting them in with larger databases on the Arctic Ocean. The intent of that project is to try to get a handle on changes in the Arctic Ocean, why the changes are occurring, why sea ice is changing, and that type of thing.

A second area is on the terrestrial side—in particular, permafrost and vegetation in the Arctic. We have several projects to determine whether the landscape is undergoing changes—whether permafrost is changing in any systematic way. We have a network of what we call permafrost observatories which are measurement sites around the state that keep track of the soil temperatures and the depth of thaw during the summer. The automated instruments are put into the ground and are battery powered so they need to be tended to about once a year. They have data loggers that record the information and there are probably 50 of those sites around the state. We also work with the Russians and have some over in Siberia as well. There are some modelers who try to put all that data into a larger framework of vegetation and climate.

The third area of focus is the atmosphere—we look at how the atmosphere of the Arctic is changing and what its connections are with the lower latitudes. What is becoming clear is that the Arctic atmosphere is not acting in isolation; the forcings from the middle latitudes and even the tropics have something to do with the changes we are seeing in the Arctic.

The fourth area is what I call trace gases: carbon dioxide, methane, and some of the other greenhouse gases as well as non-greenhouse gases that are exchanged from the surface in the Arctic. That means that terrestrial and ocean surfaces exchange those trace gases and both might be impacting the bigger picture of climate change and could be somewhat related to the methane stores below the surface. There are actually large reservoirs or stockpiles of methane in the permafrost, and then deeper down below the ocean floor are methane hydrates. If methane hydrates are released sometime in the future because of climate change, they represent potentially major consequences for the global climate. We have some biogeochemists who are measuring these exchanges of the trace gases between the atmosphere and the land surface and they are trying to get at the drivers and what might happen in the future.

The climate change we are researching has a fairly substantial component that is natural. We would say that before 200 years ago, including major climate changes like the ice ages, essentially all the climate change that happened was natural. Even in the present era when there is apparently an anthropogenic component, there is still a large natural component to the changes. Those natural changes don't just include volcanoes and solar activity, things people normally regard as natural. They also include atmospheric circulation, the wind patterns that go through changes. These changes can occur with time scales of a year, a decade, or several decades. That means that for a couple of decades the wind pattern may lock into a preferred mode that would produce climate anomalies, departures from the normal climate in a particular area. Then, that wind pattern may shift back to another mode. Some of those type changes have affected Alaska in the last 50 years. The impacts of those circulations can be substantial and can amount to several degrees Celsius, or as much as five to eight degrees Fahrenheit, over a fairly short period of several years. Those changes can be at least as large and in some cases larger than the anthropogenic component to climate change. We have to view the changes as naturally occurring ones that are superimposed on whatever humans may be doing to the climate system.

There have been some major climate impacts over the past 50 years. In Alaska, I would distinguish changes between the interior parts of the state and the coastal areas. The interior region change seems to be an earlier spring and later freeze-up in the fall which means that the warm season and the growing season are becoming longer. There are some fairly striking examples of dates of snow disappearance for example. The snow has been disappearing earlier over a good part of the state. The green up, the leafing out of the vegetation, has been occurring earlier. Here in Fairbanks, the growing season length between the last spring freeze and the first fall freeze has increased from about 80 days a hundred years ago, to around 120 days now. That is a 50 percent increase! That is something that is certainly noticeable to people around here—not just the gardeners, but people that have lived here for periods of decades.

The winter temperatures in the interior part of the state have warmed by eight or nine degrees Fahrenheit in the last 50 years. That is a big change in climate terms. Eight or nine degrees are noticeable to people as well. There are just a lot fewer -40 days than there used to be and the data shows that. When these -40° periods do come, they don't last as long as they did in the past.

There are other changes occurring in the interior, where the fire seasons, at least the extreme fire seasons, are tending to be more common. There are lots of fires and lots of area burned. This is tied in with the longer summer growing season because the chances of a good dry stretch go up substantially, and a dry stretch is what it takes to get a fire season into the severe category.

The insect infestations seem to be a real factor around here as well. There are species of insects that are working their way into the interior and the southern part of the state and doing a fair amount of damage to certain types of trees. The spruce bark beetle did a number on the Kenai Peninsula forest area in the last decade. That is an insect that requires two relatively mild winters in succession to go through its full life cycle and invade the trees. Here in the interior, there is a birch borer, a leaf miner that is doing a fair amount of damage. The birch trees are fairly widespread in the interior, and this is a real concern of the forestry community.

On the other hand, in the coastal areas the big impact seems to be tied to sea ice. The sea ice has been retreating larger distances offshore, and this condition has been in the news quite a bit in the last few years. Just this past week, we had a new record minimum for ice coverage in the Arctic Ocean. That impacts the coastal communities as it affects their access to offshore waters during the spring whaling season, for example. The communities are finding the ice is less stable because it is degrading earlier. Perhaps more importantly for the long term, the additional open water increases the vulnerability to floods and erosion along the coast. With more open water, any storm systems that come along can have more open water to build up waves. It's the waves that really impact the coastlines and the infrastructure along the coast, especially in the western part of the state. There have been some extreme storm events with coastal flooding that have not been recorded in the preceding decades. If sea level does rise over the next several decades, that will only make things worse because you will have a higher base sea level that these wave events are superimposed on.

I should add other impacts we are seeing in the marine area. There are papers on this that have come out in the scientific literature in the last three years which report that in the Bering Sea, the marine ecosystem seems to be shifting northward. In the Bering Sea and in the Gulf of Alaska, they are finding different fish and other types of marine life farther north than they have been found in the last several decades. If the northward shift continues, there may have to be a relocation of some of the fishing and processing operations.

The more serious negative impact related to the loss of sea ice will be to the marine mammals that depend on sea ice for their habitat. That group includes walrus, certain types of seals, and the polar bear. As the ice retreats offshore or towards the north, these marine mammals are going to have less access to the ice that they depend on as a platform for either reproduction or food. There are signs that the polar bears, at least in the Alaskan sector, are in that category. There are signs that walruses as well are being impacted farther south down in the Bering Sea since the ice is less common than it was a decade ago.

In fact, the loss of sea ice is perhaps the most shocking impact I have seen, and I don't think anyone would have anticipated it 10 or 20 years ago. I remember back in the 70's when the oil companies tried to supply the North Slope when the pipeline was under construction. The major supplies had to go through the Bering Strait and then past Bar-

row over to Prudhoe. Several years in a row there, the barges barely made it because the ice was essentially up against the coast all summer. It was touch and go. Here we are 30 years later and the ice is offshore by several hundred miles. You could drive an armada through there. There are some signs by mid-century that essentially all the ice in the Arctic Ocean could be gone in the summer. The melt could be complete. That's a major change in the system.

You have countries now talking about claims of the pieces of the Arctic Ocean for their own purposes because it looks like the area is going to become more viable commercially. That is an area where climate change may be having political ramifications which would not have been foreseen a decade ago.

Much of what we believe about future climate change comes from climate models. The accuracy of those models is difficult to assess because there really haven't been analogs for what we are going through right now with the change in greenhouse gas concentrations. We have not had greenhouse gases rise rapidly over a short period like they have in the last 50 to 100 years. If one steps back just a few decades back to the 1970's there was actually a downturn cooling of temperatures that went on from the 50's to the 70's. There was talk back in the 70's of an impending ice age. To take the really long term perspective, we are about due for an ice age. That slight cooling of just a degree or two back in the 50's to 70's did have the possibilities of an ice age coming on. Since then, just in one generation, we have completely reversed what we were anticipating. There is a good physical basis for this anticipation of continued warming because there is no doubt that greenhouse gases are increasing in concentration, and they do tend to have a warming effect in terms of their radiative properties. If one were a betting person, you would certainly go with the trend towards warmer conditions. We do need to keep in mind these changes that can happen over several decades. That cooling from the 50's to the 70's is a reminder that other factors can come into the picture and either diminish or enhance a warming.

I have observed firsthand some of the effects on indigenous life caused by climate change in the Arctic based on visits and conversations, and we actually have a graduate student doing a dissertation out in the western part of the state, the Koyukuk River area. These communities have reported the tendency towards a longer snow-free season that's consistent with the increase in the growing season length that the instrumental data shows. They are reporting that the snow tends to degrade earlier in the spring and that does affect their outdoor activities. In the fall, they are reporting a later freeze-up and a longer period of wet ground conditions which makes it tough to get around thereby affecting their hunting activities. Fall is a big hunting season for the Native communities.

Other pervasive reports that we are hearing are that the lake levels are decreasing. That's true not just in Alaska, but also in parts of Siberia in the last few years. One potent hypothesis for that is that in areas where the permafrost is discontinuous, lakes that are on permafrost are losing some of their water through drainage as permafrost degrades in small pockets underneath the lake. It's hard to find a lake that has become larger. You can see some of this lake degradation around Fairbanks when you fly in or out if you come in over this area between Fairbanks and the Alaska Range, the Tanana Flats, you see a lot of dried-up lakes, areas that are essentially grass with no trees that are in the surrounding areas.

Even though the energy industry is not a focus, we do have one project that is looking at the impacts of the energy industry on the northern environment, particularly in terms of ice roads in the tundra. Oil companies are the ones building the ice roads for the most part, although it is really an access issue rather than a direct energy impact. In connection with this general warming and the shortening of the winter season, the time length of the permitted tundra travel each winter has shortened quite a bit over the last 40 years by something like a half. The ground has to be sufficiently frozen to support the weight of vehicles. It used to be 200 days back in the 60's and 70's and now it is close to 100 days. Their access to areas is limited and their test wells have to be completed in a shortened period.

Our real goal with our work is to reduce some of the significant uncertainty that surrounds predictions of climate change in this present century out through 2100 or 2150. The climate models are driven by greenhouse gas emission scenarios among other things, and there is a large spread among those models about how much warming will occur here and in other areas over the next century. We have large uncertainty for how much emission rates are going to change based on policy issues, energy availability, and types of energy that are used.

Technology is clearly part of the challenge here. Right now, the thinking seems to be through mid-century that the factor that dominates uncertainty is the natural variability in the system. If we happen to run into a decade or two when a natural variation takes us the other way from the background trend, we may well have some surprises as far as the climate goes. Beyond mid-century the thinking is that these greenhouse gases are the main source of the uncertainty, so we really have a double whammy as we try to narrow down the uncertainty range. So we compare models here at the center to see which ones do the best in demonstrating sensitivities that should be relevant to greenhouse gases, such things as solar forcing or volcanic forcing.

The other aspect of this uncertainty reduction is the diagnosis of the changes that are going on right now. Things like the sea ice retreat going on even more rapidly than people had anticipated five or ten years ago. The burning question is what is really behind it. Is it warming of the ocean surface that is causing melting and direct loss in that respect? Is it a change in the in-flow of warmer water from the Atlantic? Is there something else going on? Are the clouds changing, for example? There are a number of factors that come into play here when we are trying to figure out why the ice is decreasing as rapidly as it is. There is most likely some sort of feedback going on that is tied in with the tendency for open water to absorb solar energy more than an ice covered ocean would.

We get asked if we believe that humans are contributing to global warming. I would answer that we are very certain that humans are contributing to global warming. In fact I worked with the IPCC as part of their Fourth Assessment, and they've put a 95% confidence on the likelihood that humans have contributed most of the warming. The IPCC is the Intergovernmental Panel on Climate Change, an international group that assesses climate change every six or seven years. The key phrase is there is solid evidence and unanimity of opinion of scientists that humans have contributed to the warming.

Naturally, the effects will vary by location. The warming in Alaska, for example, has been larger than almost anywhere else in the world, especially in the winter and spring as we mentioned a while ago. At least some of that warming does seem to be the consequence of a circulation shift. There is an atmospheric circulation pattern that involves the north Pacific centers of action, the Aleutian Low and the Subtropical High, which went through a shift back in the '70's that caused a jump in Alaskan temperatures of a few de-

grees. Perhaps half is due to this shift in the wind pattern. We would be stretching things to say that the greenhouse effect and anthropogenic activity is responsible for a warming of the full magnitude that we have seen in this state. There are other examples of changed circulation patterns such as Northern Europe and Northern Asia. These things are superimposed on this radiative driving that comes from greenhouse gases. It may be that there is a linkage between greenhouse gases and the circulation shifts. You will not find a solid agreement among scientists that wind patterns are going to shift in certain ways as greenhouse gases increase. We are left with this conclusion that humans are contributing, but so are the circulation shifts which at this point are left in the category of natural variability. So I would say that humans almost certainly contribute to what's happened over the past 50 years or so, but human activity is not the whole story.

Naturally, we think not only about the impacts we see, but also about solutions. I don't have any silver bullets, but I do think that the alternative energy route is the savior if there is one out there. The stimulus to develop and implement the alternative technologies should be the number one priority. We may be driven to less oil usage by availability rather than by policy. That does leave coal as a major greenhouse gas uncertainty. There's a lot of it and it has a large greenhouse footprint. The technology comes into the picture again to see if we can use coal in a relatively greenhouse-minimized way. That again is going to fall on the technological investment. We have the alternative energy sources and perhaps nuclear energy is going to need to be factored into the mix if we are going to make a dent in the greenhouse emissions.

I think stabilizing is not an unrealistic goal, and a substantial reduction is really going to require some fundamental changes in energy usage. We have a country that has certain heating requirements and it certainly has transportation requirements that are big-time both at the individual level and the public level, like aircraft transportation and that type of thing. We have to look at how transportation is one of the fossil fuel consumers. That's not going to change overnight. Large scales changes are going to be painful. So I am not optimistic of a major reduction, but I do think that with greater fuel efficiency in vehicles and building heating, we could at least stabilize without a major shock to the system.

On a local level, individuals can modify their lifestyle to have more energy efficient housing and that type of thing. My view is that individual contributions can be most effective if they are tied to the larger political arena. If we can get the message through to the legislators to act at the state and national levels, I think we may be able to do more than acting locally because the policy action on the state, federal, and international level is what is going to make the bigger changes in the large-scale emission scenarios. We are going to need guidance and more than guidance. We'll need policy and legislation from the top. It's the state and the federal levels that I am referring to. That has not happened yet. Until it does, I think people are not going to voluntarily do their little bit to the point where it will make a major difference."

Conclusion: This chapter has reported on the background and history of the climate change issue, the science of global warming and climate change, and the effects of climate change on the Arctic regions of the planet, particularly in North America. We have discussed the important role of the IPCC, and we have reported very recent findings from scientists and organizations that simply increase the alarm that climate change is happening faster and more dramatically than predicted. We have discussed the current effects of methane, and the enormous potential additional menace of methane, which if released as a feedback will only exacerbate the threat from climate change.

As societies continue to do what societies do—that is, create wealth and try to improve standards of living—while always taking the path of least resistance, the civilization that has evolved into the present is racing into a future with unsustainable practices and expectations. The results that societies have achieved, especially the "developed" countries, are the envy of the "developing" world, and are used as objectives to be achieved universally. The only problem is that the paradigms in place up until the present have seemed immutable and unlimited. We now know that they are neither. Our report on climate change illustrates but one outcome of blindly pursuing growth without allowing for all the costs.

As Lester Brown reports in "Our Global Ponzi Economy" (found on Earth Policy.org Book Bytes): http://www.earthpolicy.org/index.php?/book_bytes/2009/pb4ch01_ss4

Our mismanaged world economy today has many of the characteristics of a Ponzi scheme. A Ponzi scheme takes payments from a broad base of investors and uses these to pay off returns. It creates the illusion that it is providing a highly attractive rate of return on investment as a result of savvy investment decisions when in fact these irresistibly high earnings are in part the result of consuming the asset base itself. A Ponzi scheme investment fund can last only as long as the flow of new investments is sufficient to sustain the high rates of return paid out to previous investors. When this is no longer possible, the scheme collapses—just as Bernard Madoff's $65-billion investment fund did in December 2008.

Although the functioning of the global economy and a Ponzi investment scheme are not entirely analogous, there are some disturbing parallels. As recently as 1950 or so, the world economy was living more or less within its means, consuming only the sustainable yield, the interest of the natural systems that support it. But then as the economy doubled, and doubled again, and yet again, multiplying eightfold, it began to outrun sustainable yields and to consume the asset base itself.

In a 2002 study published by the U.S. National Academy of Sciences, a team of scientists concluded that humanity's collective demands first surpassed the earth's regenerative capacity around 1980. As of 2009 global demands on natural systems exceed their sustainable yield capacity by nearly 30 percent. This means we are meeting current demands in part by consuming the earth's natural assets, setting the stage for an eventual Ponzi-type collapse when these assets are depleted.

As of mid-2009, nearly all the world's major aquifers were being over-pumped. We have more irrigation water than before the over-pumping began, in true Ponzi fashion. We get the feeling that we're doing very well in agriculture—but the reality is that an estimated 400 million people are today being fed by over-pumping, a process that is by definition short-term. With aquifers being depleted, this water-based food bubble is about to burst.

A similar situation exists with the melting of mountain glaciers. When glaciers first start to melt, flows in the rivers and the irrigation canals they feed are larger than before the melting started. But after a point, as smaller glaciers disappear and larger ones shrink, the amount of ice melt declines and the river flow diminishes. Thus we have two water-based Ponzi schemes running in parallel in agriculture.

And there are more such schemes. As human and livestock populations grow more or less apace, the rising demand for forage eventually exceeds the sustainable yield of grasslands. As a result, the grass deteriorates, leaving the land bare, allowing it to turn to desert. In this Ponzi scheme, herders are forced to rely on food aid or they migrate to cities.

Three fourths of oceanic fisheries are now being fished at or beyond capacity or are recovering from overexploitation. If we continue with business as usual, many of these fisheries will collapse. Overfishing, simply defined, means we are taking fish from the oceans faster than they can reproduce. The cod fishery off the coast of Newfoundland in Canada is a prime example of what can happen. Long one of the world's most productive fisheries, it collapsed in the early 1990s and may never recover.

Paul Hawken, author of Blessed Unrest, puts it well: "At present we are stealing the future, selling it in the present, and calling it gross domestic product. We can just as easily have an economy that is based on healing the future instead of stealing it. We can either create assets for the future or take the assets of the future. One is called restoration and the other exploitation." The larger question is, If we continue with business as usual—with over-pumping, overgrazing, over-plowing, overfishing, and overloading the atmosphere with carbon dioxide—how long will it be before the Ponzi economy unravels and collapses? No one knows. Our industrial civilization has not been here before.

Unlike Bernard Madoff's Ponzi scheme, which was set up with the knowledge that it would eventually fall apart, our global Ponzi economy was not intended to collapse. It is on a collision path because of market forces, perverse incentives, and poorly chosen measures of progress.

In addition to consuming our asset base, we have devised some clever techniques for leaving costs off the books—much like the disgraced and bankrupt Texas-based energy company Enron did some years ago. For example, when we use electricity from a coal-fired power plant we get a monthly bill from the local utility. It includes the cost of mining coal, transporting it to the power plant, burning it, generating the electricity, and delivering electricity to our homes. It does not, however, include any costs of the climate change caused by burning coal. That bill will come later—and it will likely be delivered to our children. Unfortunately for them, their bill for our coal use will be even larger than ours.

When Sir Nicholas Stern, former chief economist at the World Bank, released his groundbreaking 2006 study on the future costs of climate change, he talked about a massive market failure. He was referring to the failure of the market to incorporate the costs of climate change in the price of fossil fuels. According to Stern, the costs are measured in the trillions of dollars. The difference between the market prices for fossil fuels and an honest price that also incorporates their environmental costs to society is huge.

As economic decision makers we all depend on the market for information to guide us, but the market is giving us incomplete information, and as a result we are making bad decisions. One of the best examples of this can be seen in the

United States, where the gasoline pump price was around $3 per gallon in mid-2009. This reflects only the cost of finding the oil, pumping it to the surface, refining it into gasoline, and delivering the gas to service stations. It overlooks the costs of climate change as well as the costs of tax subsidies to the oil industry, the burgeoning military costs of protecting access to oil in the politically unstable Middle East, and the health care costs of treating respiratory illnesses caused by breathing polluted air. These indirect costs now total some $12 per gallon. In reality, burning gasoline is very costly, but the market tells us it is cheap.

The market also does not respect the carrying capacity of natural systems. For example, if a fishery is being continuously overfished, the catch eventually will begin to shrink and prices will rise, encouraging even more investment in fishing trawlers. The inevitable result is a precipitous decline in the catch and the collapse of the fishery.

Today we need a realistic view about the relationship between the economy and the environment. We also need, more than ever before, political leaders who can see the big picture. And since the principal advisors to government are economists, we need either economists who can think like ecologists or more ecological advisors. Otherwise, market behavior—including its failure to include the indirect costs of goods and services, to value nature's services, and to respect sustainable-yield thresholds—will cause the destruction of the economy's natural support systems, and our global Ponzi scheme will fall apart.

We believe that the following interviews we conducted with **Dr. George Woodwell** in May 2009, and again in December 2009, following the United Nations Climate Change Conference in Copenhagen, makes the urgency of appropriate action to mitigate climate change quite clear.

A leading U.S. scientist whose focus has been global climate change is Dr. George Woodwell, founder of the Woods Hole Research Center in Massachusetts, an ecologist with broad interests in global environmental issues and policies.

Prior to founding the Woods Hole Research Center, Dr. Woodwell was founder and director of the Ecosystems Center of the Marine Biological Laboratory in Woods Hole and, earlier, a senior scientist at Brookhaven National Laboratory. He was also a founding trustee and continues to serve on the board of the Natural Resources Defense Council. He is a former chairman of the board of trustees and member of the National Council of the World Wildlife Fund, a founding trustee of the World Resources Institute, a founder and currently an honorary member of the board of trustees of the Environmental Defense Fund, and former president of the Ecological Society of America. Dr. Woodwell is the author of more than 300 major papers and books on ecology. He holds a doctorate in botany from Duke University and is the recipient of several honorary degrees as well as the 1996 Heinz Environmental Award and the Volvo Environment Prize of 2001. He is a member of the National Academy of Sciences and a fellow of the American Academy of Arts and Sciences

Dr. Woodwell founded the Woods Hole Research Center nearly 25 years ago after founding and leading a research institute within the Marine Biological Laboratory in Woods Hole, but came to see that the purposes of the Laboratory and the ecological world were divergent, and sought to establish his own board of trustees in a separate institution with a focus on ecology.

He had, years earlier, joined the staff of Brookhaven National Laboratory to study the ecological effects of ionizing radiation. That work involved a famous experiment in which a late successional oak-pine forest was exposed to gamma radiation over 15 years. He also led research on the persistence and effects of DDT in the general environment—how the residues moved through the environment and accumulated and affected living systems. Those findings led to a series of lawsuits in Long Island and Michigan and Wisconsin whose overall success produced the Environmental Defense Fund. The Environmental Defense Fund specifically took the toxic substances issue as its topic and has pursued it consistently and successfully over more than 40 years.

One of the issues at Brookhaven was to figure out what the environmental effects of chronic high exposure to ionizing radiation might be and how to measure them. He and his colleagues dealt with forests because forests have such a large role in defining the global environment. They picked a forest stand on the Brookhaven tract in central Long Island, New York, and installed a big source of gamma radiation.

The effect was really surprising to Dr. Woodwell, because he did not think of ionizing radiation as something that the vegetation would be adapted to or that there would be a systematic, easily defined response to it. But the response was what he called systematic impoverishment of the forest. The issue of biotic impoverishment emerged as a generality, another central law of nature caused not only by ionizing radiation, but by almost any chronic environmental change, whether toxic effects of poisons from a smelter, other systematic changes in the chemistry of environment, or a chronic physical disturbance including a change in climate. According to Dr. Woodwell, "It is the inverse of succession. Abandon a field or a garden and it will turn into forest in the normally naturally forested parts of the Earth, over a period of 50 years or so, and that forest builds up. The evolutionary pattern of course has been the same. Evolution has produced forests more and more complicated, longer life- cycled organisms and more of them, and that goes on. So evolution and succession go in one direction; biotic impoverishment goes in the other direction. It's caused by all sorts of chronic disturbance including changing the climate out from under the forest. The pattern of change is consistent and predictable."

So they worked out ways of measuring changes in the forest. One of them was to measure the metabolism—the respiration and photosynthesis of an entire forest. They could measure the accumulation of carbon dioxide in the forest on Long Island and learn how temperature inversions would affect it. "So you could see the buildup overnight—just linear buildup of carbon dioxide—and plot that hour by hour. The rate of accumulation defined the metabolism of the landscape, how many grams of carbon were being respired per unit of forest area. It was the first time as far as I know that anyone had measured the metabolism of the forest. Now, more than 40 years later, there are many techniques for making such measurements using towers, but even the idea of it was new then."

They had ways of measuring photosynthesis as well, so they worked out the equations that defined the metabolism of the landscape. They used the then-new devices that used infra-red absorption to measure carbon dioxide concentrations with great accuracy on a continuous basis. Such instruments, called infra-red gas analyzers, could practically measure a single molecule of carbon dioxide. These measurements offered new insights into nature. They were exciting times. Dr. Woodwell continued:

I became persuaded over time that the process of systematic impoverishment of natural communities was a very important transition in the world that was underway as a result of all the various disturbances that we introduce into the Earth. And once one starts thinking that way, one looks around and sees the progressive impoverishment of forests, all terrestrial systems, aquatic systems as well, and the Earth as a whole. So that's been a core observation, a new perspective, in all the things that we've done.

Early in the game, more than 40 years ago, we decided that climatic disruption was the big issue that had to be pursued systematically. ***"We've known about the buildup of carbon dioxide for more than a century."***

In preparation for the 1972 Stockholm Meeting on Human Environment, Carl Wilson, who was then at MIT, arranged a major conference at Williams College, a summer conference. This was in '72 so that conference must have been in '71 in the summer. The climatologists were there from NCAR, National Center for Atmospheric Research, and we had a big discussion about the carbon dioxide problem [emphasis added], which is what we called it at that time.

I was amazed that they decided that there really wasn't anything to be concerned about because you couldn't measure any changes in the world. The world hadn't warmed and first principles really weren't the basis on which to really do anything about it. I was incensed, really angry, and I thought that's pretty dumb. You're saying that here you've got a gun pointed at your head and it hasn't gone off yet so you don't worry about it. I was astonished that in the early 70's we were not able to get climatologists to say anything that was close to serious about the scary proposition that we were changing the composition of the atmosphere in a way that would change the climates of the Earth.

But we did know what would happen; it wasn't long at all before we had that pretty well defined. It was simply that the effect would be to warm the continental centers and dry them out. That would be a serious problem, it would happen fairly rapidly, and I wrote papers to that effect and so did others. In fact I gave testimony in the Congress in 1979 to that effect and I went recently to look up that testimony. All the things that we were saying at that time have come true. They're all true now and I'm saying the same thing now that I was saying then, that this is a big issue and how it will proceed can be predicted.

So that's happened of course and right now we are seeing droughts on every continent: droughts in central Asia, South America, Africa, droughts in North America; the Southwest is drying out, Mexico City is rationing water, the central valley of California is short of water, Arizona's forests are drying out. Bark beetles are rampant because as the trees suffer under drought they become vulnerable to invasion by bark beetles in particular, which are good at detecting hardship in trees. The same thing is happening and has happened over the past 10 years in southeastern Alaska, and the frequency of fire across the Russian boreal forest of Asia is rising as is frequency of fire across the North America boreal forest.

"You're saying that here you've got a gun pointed at your head and it hasn't gone off yet so you don't worry about it."

Respiration is very sensitive to temperature; photosynthesis is not. Respiration does not respond to light. Photosynthesis requires light and occurs only in daylight when the moisture conditions are correct. Respiration goes on all the time. But ***raise the temperature a small amount and the respiration of the whole landscape rises, not just*** *the respiration of trees, but the decay of organic matter in soils and the respiration of all plants. So changing the temperature is a big deal, a big, big thing.*

It has little effect on photosynthesis, but other disruptions do affect photosynthesis, and most do not improve it.

They are saying now that we could reduce the CO2 emissions by 80 percent by 2050 and keep the CO2 concentration in the atmosphere at 450 ppm or below. They suggest that such a level would be safe. That is simply not true. ... going to 450 ppm is totally unacceptable.

It is certainly true that the continental centers are warmer; they are drying out and we're having increasing drought, serious drought right now. The warming in the high latitudes also puts all those pools of carbon in the Arctic soils and in the boreal forest into play. Warming them up tends to speed their decay and to dump their carbon stores into the atmosphere. The carbon comes forth as both carbon dioxide and methane, the product of anaerobic respiration. Those additional emissions make the problem worse. So the warming feeds on the warming, there is no question about that, and there are several ways that that happens.

It is a frightening proposition, and it is neglected in most of the current appraisals. So what can be done is not being thought of in a strictly biophysical sense. It's being thought of in an economic and political sense, and the politicians and economists make compromises with the biophysics that just cannot be made.

They are saying now that we could reduce the CO2 emissions by 80 percent by 2050 and keep the CO2 concentration in the atmosphere at 450 ppm or below. They suggest that such a level would be safe. That is simply not true. The CO2 content of the atmosphere at the moment is 387 ppm. We have an additional warming built into that 387 ppm, yet unrealized. If we were to stabilize the atmosphere at 387 ppm carbon dioxide, there will be a further unknown additional rise in temperature. We already have unacceptable effects. A further warming will be devastating. So going to 450 ppm is totally unacceptable. It really leads to chaos and it will probably lead to runaway carbon dioxide emissions as large pools of carbon in forests and soils become mobilized.

Present total emissions of carbon are about ten billion tons of carbon a year. That's about eight and half billion tons from burning fossil fuels and about one and half billion tons from deforestation. We have agreed under the 1992 Framework Convention on Climate Change to join with the rest of the world in stabilizing the carbon dioxide content of the atmosphere at levels that will protect human interest and nature. And that's clearly at a level below what the carbon dioxide content of the atmosphere is at the moment. So we are beyond our own agreement under that treaty. The US has ratified the Framework Convention on Climate Change—not the Kyoto Protocol, but the Framework Convention was ratified by virtually all nations and is the law of the land in the U.S.

So can we reach stability? Well the current imbalance, the ten billion tons, is leading to an annual buildup in that atmosphere of roughly five billion tons. It varies—sometimes more, sometimes less than that year by year—but it is rising. So the immediate challenge is to get rid of emissions in the amount of five billion tons. We have to reduce global emissions by that much to stabilize at 387 ppm. That's only the first step of course, but how could we do it?

We have to do it, and there are only two ways no matter what they say about alcohol, coal, and all the other things they are talking about. There really are only two ways to deal with billions of tons of carbon, an enormous amount of carbon. Those have to do with managing forests and controlling the emissions from burning fossil fuels. Deforestation is producing about one and a half billion tons of carbon annually. If we were to decide as a world that all the primary forests of the Earth should be preserved, we would immediately reduce global emissions by 1.6 billion tons of carbon annually. That decision would mean that we would not replace any more primary forests with agriculture nor would we destroy them for any other purpose. There would be many advantages in addition to saving one and one half billion tons of carbon emissions.

If we then turned and said we must restore forests in the normally, naturally forested parts of the Earth to the extent of a million to two million square kilometers, we would remove another billion tons of carbon from the atmosphere annually.

So we can get two and a half billion tons out of the five billion tons simply by managing forests. And then if we could reduce the use of fossil fuels on a global basis by two and half billion tons, or about 25%, we have it. So that's possible too, but it would take leadership on the part of the United States. The United States would have to say we're going to make a major contribution to this objective in the short term. So it takes Obama's standing on the steps of the White House and asking the nation to join in a major change in how we do things and offer leadership to the world.

The problem we face is the feedbacks. The feedbacks are largely positive feedbacks of the warming of the Earth: the warming makes the warming worse. There are feedbacks involving the oceans—the oceans absorb roughly two billion tons currently of carbon because of the differential concentration between atmosphere and surface water of the oceans.

As the surface water warms it holds less carbon dioxide, so warming the oceans reduces that net flow of carbon from the atmosphere into the oceans. And of course if we stabilize the concentration of carbon in the atmosphere that difference will decline... and the flow into the oceans will be reduced as well. Warming the oceans reduces the capacity of the oceans for absorbing carbon. Warm it enough and it will emit carbon into the atmosphere, and of course, as I said before, warming the boreal forest increases respiration of trees and increases the respiration (decay) of organic matter in soils.

There is a sufficient pool of carbon in the soils and in the trees of the boreal forest to flood the atmosphere with carbon. Boreal forests probably carry on about a third of the total respiration of the landscapes of the world, which is of the order of a hundred billion tons of carbon transferred a year. So that's thirty billion tons. Increase the respiration by 10 percent and that's three billion tons of additional carbon just right there. It is going to come out of the forest. So that's big business and that's why one realizes that this business of changing the temperature is not a trifling matter.

We have about 6.8 billion people on the planet right now, headed toward nine billion or more, competing for food in a world in which the continental centers are drying out, when the big agricultural regions are near or beyond their limits for water, when we're heavily reliant on an industrial agriculture that is heavily reliant on fossil fuels and, for that reason alone, fundamentally unstable—certainly unstable in the face of shortages of water—and we march on.

Then I have a picture of the southern Amazon basin showing the forest being eroded away by the expansion of industrial agriculture to produce soy. Those forests have trees that root as deeply as 40 to 60 feet. So they're tapping a soil profile that is really tremen-

dous, and has large reserves of water and nutrients. Do away with the forest and replace it with agriculture and we're doing away with this big machine which evaporates water into the atmosphere and feeds the atmospheric circulation of the world, and replacing it with soy, which is a shallow-rooted annual crop and doesn't produce all that water into the atmosphere... or the cooling. Walk out of that cool tropical forest that's moist and has maybe five different layers of tree leaves in it absorbing the solar energy into one of those open fields and the weight of the sun is just incredible. In the stifling heat one wonders how soy can survive in that circumstance, but it does. Realize that this is a totally different climatic regime.

Looking at a landscape that's going from forest to industrial agriculture in the tropics is looking at the landscape that's going from cool to hot—from cool and moist to hot and dry. And not only that, but it affects the neighborhood, the region and the global circulation of the atmosphere. This is not a trifling change. We're turning thousands of square miles into industrial soy production, probably a short-lived phenomenon because many crops in the tropics last for just a few years before nutrient deficiencies, diseases, or market fluctuations catch up with them. Restoration of the forests may not be possible at all, certainly not in time of interest to this civilization. We are making a Faustian bargain in destroying forests for commercial purpose.

I am describing the biotic impoverishment of the tropics. Turning it from forest into industrial agriculture destroys the forest, which is permanently destroyed as far as we're concerned, and it's not going to recover in a short time of interest to us. It dumps the carbon into the atmosphere and changes the climate locally and regionally and globally. Allowing these transitions is foolish beyond comprehension.

So I come back to the absolute necessity for stabilizing the composition of the atmosphere at the moment and then moving beyond that to reduce the atmospheric burden. I see no way to get to that point without having a revolution in how we view the Earth. We need a new view of the Earth, a new world view in which we set aside, at least for the moment, politics and economics and decide that we absolutely have to stabilize the human environment. We really have to stabilize the composition of the atmosphere and move toward long term stability, which is lower CO_2 content, to restore our climatic system to stability.

We have to do that substantially immediately. That means that we put ecological considerations above economic and political considerations. That's going to be awkward for at the moment we are operating on a model in which we assume that the Earth is still very large in proportion to the demands, and very resilient.

Failure to make this transition in perspective is chaos as far I'm concerned. It is not chaos sometime in a century or so. It's chaos, progressive chaos, now. And if one wants examples of it, look around the world. Look at Somalia, which has no government and substantially no economy and is being racked by drought, and so are the other central African nations. Kenya, for instance, cannot preserve its parks because people outside the parks are so numerous that they do not have a place to live and they have to go to the parks to steal the wood and water. They're having a drought and they're talking about electric fences around the parks to keep people out.

Haiti in the western hemisphere is in a political, economic and environmental abyss. It's not possible for Haiti to cure its environmental, economic, and political problems internally. There's no way an economy can be rebuilt in Haiti without restoring a func-

tional landscape. Haiti has a totally dysfunctional, completely impoverished landscape, with no forests. It has agriculture driven to thirty-degree slopes that cannot retain agriculture for more than a year or so. They erode away the next time the rain is heavy, and the rain is heavy all the time.

The rivers run in a different place every time it rains. The island nation with seven million or more people is over-populated, and regular floods wash out new sections of the slums that grow up in the valleys, and people drown in each rainstorm. The only way to restore Haiti is to have some outside force with money come in with a plan and displace people from the land, and pay them. They have to be supported and subsidized, as a functional landscape is restored to the point where an economy can be established that will support a governmental system. Haiti has not had a stable governmental system in decades, many decades. I look at it as the Haitian Abyss, where we're headed as a world unless we can find our way out.

It portends genuine anarchy, and anarchy is developing of course—Pakistan, Afghanistan, and Somalia. Of course in some of those cases you can say it's political failures, and it is political failures, but the political failures lead to environmental failures, and the environmental failures lead to economic failures which add to the chaos. And pretty soon there is no way of restoring the economy or restoring the landscape, no internal way of doing it. So we have to look for outside forces, and outside forces are not going to come to the Earth and straighten it out if we get the whole thing in a mess, which we're doing fast.

In 600,000 years, for which we now have a record that goes back 800,000 years, the carbon dioxide concentration of the atmosphere didn't exceed roughly 284 ppm. It was less than that until roughly 1885. The 1900 level was well under 300 ppm, so we should go back to that and operate from there. They talk about sea level changes being the most frightening things. Sea level change is a frightening matter and sea level was 300 feet lower than it is now ten thousand years ago right here. And Georges Bank was exposed, but sea level change is about four millimeters per decade. That's trifling in comparison with the changes in climate that are affecting us now.

There is a resistance by the public to accept the things I am talking about, but I think the oil companies did us real dirt. The Global Climate Coalition spent oil company money. Exxon and others spent tens of millions of dollars, undermining the basic science of climate, and the scientists who supported that information, and they did it very effectively. It was one of the most powerfully effective public relations campaigns ever carried out, and the residue of that is what you see. It was a scurrilous program, absolutely scurrilous.

They are still doing it to a lesser degree by just raising questions. I think they have abandoned the original coalition, but Exxon is still advertising that they are the sources of the energy that drive the industrial world, and they have to be supported, and they want to drill more wells and want access to more places to drill and so on. There is money to be made there, and they aren't backing away from that money. They are not saying that we're going to become the wind company or anything like that. They're saying that they are going to be the oil company, and the oil company is going to supply oil for the foreseeable future, and there is no serious problem. They are just like those heads of the tobacco companies that went to Washington and said that they did not believe that smoking caused cancer. They knew better—venal corporate executives at the worst.

The oil companies have done it. The coal companies are with them, telling the public we can have "clean coal". **There is no such thing as clean coal, and not only is there no such thing as clean coal, there is no such thing as wholesome coal. All you have to do is look what's going on in the southern Appalachians to ask whether coal can be produced in a wholesome way.** *It cannot be, and it should be done away with immediately—outlawed. There are things we do outlaw such as murder. Industrial activities that destroy the earth are destructive of people and must be outlawed in the public interest.*

   At the moment we are headed for a runaway greenhouse effect *as we warm the Earth, and the ocean doesn't take up as much carbon; as we warm the Earth and the forests decay more rapidly—burn up, trees die and decay as climate moves out from under them; as the organic matter in soils decays more rapidly and dumps carbon. Three billion more tons of carbon into the atmosphere every year is an impossible challenge to the world.*

   The only possible new world requires cooling the Earth, and cooling the Earth can only be done by reducing the use of fossil fuels and managing forests. That's the only way that we can handle billions of tons of carbon—everything else is make-believe. It's fun to make-believe about alcohol and other "bio-fuels" but all are trifling in total. Renewable energy is not make-believe but it's a new world. It doesn't work as the same world powered with renewable energy—it's part of a new world where we live differently.

   The difficulty is that we have to live and work in the context of our time. We can work to change it, but in the context of our time it's not really possible to live without an automobile. Plug-in hybrids will help, but we do not have to produce the electricity they need with fossil fuels. We can produce it with wind machines and with solar panels on the roof. This entire Woods Hole campus burns no fossil fuels. In fact, we burn nothing. We shall soon have a 100 kilowatt wind turbine operating. We expect to be producing more energy than we use. And if we do things my way, we shall have a fleet of small electric cars that will be charged by the excess energy that we produce with our wind turbine. The staff will commute to work in those cars.

   A further concern that becomes more severe as the climatic disruption proceeds is methane. Methane clathrates: http://www.techimo.com/forum/debateimo-politics-religion-controversy/215984-methane-clathrates-melting.html *store very large quantities of methane in shallow seas in Arctic regions. The overall warming may be starting to free these hydrates now. Atmospheric methane concentrations are rising again. They dropped for a long time, but they're going back up and nobody quite knows why. My own guess is the rate of anaerobic decay in marshes and bogs in the higher latitudes is rising. The major source of methane right now is this anaerobic decay, but it's also true that the clathrates are highly vulnerable to a warming of coastal waters. (Scientist) Gordon McDonald used to argue that all the carbon dioxide in the atmosphere had come from methane earlier and he may have been right. There is real concern that present warming is mobilizing clathrates and contributing a further strong positive feedback.*

   I don't think that we can address these problems any longer without addressing the population problem. Six to seven billion people are too many people for this small world. We ought to be headed for three billion or maybe two billion on a global basis and certainly two hundred million in the U.S. When we talk about immigration we ought to be talking about immigration for what purpose, and of how many, and aimed at some number as an objective. I would argue that it's not 300,000,000, it certainly isn't 400,000,000, and it's much more likely that it should be 200,000,000, a much more sensible number if we wish to offer our children reasonable opportunities and a potentially acceptable and continuing level of civilization. We're interested in the welfare of our progeny, not just their existence. There isn't any problem in the world that isn't made worse by larger numbers of people.

Some people are talking about geo-engineering as a way out of our problems—things like clouds of plastic in orbit around the Earth. I think those efforts will make more trouble than can be repaired in any number of lifetimes. Those who advocate such silliness forget that the environment is an evolutionary product, maintained by living systems that depend on the continuity of their historically stable environments. Any chronic change produces increments of impoverishment that are cumulative and destructive of all we require in life and environment. I would not allow such arguments a moment's attention.

Much hinges on what the scientific community does with the immediate challenge, the climatic disruption and the progressive slide toward the Haitian Abyss. It can be defined lucidly enough to catch the public imagination and generate a new view of the world; the transition will be underway from the bottom up. Scientists and others have no great trouble envisioning a totally different world in which the objective is preserving the human habitat. The economic and political aspects of it become secondary, at least for the moment, and the basic rules of biophysics are defined and celebrated.

The principles of politics and economics are not natural laws. They are derivative, malleable subsets of hard and fast environmental facts and principles that, ignored or infringed, extract an inexorable toll from the human circumstance. That toll is measured in elements of life itself: water, air, land, and opportunity to live in a wholesome and nurturing environment that is systematically sustained and not continuously eroding and fusing into larger neighboring necrotic environments.

We need a new context, a new model of the world, and the new model is to accept that the world is small, and it's a biological system, and the rules for running a biological system are really quite narrow. They don't include unrestricted operations by commerce or industry that change the basic chemistry of the Earth or metaphysics of the Earth or anything else. Industries have to be housebroken to this new world, and we can bring that about.

There isn't any reason at all that we cannot say that the fundamental rule is no toxic releases at all, no changes in the chemistry. If you build something you can un-build it, if you make a toxin you have to account for it before you turn it loose, and when you build things you have to decide what the end point is going to be. It isn't a pile of junk, it's not plastic in the middle of the ocean, it's recycled and one way or another, you're responsible for it. Where does it go? You have to take care of that. We can do all that. We can build for reuse, build forever. Build not for waste but for containment.

It's a different view of the world, but it will come out of the scientific community only if we can get together and produce it.

The other way is chaos in a short time.

In looking at the outcome of the much-anticipated UN Climate Change Conference in Copenhagen that just concluded, one can hardly be anything but disappointed at the product. The issue of a warming planet has been around for 30-40 years. In fact, I was writing about it in 1979 as a serious problem, and it was in the report of the Council on Environmental Quality, published in 1980 by Gus Speth that was called the Global 2000 Report.

In that report we said this is a problem that has to be addressed, and should be addressed. We've wasted all that time, and right now we're down to having the effects of the warming conspicuous with the drought on every continent, people being moved off the land, and having to move off the land in Central Africa. We're looking toward even drier places in our own Southwest, and people in Mexico are anxious to leave too, and would come into the United States if they could. Central Asia has its own drought. Central South America has its drought. Australia is into disaster. They've lost their rice crop. And, so we have already serious environmental effects of he continued warming of the earth. And so out of Copenhagen we have a no-agreement at all to anything concrete.

Even the non-binding agreement to set up protections to limit the warming of the earth to two degrees is totally unacceptable. And that's not an additional two degrees from 2009; it's two degrees counting the changes since the Industrial Revolution. And we've already increased 7/10 of a degree centigrade. A two degree rise is just absolutely intolerable.

We already have serious problems. If we allow the present circumstance to continue, we will melt all the glaciers and the world will disintegrate around us. If we allow it to go up by another degree and 2/10 or thereabout, that will simply accelerate the degrading transitions. And, there is no reason at all—no way at all that this civilization can survive that sort of change in its basic environment. So, I'm not at all pleased with what came out of Copenhagen, and I think the scientific community has to say forthrightly this moment that this won't work. It will absolutely have to fall together and stabilize the composition of the atmosphere and reduce the worst of the causes of the rise in CO2. Some people are calling for 350 ppm of CO2 as the absolute limit, but that also won't work. Even so, it's a lot better than allowing the atmospheric burden of CO2 to rise toward 500 ppm.

So, I'm unhappy with what we have not been able to do. Mr. Obama went to Copenhagen of course without any real strength offered to him by our Congress, and did what he thought he could do. And I suppose if he had gone there and offered genuine leadership, the Congress would have revolted even worse. I suppose that is what he feared, and so he did a fairly mild thing, which he could do. On the other hand, he could have gone there and said "Well, look, the world has a serious crisis. I recognize the dimensions of the crisis. My hands are tied by a recalcitrant Congress, but if I had my way, here is what we should do." And then because he knows he has a science advisor who knows, they all know the seriousness of the challenge. But he chose not to do that. That was a political decision, of course, and it may be a more powerful decision to lead the Congress than he would have had otherwise, but I have a hard time believing that. At that moment we didn't get what we needed.

Obama could lean out ahead and use the EPA's right to regulate CO2 as a pollutant if he is willing to take chances. Of course, if he moves strongly and the Congress does decree, they could take action to tie his hands. But my own view is that he should go absolutely as far as he can. He should push the limits. He has to, because the environmental limits have been pushed beyond any reasonable level, and we've wasted all the time that we have had to fiddle around and we have fiddled around and not done anything. We haven't even experimented in reducing the use of fossil fuels or stabilizing forests globally. Those two things are the only tools we have that are big enough to have an effect.

But getting the needed changes comes down to a political process. I really am not an expert of course in the political process, but I do realize that the political process has deviated far from what scientists think will work in the world. So we in the scientific community have pushed in every way possible to get the political machinery working in the right direction.

Just what course to take is hard for me to say. I might turn the whole issue around the other way and say, "Well, instead of arguing about who should have the right to poison the earth more, we should be arguing about how to proceed with alternative sources of energy."

If we were to subsidize the development of renewable energy and decide that hydrogen would work, as I said to you before, we could have a major subsidized program for the development of hydrogen as an energy storage mechanism, and ways of using hydrogen which would displace the interest in fossil fuels. We could do that if it were well subsidized it would be the way to go in everyone's mind. And then, just forget about poisoning the world with oil and coal.

Look at what Thomas Friedman has been saying. He's been going down that line for some time and he is very instructive and right. I have to say I favor taxing the hell out of fossil fuels—just plain brutally taxing it with a tax that's going to get worse and worse. Lay it all out ahead of time with a dollar tax on gasoline and next year it's going to go to a dollar and a half and the next year it will go to two dollars, and so on.

That's what we have to do and just tell the world that we're doing away with fossil fuels and it's going to come fast. Then those who have to use it will know, if you have to run your tractor on fossil fuels like diesel for a while, pretty soon we'll have a hydrogen substitute for it and it'll work. But maybe you can use biofuels for essentials like a diesel tractor on a farm. But what the hell? We need to figure that out.

In a sense this approach is command and control. It's saying that we are going to finance this transition—this transition is going to occur, and we're going to encourage it in every way we can. We'll do it financially; we'll do it by law, and so on. That's what governments are for. Governments are to function in the public interest. The public interest at the moment is very clear. We have to have a stable earth, an earth that you can continue to live on and feed seven billion people, and so on. All these things.

A major part of the problems in getting to solutions is that so many people are in denial of well-known facts. Attempting to cancel out all of the data on the climactic changes that we have accumulated over the course of the last century is to turn the earth upside down. It's the equivalent of denying gravity, that the sun will rise tomorrow at any time at all, and so on. You can't do that; you just absolutely cannot neglect the fact that we have added 30% to the carbon dioxide burden of the atmosphere and a whole series of other heat-trapping gases to the atmosphere. And that these things just on first principle warm the earth. Those first three sentences in brackets should be bolded and separated, very important!

Second, you can't deny that glaciers are melting, that the earth is warming, the sea level is rising, that the climates are changing, that the distribution of birds and plants is changing, that agriculture is being affected, that the things we are seeing now were predicted, predictable and now observable changes in the climates of the earth. All this was known 30 years ago, so I have no patience at all with people who are substantially saying well the earth isn't round, it's flat.

Back to Copenhagen, there's one other aspect of that meeting that I think was perhaps the most constructive was the emphasis on forests. We and others emphasize the fact that deforestation is producing roughly 20% of the total carbon released into the atmosphere. And stopping deforestation is a major objective currently. Now stopping it will reduce the emissions of carbon from deforestation and that's one and one-half billion tons a year of carbon, which is very significant on a global basis.

So we have pointed out that management of forests in such a way as to preserve the primary forests of the earth globally would be a very constructive step. We know that steps can be taken to favor the preservation of tropical forests using this process which is called by the acronym REDD: Reduced Emissions from Deforestation and Degradation. And that has gained a lot. It is pretty well understood that it should be possible to pay people who might turn their forests into agricultural land for not doing that. And in Brazil it seems to be working. Now whether that's a long-term wholesome way of preserving forests, I'm not prepared to say because I don't really believe that we should have to pay people to do what's right for the world. That should happen for other reasons. Many things that are not economically attractive to us should be done because they are right for the world.

Another very important accomplishment that, alone, was worth the trip to Copenhagen, was Obama's work with the prime minister of China to agree to more transparency in their efforts to reduce the amount of greenhouse gases per unit of production. That was a very good thing and he could do it where no one else could.

Overall, I think he did a good thing by going to Copenhagen, and getting what he could get. He didn't go there with enough support from our own Congress to do what needed to be done. And as I said, he made the judgment that he couldn't lead the Congress, but I tend to think these problems are serious enough that we need that bold leadership.

His approach to climate change is like his approach to the healthcare bill. It seems to me that he has been a little too relaxed. Maybe he did a lot behind the scenes, but he didn't get out there and use the bully pulpit for what he could have used it for. I think he has more power than he thinks he has.

As I said before, I think it is very important that the scientific community state very clearly at the moment how serious the issue is so that 10 years from now our grandchildren won't look back at us and say why were you guys asleep? I want them to know that we were not asleep. We did the best we could and it was politicians who were sufficiently incompetent or corrupt to avoid taking the steps that needed to be taken.

It has been said that the only force in modern society that is large enough and powerful enough to tackle climate change is business. That is, when the economics of action to combat climate change outweigh the economics of inaction, business interests will embrace climate change in order to profit from it. So, while the science of climate change attempts to explain what is happening, the economics of climate change may ultimately decide what is done.

Dr. Jason Shogren is the Stroock Distinguished Professor of Natural Resource Conservation and Management and Professor of Economics at the University of Wyoming. His research focuses on the behavioral underpinnings of private choice and public policy, especially for environmental and natural resources. By Royal Appointment, he served as the King Carl XVI Gustaf's Professor in Environmental Science, Umeå University, Sweden, for the 2007-08 academic year. In 1997, Shogren served as the senior economist on the Council of Economic Advisers in the White House in the run-up to the Kyoto conference and also has served on the IPCC. He is also an editor of several natural resource and economics journals. Recent publications include Environmental Economics (Oxford University Press) and Endangered Species Protection in the United States (Cambridge University Press)

As an economist, if I had the power to mandate the policies modern societies must use to respond to climate change, I would impose either a carbon tax, or a cap-and-trade system for carbon. A green tax, or carbon tax, and cap-and-trade programs are in theory the same thing. One fixes the price and one fixes a quantity, respectively. That is, a carbon tax fixes a charge per every unit of carbon, and cap-and-trade fixes a total level of carbon emissions. In theory we should end up at the same place as long as the supply and demand curves for carbon are the same.

I've found that the choice imposes a different risk on the economy and the environment. If you pick a carbon tax, you essentially fix the price and allow quantity to vary under different supply and demand conditions, which for an economist is not a big deal. But if you are a climate scientist and thus worried about thresholds, you are concerned that those quantities may get too high and potentially exceed some threshold which could trigger a catastrophe.

If you are interested in fixing the total quantity of carbon allowed, then the price of carbon must be allowed to vary, and that shifts the burden onto the economy. That will generally upset a few businesses because under this scenario you can have flexibility to buy all the carbon you need, but at the cost of not really knowing what that price will be. In this sense, this method of regulation is a little less certain.

For a long time, economists promoted both policies. Cap-and-trade was promoted as a way to satisfy an environmental target and to have a relief valve, which would be the flexible price. When the idea first started out in 1966, it was thought of as a little radical. Over the years, it has become a favorite of environmental groups just because it puts and enforces a hard target on the cap.

Another advantage of cap-and-trade is that the total allowed emissions can be reduced over time, which is much easier politically in some people's opinions, than a tax-- we all know how people recoil from taxes. Even though they are the same, you do not have to call it a tax—you can call it cap-and-trade. But a lot of politicians who oppose cap and trade have turned to calling it "cap-and-tax."

What is interesting from an economist's perspective is that setting the tax is a lot more straightforward than having a global quantity permit, because individual countries can set a tax of their own choosing and they are not so much relying on the idea of a global trading market for carbon. It can become a political football like currency exchange rates have recently.

If the cap really is binding, then everybody is going to need a carbon permit to do about anything. Every time you turn on the lights, start a car, eat a meal, chop down a tree, you are releasing some kind of carbon, so it becomes a global currency. For a lot of economists, the idea of creating a global currency, with its administration, the transaction's costs, and the enforcement of it become so overwhelming that it's not clear that it will be the most effective system. Not all economists agree, of course, because we don't have a whole lot of experience with a global cap-and-trade.

The United States does have experience trading sulfur permits, but that is not global. That was just in the U.S., so enforcement has not been an issue. But, if we formed a global market with say, Russia, China, India, the U.S and Japan, and if someone violates it, what is the punishment? Do they pay a fine? Do they get sanctioned? What if they don't pay the fine? Obviously, the issue become very sensitive geopolitically.

When you have global trade with just normal market goods, there are plenty of issues in terms of human rights and labor and how it is produced and the pollution it sends elsewhere. Now if you are thinking about something like carbon traded on a global market, the potential transaction costs become huge.

Because of these issues, there is a certain segment of economists who have promoted the idea of "Let's just put a price on it." There will be some variability in the amount, but we can at least get the tax up and running at a national level a lot easier, and you should accomplish the same goal if you are setting the tax at a level to change behavior, not just to raise revenue.

That is the other criticism of the tax. Except in certain Scandinavian countries, the taxes have been set so low that it has been mainly just revenue raisers, not high enough to change behavior. Of course, you could say the same thing about the very loose cap-and-trade systems like they have in Europe. The price is too low.

Much of the information provided about climate change to the public has come from the Intergovernmental Panel on Climate Change founded in 1988. I was lead author for one chapter of the Third Assessment Report published in 2001.

The recent furor about "climategate", regarding some leaked emails was bound to happen. Scientists are human, and they are bound to say a few things that are not on the dance card.

You can then use a "multiplier effect" and magnify a few statements out of thousands. There is nothing new about that, and scientists are a little naive about what happens in the political arena. If you leave one shred of dangling red meat out there, it will get picked up on. [Since Dr. Shogren's interview, an independent (not part of the IPCC) British blue-ribbon panel tasked with looking into "climategate" has concluded that computer hackers who "discovered" the scientists allegedly trying to cover up mistakes blew the whole issue out of proportion, and that the scientists at East Anglia University committed no improprieties and cast no doubt on the science of global climate change.]

Also recently, the outcome of the Copenhagen meetings was in a way unavoidable, because even though China is doing a lot in some aspects of energy production, they are also trying to grow their economy at 10 percent per year-- there is no way they will want to slow that down.

From what I've read, they are investing significantly more than we are in renewables. They are investing especially in hydro, with the Three Gorges Dam project. It they beat us to the technology punch, and they can get the patents on cheaper, better, faster energy sources that are less carbon-intensive, we will obviously be disadvantaged. We may end up buying not just clothes, goods, and services from China, we will be buying our technologies from them as opposed to the other way around.

The countries at the bottom of the global income bracket look around and sees how we got rich off of carbon, and they want the same standard of living and the same options. To me, getting China and India to agree to binding reasonable cuts is our biggest challenge. Now, flip this around, and Asians can claim that the U.S. isn't on board. In general we don't have a lot of leverage. Europe has been the leaders on this, and they don't have a lot of leverage over us or Asia.

Economists think about these matters in terms of costs and benefits. The best cost estimates to control carbon I've seen have ranged between one and two percent of Gross Domestic Product. For that kind of insurance, is it too much for people to ask? Probably not. Then again, no one has been willing to step up. The Stern Review on the Economics of Climate Change is a detailed study released in 2006 that basically concluded that spending one percent of global GDP annually starting now is necessary to avoid a loss of 20 percent of global GDP later. If you believe in the argument on climate change variability having a fat-tail distribution of damages, this does not even represent the worst case scenario. If we have a catastrophe with global climate change, 20 percent may be a down payment.

Given the intense power of the coal and fossil fuel industries, the big debate domestically was about whether the policies that we were promoting like Kyoto would sell politically. From an economist's perspective, we argued that it was better to put incentives in place so that when the capital stock (like power plants) of these companies turned over, it turned over in a way that was more carbon-friendly, even carbon-reducing. That might entail a plan that takes 30 or 40 years as big power plants and automobile fleets are replaced with something more efficient.

One idea is to use the current financial crisis as a lever to promote the "global green new deal." One of my colleagues here at the University of Wyoming who worked for the United Nations created a report on how you could have this triple bottom line by using the financial crisis and stimulating the economy by investing in not necessarily more bridges and roads, but by building high speed rail, things that would get jobs started, reduce energy dependence, and reduce climate change risk.

The big picture for me is that there are four points that I always come back to when trying to understand costs, benefits and trade-offs:

First, what are the chances of a real catastrophe if we continue business as usual? That will definitely change how we think about benefits of climate policy.

Second, on the cost side, it comes down to how we engage the emerging economies to make reasonable and binding cuts. Naturally, that applies to the U.S. as well.

Third, do we allow businesses to find low cost solutions as a result of the free market? Will we have flexibility in the system, so that we can find the lowest-cost solutions to hit the target?

Fourth and last relates to energy efficiency and the rate of adoption. We cannot be overly optimistic and think that we can get 25 percent of the way to our goal as people voluntarily begin to reduce energy consumption. Will I just decide to do it, or do I need an increase in energy prices to get me on board? That's where economists can be part of the dismal sciences when we say people are not necessarily going to change for the right reason.

Those four points: catastrophe, the emerging economies, flexibility for low cost solutions, and adoption of energy efficiency will help you determine whether you think climate change policy is appropriate.

Reference List

Alaska Department of Natural Resources. (2008). JICC Report as of 8/18/04.

American Geophysical Union. (2008). Position on Climate Change. Retrieved July 26, 2009, from http://www.agu.org/outreach/science_policy/positions/climate_change2008.shtml.

An accurate picture of ice loss in Greenland. (October 10, 2008). Science Daily. Retrieved August 31, 2009, from http://www.sciencedaily.com/releases/2008/09/080930081355.htm.

Barnola, J.M., Raynaud, D., & Lorius, C. (2003). Historical CO2 record from the Vostok Ice Core. Laboratoire de Glaciologie et de Geophysique de l'Environnement, Cedex, France.

Barkov, N.I. (2003). Arctic and Antarctic Research Institute, St. Petersburg, Russia.

Begley, S. (August 3, 2009). Newsweek. P. 30.

Bernstein, L., P. Bosch, O. Canziani, Z. Chen, R. Christ, O. Davidson, W. Hare, S. Huq, D. Karoly, V. Kattsov, Z. Kundzewicz, J. Liu, U. Lohmann, M. Manning, T. Matsuno, B. Menne, B. Metz, M. Mirza, N. Nicholls, L. Nurse, R. Pachauri, J. Palutikof, M. Parry, D. Qin, N. Ravindranath, A. Reisinger, J. Ren, K. Riahi, C. Rosenzweig, M. Rusticucci, S. Schneider, Y. Sokona, S. Solomon, P. Stott, R. Stouffer, T. Sugiyama, R. Swart, D. Tirpak, C. Vogel, & G. Yohe, (2007). PCC Climate change 2007: Synthesis report. Valencia, Spain: IPCC.

Bernstein, L., P. Bosch, O. Canziani, Z. Chen, R. Christ, O. Davidson, W. Hare, S. Huq, D. Karoly, V. Kattsov, Z. Kundzewicz, J. Liu, U. Lohmann, M. Manning, T. Matsuno, B. Menne, B. Metz, M. Mirza, N. Nicholls, L. Nurse, R. Pachauri, J. Palutikof, M. Parry, D. Qin, N. Ravindranath, A. Reisinger, J. Ren, K. Riahi, C. Rosenzweig, M. Rusticucci, S. Schneider, Y. Sokona, S. Solomon, P. Stott, R. Stouffer, T. Sugiyama, R. Swart, D. Tirpak, C. Vogel, & G. Yohe, (2007). PCC Climate change 2007: Synthesis report: Summary for policymakers. Valencia, Spain: IPCC.

Blades, M. Blast from the past—James Hansen 1988, Daily Kos, January 14, 2008. http://www.dailykos.com/storyonly/2008/1/14/32422/5770

Brown, L. (2009). Our global ponzi economy. Adapted from chapter 1. New York: W.W. Norton & Company. (Found on Earth Policy.org Book Bytes), at http://www.earth-   policy.org/index.php?/book_bytes/2009/pb4ch01_ss4.

Climate change and Arctic impacts (n.d.). CIEL. http://www.ciel.org/Climate/Climate_Arctic.html.

Connor, S. (September 23, 2008). The Methane Time Bomb. Techimo. Retrieved July 26, 2009 from: http://www.techimo.com/forum/debateimo-politics-religion-controversy/215984-methane-clathrates-melting.html.

CO2now.org. (2009). CO2 Home Page. Retrieved November 2, 2009 from http://co2now.org/index.php?option=com_frontpage&Itemid=1

Delft University of Technology (2008, October 10). An accurate picture of ice loss In Greenland. ScienceDaily. Retrieved November 2, 2009, from http://www.sciencedaily.com /releases/2008/09/080930081355.htm.

Fairley, P. (2009, September). Sorting out soot. Discover Magazine, pp. 12-13.

Global Carbon Project (July 6, 2009). Super-size deposits of frozen carbon in Arctic could worsen climate change. ScienceDaily. Retrieved August 21, 2009, from http://www.sciencedaily.com/releases/2009/06/090630132005.html

Global warming puts the Arctic on thin ice (2005). Natural Resources Defense Council. Retrieved July 2, 2009, from http://www.nrdc.org/globalwarming/qthinice.asp#.

Gray, V. (1999, February). Greenhouse Bulletin No 120.

Hansen, J., A. Lacis, V. Oinas, R. Ruedy, & M. Sato, M. (2007). Global warming in the 21st century: An alternative scenario. New York: Goddard Institute for Space Studies.

Hansen, J., M. Sato, R. Ruedy, K. Lo, D. Lea, & M. Medina-Elizade, (2006). Global temperature change. Proceedings of the National Academy of Sciences of the USA. Washington, D. C.

Huffington Post. (2008, November 24). Twenty years later—tipping points near on global warming.

Keeling, R., S. Piper, A. Bollenhacher, A., & S. Walker, (2008, May) Carbon Dioxide Research Group, Scripps Institution of Oceanography, University of California, La Jolla, California, USA.

Loya, W. (2009, June). Climate change implications for Yukon Flats National Wildlife Refuge. The Wilderness Society. Retrieved November 3, 2009, from http://wilderness.org/files/Yukon%20

Flats%20Refuge%20Climate%20Implications.pdf

Madrigal, A. (May 28, 2008) Could methane trigger a climate doomsday within a human lifespan? Wired Science. Retrieved August 31, 2009 from http://www.wired.com/wired-science/2008/05/could-methane-t/

Maislin, Mark. (2009). Global warming: A very short introduction. New York: Oxford University Press Inc.

Mrasek, V. (2008). A Storehouse of greenhouse gases is opening in Siberia. Spiegel Online. Retrieved July 5, 2009, from http://www.spiegel.de/international/world/0,1518,547976,00.html.

NASA. (2009). New NASA Satellite Survey Reveals Dramatic Arctic Sea Ice Thinning. GREEN CAR CONGRESS. Retrieved September 1, 2009, from http://www.greencarcongress.com/2009/07/nasa-20090708.html

Natural Environment Research Council. Plants absorb more carbon dioxide under polluted hazy skies. ScienceDaily (April 23, 2009). Retrieved September 7, 2009. www.sciencedaily.com /releases/2009/04/090422132829.htm.

Natural Resources Defense Council. "Global warming puts the Arctic on thin ice." Retrieved July 2, 2009. http://www.nrdc.org/globalwarming/qthinice.asp#.

NOAA. (2008). Earth System Research Laboratory. Retrieved July 5, 2009, from http://www.esrl.noaa.gov/gmd/ccgg/trends/.

Pew Center on Global Climate Change. (2009). Global warming and the Arctic FAQs. Retrieved July 2, 2009, from http://www.pewclimate.org/global-warming-basics/faq_s.

Queen's University (August 9, 2005). Ice shelf disintegration threatens environment. Queen's Study. ScienceDaily. Retrieved December 22, 2008, from http://www.sciencedaily.com/releases/2005/08/050804123855.htm

Rejcek, P. (October 3, 2008). House call. The Antarctic Sun.

Revkin, A, & Krauss, C., (2009, October 15). Curbing Emissions by Sealing Gas Leaks, The New York Times.

Romanovsky, V. (2009). Clean Air Cool Planet; Interview with Dr. Vladimir Romanovsky, of the Geophysical Institute, University of Alaska, Fairbanks, AK. Retrieved August 31, 2009 from http://www.arcticwarming.net/node/70.

Roosevelt, M. (February 20, 2009). Bubbles of warming beneath the ice, Los Angeles Times. Retrieved July 2, 2009 from http://www.latimes.com/news/science/environment/la-na-global-warming22-   2009feb22,0,646220.story.

Sagan, C. (1980). Cosmos. New York: Random House, Inc.

Shin, L. (July 2, 2009). Thawing permafrost could emit massive amounts of greenhouse gases, Retrieved August 31, 2009 from http://solveclimate.com/blog/20090702/thawing-permafrost-could-emit-massive-amounts-greenhouse-gases

Stang, D. (2009). Trends in Atmospheric Methane. Retrieved November 2, 2009 from http://zipcodezoo.com/Trends/Trends%20in%20Atmospheric%20Methane.asp.

UNEP YEAR BOOK. (2008). Retrieved July 2, 2009, from http://www.unep.org/geo/yearbook/yb2008/, p. 43.

University Corporation for Atmospheric Research. (n.d.). The greenhouse effect. Retrieved November 4, 2009, from http://www.ucar.edu/learn/1_3_1.htm

University of Alaska at Fairbanks. (2009). http://www.alaska.edu/uaf/cem/ine/walter/

University of Miami Rosenstiel School of Marine & Atmospheric Science. Strong evidence that cloud changes may exacerbate global warming. ScienceDaily (July 24, 2009). Retrieved September 7, 2009. www.sciencedaily.com /releases/2009/07/090723141812.htm.

US Fish and Wildlife Service. (2009). Retrieved Septermber 4, 2009. http://www.fws.gov/Refuges/profiles/index.cfm?id=75635

Walter, K., Zimov, S., Chanton, D., Verbyla, D., & Chapin, S. (2006). Methane bubbling from Siberian thaw lakes as a positive feedback to climate warming. London, UK: Nature Publishing Group.

Weart, S. (2007, July). The Discovery of global warming, American Institute of Physics, Melville, New York.

Global Warming, Coleville River style

Thomas Napageak, Nuiqsut

Glenna Tetlichi, Old Crow

Sue Oliver, Ft. McPherson Gikhyi

I want to be sure that your readers understand that my life is very interesting, and I have a lot to live for in this community. This is where and how I want to live. It's pretty hard to live here at the cost of everything. But there is no price tag on my life. I want to live as free as I can subsistence-wise, and I want to keep my people and our tradition going.
Thomas Napageak, Kupa, of Nuiqsut, Alaska

Chapter Six
This I Believe

This concluding chapter reprises the issues of the previous five chapters. What are the common threads, both for voices in the same chapter, as well as between voices crossing chapter lines? Clearly, this area of the Arctic is a complex place, and our ability to understand it depends on our careful listening to its many voices.

Daniel Quinn, in his now classic book, Ishmael, asks the reader to accept that a gorilla (Ishmael) can communicate with humans-- in the book's case, a person known simply as "the pupil." The all-knowledgeable Ishmael leads the pupil through an in-depth, highly critical examination of humanity and explains how humans have set themselves apart from all other living things. The pupil comes kicking and screaming into the realization that humans need to change their ways and remember that they are indeed not gods who decide what species will live and die in order to make things easier for themselves. The pupil, at the very end of the book, asks Ishmael a leading but as yet unanswered question. "What do I do if I earnestly desire to save the world?"

The wise Ishmael gives the pupil a program to do just that. First, he says modern humans need to stop killing the people who have for thousands of years lived close to the land. Secondly, we must stop playing god, thus stop making decisions of who should live and who should die. And finally, we must each teach a hundred what we have learned.

This Quinn classic in essence makes our case for us, the authors of this book. We must listen closely and carefully to what few voices are left that live as a part of nature. If we do not do this, and we eradicate these highly knowledgeable peoples, we do so to our own detriment.

The Wisdom of the People of Two Worlds:
Chapters Two and Three

At first, we conceived of Chapters Two and Three, the Gwich'in caribou people and the Inupiat and Inuvialuit whalers, as perhaps having different views of the world, and perhaps different common threads. Counter to our own naivete, the common threads were essentially the same. Thus we found that the place of reverence of the caribou and the whale, each the charismatic representative of the very lifeline of the people, were in many ways, almost identical. Not surprisingly, the one Inupiat group which had caribou at its center, the people of Anaktuvuk Pass, Alaska, were in some ways more like Gwich'in than Inupiat.

The Inupiat, the Inuvialuit and the Gwich'in people of the Alaskan and adjacent Canadian Arctic probably come as close to living their original lifestyle as any Native people in North America. Their close connection to the land is amazing to anyone visiting or reading about the area for the first time. Whether it's the caribou or the whale, there's an unquestioned connection that most Americans and Canadians from down South have difficulty understanding.

On the other hand, these Native people, with the help in some cases of their friends from the South, have adopted and adapted to many of the ways of those friends. Snowmobiles, four-wheelers, trucks, air travel, high-powered rifles, and motor boats are some of the main items that have become a prominent part of the Native tool kit. Satellite television and all the related means of entertainment and communication including computers are present in every village.

Education is two-pronged. While many villages have K–12 (or at least K–9) educational offerings similar to those in the South, there is a constant and very healthy concern with integrating traditional knowledge of the land into the curriculum. And if the Native student is to go beyond high school, Whitehorse, Fairbanks and other, more southern cities are in the cards. For those who choose to go or must have a part of their education in the South, there is an ability to move back and forth between the two.

Mixing and matching two worlds of education and life

Gwich'in Glenna Tetlichi spent her first 15 years in Old Crow, Yukon, and learned the traditional Gwich'in ways. Her dad was the skilled hunter, Donald Frost, who provided well for his family. At age 15, Glenna had to leave Old Crow, which provides only grades one through nine. She moved to Whitehorse to attend high school. She found the transition very difficult, as she went from the top of her class in Old Crow to near the bottom in Whitehorse. But she survived and more.

She stayed in the South for a total of 20 years, only coming back to Old Crow on holidays and certain critical times for family obligations. But she knew that she would get "that call to come home." Glenna got married, and her husband Joe and she had two boys. From 1996 to 2008, they lived in Old Crow. The boys were taught by Joe the art of hunting and fishing. Glenna says,

"Actually, they (the boys) enjoy it all very much…. Sometimes, we will have to take them out of the classroom for a day or so to get that out of our 12-year-old's system. It's very hard to strike a balance between school and bush, especially during caribou season."

In 2008, they moved to Whitehorse so that their boys would be able to start Whitehorse schools and still be with their parents.

Thomas Napageak, Inupiat name Kupa, is a bit more traditional than the Tetlichis, at least at the tender age of 26. He is the young whaling captain, who loves the bush lifestyle. He was trained as a whaler by his father, Thomas, Sr., and became a whaling captain when his father became too old. Kupa says he plans to take his two daughters whaling when they get older, as there may be a time if something happens to him that they will have to provide for themselves. He is currently training some boys in Nuiqsut to whale.

But Kupa sees the importance of the formal education, especially if traditional knowledge is integrated into the local high school curriculum. He says that he has received a good education in both the bush and formally. He always kept a subsistence journal, being required to write one page of this diary each day, and being graded on the result.

The ever-upbeat Kupa says he doesn't know exactly where his future is headed, but for his next challenge, he wants to get into politics. He says,

"I want to help this village keep putting its foot down and maintain the subsistence that we have around here.... But no matter what I do for employment, there's no question that I will continue whaling, hunting and fishing."

Dennis Allen is an Inuvialuit/Gwich'in person from Inuvik who has taken a somewhat different path to balancing the lifestyles and the education. He grew up learning the traditional Inuvialuit ways from his late father, Victor. His father was a great whaler and taught Dennis much of that traditional practice. But when Dennis turned 17, he was able to jump from school to a high-paying job in the Mackenzie Delta "oil patch." Till he was 30, he led the high-flying, wild lifestyle of a young, single roughneck oil worker.

But at that age, he decided there was more to life. He enjoyed writing songs and expressing himself artistically. He felt the strong call to go back to school, so he left the "oil patch" for good.

After several years in college in Calgary, Alberta, Dennis went to work in the TV industry. He worked for the CBC on the hit drama, North of 60. His first adventure in writing his own film was called Someplace Better, a partially autobiographical drama about the two worlds of Native and non-Native life. His second film was about a special march that a Native Dene group did and was titled Walk a Path to Healing. Dennis, continuing his autobiographical work has created his latest film, My Father, My Teacher.

Dennis, his wife, and two young children now live in Whitehorse, where he is further pursuing his career in film. Check him out at www.mackdelta.com.

Darius Elias, as we saw, is a Gwich'in man in his 30's who is now a member of the Yukon Legislative Assembly. He grew up very traditional, being raised by his activist mom (Norma Kassi, one of four Canadian representatives on the Gwich'in Steering Committee) who moved between Old Crow and Whitehorse, and his grandmother Mary Kassi, who taught him the traditional ways up in Crow Flats above Old Crow. One June he was with his grandmother at camp in Old Crow Flats when she told him things had to change,

"Sonny, you gotta go to school. You can't come here next year." I remember the pain I was going through when she told me that. I thought about it all year until March of the next year. She sat me down and told me that I will lead someday, and that I have to learn the Western society. "You have to learn the other way," she said, "so you can talk like they talk and so you can write like they write."

Darius says he now realizes that she wanted him to go to school so that one day he could save the caribou. He wasn't to see his beloved Crow Flats for 10 years.

After graduating from high school in Whitehorse, Darius went on to college for four years and got a degree in business. He later went on for a degree in Natural Resources and returned to Old Crow with a family. He went to work at the newly formed Vuntut National Park as the park warden. He says he tried to "strike the right balance" between the traditional Gwich'in ways and how it is in the outside world. He pledges to teach his lessons to his two boys, Johnny and Bhodi and his two daughters, Rachael and Heather.

Guarding the traditional life

Darius Elias' life provides a good transition from education and life in two worlds to protecting the Gwich'in lifeline, the Porcupine Caribou Herd. In addition to his leadership roles in his home community of Old Crow and representing Old Crow in the Yukon Territorial Assembly, he has traveled to Washington, D.C., to help protect the caving grounds of the herd.

On the Alaska side of the Gwich'in nation, one of our interviewees stands out for her staunch and life-long fight to protect the U.S. calving grounds of the Porcupine Caribou Herd, the Arctic National Wildlife Refuge coastal plain. That person is **Sarah James** of Arctic Village. She grew up on the land with her mom, dad and siblings, in Arctic Village and Fort Yukon.

She began her education in Arctic Village in 1955 with the first teacher the village ever had. Four years later, she went to boarding school in Oregon for a period to learn English, where she got a high school diploma in six years. Life in Oregon did not suit Sarah, but she got through it.

When she returned to Old Crow, she became concerned with protecting the caribou. She speaks of how the caribou have "revived" her people time and time again and of their special relationship to the caribou.

"So we have that spiritual connection. If it wasn't for the caribou, then we would starve…. Anything that saves the tribe, we take that as sacred to our life. That's how it is with caribou to us."

In 1988, the entire Gwich'in nation (15 villages) came together for the first time in over 150 years in Arctic Village to decide how to protect the caribou. She tells of the fateful decisions made by the tribal elders and chiefs, and of how she was one of four Gwich'in from Alaska to be chosen to serve for life as a leader of the Gwich'in Steering Committee.

After 21 years, Sarah is still very much a leader of the Committee. She speaks of fighting a battle in the U.S. Congress, with some big victories, and some small. She feels they could not have done this without their friends in the Lower 48. They have indeed become very adept at making friends in the South.

Her efforts have been inspirational as well as successful. In 2002, she and two other Gwich'in leaders, **Jonathon Solomon** of Fort Yukon, Alaska, and **Norma Kassi** of Whitehorse, Yukon, won the Goldman Environmental Prize for their many efforts to save the caribou.

Going back to Kupa (Thomas Napageak) of Nuiqsut, Alaska, we find the fire to protect the whale and his people's right to hunt them much the same as Sarah James' with the caribou. He speaks of all the problems with offshore drilling and of his strong opposition to the practice.

While Kupa is young and has not traveled much as yet, he is very interested in politics, and that may well lead to trips to the South to protect Inupiat whaling. His statements belie a potential future as spokesman for his people.

"My point of view[about offshore drilling] is that these people are in it for the money. I might be wrong, that's what it appears to me. If they offered me money instead of going out whaling, I wouldn't take it. Where would our tradition be? Where are we going to be?"

A similar sentiment for protecting tribal subsistence was expressed by **George Paneak**, the mayor of Anaktuvuk Pass, Alaska. In March of 2007, the U.S. Bureau of Land Management held a public meeting in Anaktuvuk Pass to discuss coal and heavy-metal mining west of the village. They brought maps and explained where the coal and other metals were. He knew they would have to build a road. He goes on,

"That really concerned the residents. How would it affect the herds? Would they find a different route, or would they not exist anymore in that area? We heavily depend on that herd. That's our meat. And you know, even if it meant jobs, we were really concerned about the road that would transport the hard-rock."

The Bureau of Land Management went home without an agreement, but George feels they may come back later, maybe 10-15 years down the road.

Lorraine Peter, a Gwich'in person from Old Crow, Yukon, found an important calling of her life to go South to the Lower 48 with Lenny Kohm to tell people about her life out on the land and the importance of protecting the caribou.

"One time [in camp], I heard a noise outside. I went to the door, which was just a blanket covering the tent, and I opened it real slow because I could hear other noises. I figured it was probably caribou and I peaked out the doorway, and there was about 200 caribou going past my mom's tent.... I shared that story when I did my very first talk traveling with Lenny. I don't think there was a dry eye in the house."

Indeed, Lorraine and many other Gwich'in people have likewise expressed their deeply-felt feelings and first-hand experiences of life in the Arctic directly to citizens of the Lower 48. Their passion and commitment have made a significant difference in stopping every attempt to open the Arctic Refuge coastal plain to oil and gas exploitation.

An important part of the effort to protect the whale and the caribou are the words that the people use to describe their deep connection to these cultural icons. Three of our book's subjects, one an Inupiat and two Gwich'in, give an especially good impression of the deeply held feelings.

Roger Kyikavichik of Old Crow gives us an excellent explanation of the importance of the caribou to the Gwich'in people. He tells us the Arctic Refuge coastal plain is so sacred, that his people are not allowed to ever go there. Darius Elias tells us that his people believe that their heart is half caribou and the caribou's heart, half Gwich'in.

Roger tells us of the importance of caribou meat.

"If you can't go out to your freezer and pull out caribou meat, you will be sad and sick, spiritually, mentally and physically sick."

Young Inupiat whaler from Kaktovik, Alaska, **Jules Lampe,** gives us an idea of just how emotional whaling is for him.

"I'll tell you, when you take a whale, it's really exciting. It's heartwarming, and it's, it's ecstasy! It's a really good feeling to get a whale and see everybody happy to have another year's worth of food."

My home, my heart

For the Native people of the Arctic, the deeply emotional feelings for either the caribou or the whale do not necessarily extend to the other. Anthropologists have found that essentially every culture sees protecting their own as central. While the Gwich'in as we have seen revere the caribou, while they may have a soft place in their heart for the whale, they are not willing to devote their life to protecting it. None of their villages are near the coast, and the whale plays no part in their subsistence.

The Eskimo people, on the other hand, are in most ways a mirror image of the Gwich'in. Since the whale is the most charismatic and important animal in their world, with some exceptions, they see protecting the whale as much more significant than protecting the caribou. One major exception are the Inupiat people of Anaktuvuk Pass, Alaska, which is located 200 miles from the coast. Their main subsistence food, as we have seen, is the caribou of the Western Arctic Herd. Thus, the reaction of the mayor of the town, George Paneak:

"Times change. But they [the U.S. Government] need to know that to my people, the caribou is a lasting thing."

Further, while a number of people from Kaktovik, Alaska, are concerned about drilling in the Arctic Refuge coastal plain of which they are a part, they are uniformly quite upset about offshore drilling's effects on the bowhead whale's migratory path. The caribou provide a significant part of their diet, but nothing like the three bowhead whales they are allowed to take every year for their village.

While this attitude on the part of the different Native people in the Arctic may not be particularly surprising, a failure to recognize these important differences has led to unfortunate misunderstandings in important policy decisions in the Lower 48. Here is an excellent example as verbalized by North Carolina activist Lenny Kohm. Lenny had brought Glenna Tetlichi of Old Crow to a critically important meeting with Republican Congressman Gillcrest. Two environmentalists had given their take on the question of drilling in the Arctic Refuge coastal plain, and the Congressman's next question was addressed to Glenna. It concerned two Inupiat women who had come to his office supported drilling.

"I am curious; if those women were sitting here right now, Glenna, what would you ask them?" ... She stopped for a minute, thought about it, and said, "I would ask them, when your children come to you and ask you who they are and where they came from, what are you going to tell them?"

The congressman responded, "As long as I am in this Congress, I won't let anything happen to where you live or the people you love."

And indeed, Congressman Gillcrest has voted consistently to protect the caribou. While this is an incredible story of a passionate woman giving a compelling, first-person answer to a congressman's question, unspoken was the lack of understanding that the Inupiat women did not have the stake in protecting the caribou that Gwich'in Glenna had. Had the issue been offshore drilling, the attitudes of the two cultures' representatives may well have been reversed. While clearly not the case with Congressman Gillcrest, no doubt politicians have taken advantage, using this cultural sleight-of-hand to support an argument.

Those Who Come for Business and Pleasure: Chapter Four

The one most obvious trait that all of the non-Native people whose interviews we published possess is the sheer love of and dedication to the Arctic area. Some have lived in the Arctic part of the year or year-round for 20-30 years, and some visit whenever they can.

In all cases, these people are activists of one description or another, working for the betterment of the Gwich'in and/or Eskimo of the region. Importantly, they all bring either certain skills or proximity to political power, two connections that tend to be in short supply on the ground in the Arctic of Alaska and adjacent Canada. Bush pilot Dirk Nickish and Arctic wilderness guide David van den Berg are both prime examples. David fell in love with Alaska and the Arctic over 20 years ago. His years as a back-country guide on the North and South Slope have led him to advocate protecting the land and the people of the Arctic as the head of an environmental organization in Fairbanks.

Bushpilot Dirk Nickish, an economist by education, takes a look at the petroleum industry's promises and finds them coming up short. He sees no positive effects of drilling. When Alaskans tell him that the oil companies are responsible because it's in their best interest to do a good job, he chalks those claims up to great advertising campaigns. He says both Exxon and BP have repeatedly shown that "they would rather pay fines than comply with regulations.... For them, it's just a little PR blip that gets covered up, and then they get to negotiate the fine."

Biologist Geoff Carroll has made perhaps the largest commitment to the Arctic, having spent most of the last 30 years of his life in Barrow. His role in population studies of the bowhead whale has greatly benefited the Inupiat, allowing a larger annual quota of the whales. All three are well-known over the region by many of the Native people.

Arctic activist Lenny Kohm has dedicated the last 20-plus years of his life to protecting the Arctic National Wildlife Refuge by rallying the Gwich'in themselves to come to the Lower 48 to tell their story first-hand to influential citizens. Shirl and Bill Thomas have strongly supported the Arctic Refuge in their Sierra Club work, based on their numerous trips to the region. Sue Oliver, as we have seen, dedicated almost four years of her life to her beloved Fort McPherson Gwich'in congregation.

Wilderness guide Laura Beebe has led groups of young people for years into some of the wildest parts of the region that include Native villages such as Anaktuvuk Pass, Alaska, and has taught the Native children in some of the villages. Itai Katz is an Israeli man who has married into Gwich'in culture in Tsiigehtchic, Northwest Territories. He has brought with him a penetrating concern for protecting Native interests in the Mackenzie Delta area from the development of a natural gas pipeline. Finally, Dave Harman, after a 2004 trip of personal discovery to the Arctic, has written all or parts of two books about the region, including this one.

The Warming of Arctic North America: Chapter Five

While the Native people resolutely teach their children and grandchildren the traditions, the spiritual connection, and the skills of living beautifully from what the earth provides, and while the Native people fight to protect and preserve the ecosystems that support them from the ravages of petroleum development, an insidious threat is rising that is bigger than threats from the oil wells, the toxic spills, the ice roads, and America's thirst for oil-- global climate change.

We now know that unnatural warming of the planet has been underway for almost 200 years, at first very slightly and almost immeasurably, and now more dramatically, very measurably, and is accelerating. Scientists pin the blame for the warming on the inexorable rise of carbon dioxide in the atmosphere, caused by burning fossil fuels and by the rapid deforestation of the planet. It's ironic that the discovery that petroleum and coal could power machines to do work for us would also poison our atmosphere and warm the planet.

A molecule that exists today as only 387 parts per million, or less than 4/100 of 1% of the atmosphere, blocks warmth caused by the sun from radiating back into space. Atmospheric carbon dioxide is now at a level that is the highest in at least the last 650,000 years, and continues to rise. And, temperatures have been rising along with the carbon dioxide levels.

The warming caused by carbon dioxide is unleashing a new menace that may be more potent and more dramatic, and is just being studied and understood by scientists-- methane. Paradoxically, the frozen north that is warming so rapidly holds locked away in its freezer chest called the permafrost, enormous amounts of organic material that have begun to decompose now that warming temperatures melt the permafrost to deeper and deeper levels. Where the decomposition is done in environments without the presence of oxygen, like the bottom of Arctic lake beds, it produces methane, a greenhouse gas that is 20 to 25 times more potent than carbon dioxide in blocking the heat from escaping the Earth. So, the methane production is a feedback from other warming.

In a very real sense, the warming is causing more warming, a spiral. The magnitude of this spiral, and how fast it will increase, is not known with certainty. What is known is that predicted worst-case outcomes from increasing atmospheric carbon dioxide and methane portend unimaginable changes to the earth and its web of life.

And actual results coming from studies consistently report more warming and more melting than previously estimated. As Newsweek's Sharon Begley recently reported, "Although policymakers hoped climate models would prove to be alarmist, the opposite is true, particularly in the Arctic."

As we have seen and heard, climate change is real, it is underway, and the Arctic region is feeling it sooner and more dramatically than virtually anywhere else on earth. While the Earth warmed on average 1° F during the Twentieth Century, the Arctic regions warmed 4-5 F° just in the last half of that century. The Arctic is warming more rapidly than the other parts of the planet because warmer temperatures melt snow and ice cover, exposing open water, soil and foliage, which in turn absorb more heat from the sun. Some scientists now believe that the primary reason for the rapid warm-up, however, is the amount of soot that wafts from the South from coal burning, and diesel engines, settling on the snow and ice, causing it to rapidly warm and melt, leading to more warming and melting.

Conclusions of the Intergovernmental Panel on Climate Change, plus our reading of current and past research studies, as well as our interviews with scientists convince us that the Earth is warming and that climates are changing. There is little doubt that human activity is the predominant cause. But the nature of the scientific method and the flux of studies and data lead scientists to be conservative by nature as the body of knowledge progresses. This conservatism motivates scientists to reserve judgments and withhold some conclusions about climate change, because the relationship between carbon dioxide, soot, and methane, versus atmospheric circulation, ocean circulation, cloud cover and solar cycles, all implicated in the warming, are not yet completely deduced. Yet, other scientists and the indigenous people of the Arctic are no longer in doubt now about what is coming, and the evidence seems to say that the changes are coming rapidly.

Gwich'in native, Darius Elias, is living with the rapid changes.

"The caribou migrations have changed, the caribou patterns have changed, and we are seeing a lot more parasites on the caribou, and we are seeing insects we have not seen before. Also, there are pelicans arriving. The vegetation is growing up the side of the mountains. On the coastal plain, the dwarf birches are just invading from the mountains at a very rapid rate,

which is also alarming.

Dr. George Woodwell, founder of the Woods Hole Research Center makes this dire warning,

"At the moment, we are headed for a runaway greenhouse effect as we warm the Earth, and the ocean doesn't take up as much carbon; as we warm the Earth and the forests decay more rapidly—burn up, trees die and decay as climate moves out from under them; as the organic matter in soils decays more rapidly and dumps carbon. Three billion more tons of carbon into the atmosphere every year is an impossible challenge to the world."

We now know that we cannot wait any longer to take action.

Darius Ellias, Bishop MacDonald and demonstrators at Arctic Refuge Action Day

The reality of the disappointment from the Copenhagen Climate Conference in December 2009 makes it more urgent than ever for the scientific community and average citizens alike to mobilize to overcome the influence of special interests that have enormous power in the U.S. Congress because of the power of money. But as environmentalist Lenny Kohm says, "You are the most powerful person in Washington." Congress just needs to hear from you before it's too late.

Postscript

President Obama releases his offshore drilling plans for the next ten years

On March 31, 2010, just before Arctic Gardens went to press, President Obama released his plan for U.S. offshore drilling for the next 10 years. He announced that areas off the East Coast of the US and off the north coast of Alaska that are not yet available for petroleum exploration and drilling would be studied to determine such activity's effects on tourism, the environment and national security. The Beaufort and the Chukchi Seas constitute an area of 130,000,000 acres, which is larger than the landmass of California. Leases in 2005, 2007, and 2008 that constitute 2,800,000 acres have already been let, and exploration may begin there soon. The median estimate of undiscovered, economically recoverable oil

in the entire 130,000,000 acres is about 10.6 billion barrels, or about 16 months of U.S. crude oil needs if that were the only supply.

The State of Alaska supports offshore drilling activity. It is particularly interested in production in the Arctic that could augment the declining throughput in the pipeline from Prudhoe Bay, the revenues from which pay for much of the state's budget and an annual citizen allocation.

For the Beaufort Sea, tracts leased in two recent sales in 2005 and 2007 have not yet been explored partly due to litigation, and that exploration may be begun as early as this summer if concerns of the Inupiat Eskimo whalers can be satisfactorily resolved. The areas open for exploration are in the vicinity of the path of the semi-annual bowhead whale migration, and the concern is that petroleum exploration and drilling would change the whale's path so that the whaling boats of the Inupiat could not reach them. This would deprive these Native Americans of their most important food resource over the last several thousand years. The Department of Interior says that results from anticipated exploration and ongoing research into oil-spill clean-up capability in icy waters will inform future decisions to proceed. As yet, the Obama Administration has not publically expressed concern about the potential threat of large changes to the whale migration patterns. Other areas in the Beaufort will be considered for exploitation in the 2012-2017 time period.

The Minerals Management Service estimate of undiscovered, economically recoverable resources for the Beaufort Sea Program Area is 2-7 billion barrels (Bbbl) of oil and 3-20 trillion cubic feet (tcf) of natural gas. Information acquired from exploration activities would serve to reduce the level of uncertainty in resource estimates for both leased and un-leased areas.

The Beaufort Sea on the east is divided from the Chukchi Sea by a northerly drawn line from Point Barrow, Alaska.

Tracts leased in the Chukchi Sea in 2008 have not yet been explored due to ongoing litigation. Like the Beaufort, other areas of the Chukchi Sea will be considered for leasing in the 2012-2017 time period. The Minerals Management Service estimate of undiscovered, economically recoverable resources for the Chukchi Sea Program Area ranges widely from 0.15-12 Bbbl of oil and 0.5-54 tcf of natural gas.

As the various media and official government releases are read, one cannot but be impressed with the lack of any mention of the potential for the off shore petroleum exploitation to adversely affect the long-time subsistence practices of the Inupiat Eskimos. A desire to minimize impacts to tourism, the environment and national security are the concern, to the exclusion of an impact that has the potential to destroy an ancient culture that has managed to integrate itself into the modern world through technology, but without losing its identity as a people. Hopefully, this form of nothing less than cultural genocide will be stopped before we sacrifice another Native American culture for our culture's addiction to money and petroleum.

Artic Gardens Image Credits